THEOLOGY
AND
NARRATIVE

THEOLOGY
AND
NARRATIVE:
A CRITICAL INTRODUCTION

Michael Goldberg

Abingdon
Nashville

THEOLOGY AND NARRATIVE: A CRITICAL INTRODUCTION

Copyright © 1981 and 1982 by Michael Goldberg

Library of Congress Catalog Card Number: 82-4050

ISBN 0-687-41503-9

Scripture quoted, with a few minor changes by the author, is from A New Translation of the Holy Scriptures According to the Masoretic Text (New Jewish Version). Philadelphia: Jewish Publication Society of America, 1962, 1978.

Selections from *God of the Oppressed* by James H. Cone, copyright © 1975 by the Seabury Press, Inc., are used by permission of Seabury Press and The Society for Promoting Christian Knowledge.

Excerpts from *Situation Ethics: The New Morality* by Joseph Fletcher, copyright © MCMLXVI W. L. Jenkins, are used by permission of Westminster Press and SCM Press Ltd.

The quotation from *The Way of All the Earth* by John S. Dunne, copyright © 1972 by John S. Dunne, C.S.C., is used by permission of Macmillan Publishing Company and Sheldon Press.

Selections from *The Self in Transformation: Psychoanalysis, Philosophy, and the Life of the Spirit* by Herbert Fingarette, copyright © 1963 by Basic Books, Inc., publishers, are used by permission of Basic Books, Inc., publishers, New York.

Lines from *Brother to a Dragonfly* by Will D. Campbell, copyright © 1977 by Will D. Campbell, are used by permission of the Continuum Publishing Company.

The quotation from *The Politics of Jesus* by John Howard Yoder, copyright © 1972 by William B. Eerdmans Publishing Company, is used by permission.

MANUFACTURED BY THE PARTHENON PRESS AT
NASHVILLE, TENNESSEE, UNITED STATES OF AMERICA

FOREWORD

This book grew out of my interest—as well as that of a lot of other people—in 'narrative theology.' Wherever one looked recently, it seemed as though ever greater numbers of books and articles were calling our attention to the significance of stories for theology. Yet at the same time, one could not ignore the ever-increasing feeling that most of these works were unjustifiably sidestepping the critical issues involved: judgments of truth, assessments of rationality, questions of method. It's issues such as these this book is intended to address. As such, the book is more a work in the philosophy of religion than an actual piece of constructive theology. However, I believe that what the book has to say can indeed provide a strong foundation for a constructive theology—whether it be a Jewish one I hope to write one day or another kind of theological enterprise someone else might choose to embark on.

This book began as a doctoral dissertation at the Graduate Theological Union in Berkeley. It has undergone several revisions along the way, and along the way, several people have helped me keep the project on track. I was very fortunate to have had the guidance and advice of Peter R. L. Brown, Robert McAfee Brown, and John T. Noonan, Jr. Their varied religious backgrounds and scholarly interests gave me a broadened perspective from which to see and confront the problems posed in the book, and for this gift of theirs to me, I am truly grateful. Additionally, my debt to Stanley Hauerwas ought to be apparent throughout the book. His comments and suggestions to me, like his writing generally, always seemed to have the ability both to stimulate my mind and touch my heart. Above all, I must thank James McClendon—for his wisdom, for his patience, for himself. He has not only been my teacher and mentor, but he has also been my friend, and in Jim's case, friendship turns out to be one of the world's goods that is truly good after all.

I would also clearly be remiss here if I did not thank my wife, Myrna. Although she does not think of herself as a religious person, she has taught me better than anyone I know about the biblical virtues of steadfastness and fidelity. Her constancy in putting up with me and my frustrations on all those days when nothing seemed to come, her faithfulness in encouraging me despite the disappointments on all those other days when what came wasn't what I wanted, gave me the strength and courage to go on. From the day of our marriage to this day in our marriage, Myrna's presence has continually reminded me of the way God has blessed my life.

And in the last analysis, it is to God I must give thanks for all these people and their help and for keeping me alive, sustaining me, and allowing me to reach this good time.

Michael Goldberg

Shevat 23, 5742
February 16, 1982

Note to reader: In this book, double quotes (" ") are used for all quotations except for quotes within quotes (" ' ' ") and 'scare' quotes.

To my mother

CONTENTS

I

INTRODUCTION:
'PROLOGUE TO THE STORY'

Consider the following statements about the relationship between theology and narrative:

> Narrative or *story* is a means of expression uniquely suited to theology. . . .[1]

> Narrative is a perennial category for understanding better how the grammar of religious convictions is displayed and how the self is formed by those convictions.[2]

> There can be . . . hardly anything that theology needs more than the religious experience that is expressed in the symbols and stories of the people. It needs this heritage very much if it is not to die of hunger because of its own concepts which are so seldom an expression of new religious experience and which so often simply reproduce the expressions of earlier experiences.[3]

11

All of these statements have one thing in common—the claim that the religious convictions which are at the heart of theological reflection depend on narrative for their intelligibility and significance.

That claim is certainly at the core of two recent theological works: *Diving Deep and Surfacing* by the feminist writer Carol P. Christ and *God of the Oppressed* by the black thinker James H. Cone. While Christ argues that women, lacking stories truly expressive of their own experience, have simultaneously lacked an authentic way to understand themselves, the world, and the "great powers" of the universe, Cone maintains that many theological accounts of such themes as oppression, liberation, and God's activity in human life have been inadequate, owing to their failure to attend sufficiently to the biblical stories of the Exodus and the life, death, and resurrection of Jesus Christ. What support do these two theologians bring to justify their assertions, and how strong is it?

One of the important underpinnings for Christ's work comes from the writings of Stephen Crites, who has observed that

> A man's sense of his own identity seems largely determined by the kind of story which he understands himself to have been enacting through the events of his career, the story of his life.[4]

Building on that theoretical foundation, Christ adds:

> Women's stories have not been told. And without stories there is no articulation of experience. . . .

Without stories [a woman] cannot understand herself.
Without stories she is alienated from those deeper
experiences of self and world that have been called
spiritual or religious. . . . The expression of women's
spiritual quest is integrally related to the telling of
women's stories. If women's stories are not told, the
depth of women's souls will not be known.[5]

Christ lays part of the blame for this dearth of women's
stories at the feet of men, who have traditionally been the
storytellers in Western culture. The tales that these men
told tend to cast the male in the role of central character
on whom the action turns and simultaneously to relegate
women to the status of "bit players."[6] In Christ's opinion,
such male-dominated stories, by portraying women,
their lives, and their experiences as significant only in
relationship to the 'more important' activity of men,
imply that in and of themselves, the life experiences of
women contain nothing of value or substance. Additionally, these male-biased stories, through their tendency to
depict freedom in terms of the transcendence of the mind
over the body and the spiritual over the physical, are
largely responsible, in Christ's eyes, for the kind of
philosophical dualism characteristic of Western consciousness and the kind of omnipotent and remote deity
typical of such Western religions as Judaism and
Christianity.[7] If one primary function of stories is to
provide an orientation to the world, then at least so far as
Carol Christ is concerned, the male-centered stories that
women hear can only be profoundly disorienting.

Christ's own prescription for setting things straight

thus becomes virtually self-evident: it is time to attend seriously to the stories *women* tell. In *Diving Deep and Surfacing*, she follows that prescription through an incisive discussion of the stories reflected in the writings of such diverse figures as Kate Chopin, Margaret Atwood, Doris Lessing, Adrienne Rich, and Ntozake Shange. She concludes that stories such as these, arising from an "experience of nothingness," provide a basis for women "awakening" to the "great powers" which are the ground for a new identity and orientation in the world. This awakening, she contends, is capable of overcoming the old dichotomies of reason and emotion, nature and spirit, body and soul, and thus might culminate in

> a new understanding of being human, in which the body is given a more equal footing with the intellect and the human connection to nature is positively valued at the same time that the awesome (but not unlimited) human capacity to manipulate and control nature is recognized.[8]

Christ believes that through the telling and hearing of women's stories and the subsequent reappraisal of their experience, a transformation in attitudes and values would very likely result. She notes, for example, that men's stories usually portray nature as an obstacle to be overcome or as inert matter to be manipulated. By contrast, women's stories, reflecting their experiences of the natural functions of their bodies such as menstruation, childbirth, and menopause, could serve as the basis for a religious outlook which gives such functions positive value, thus leading to renewed reverence for nature and possibly even to solutions to current ecological problems.[9] In that event, with women's stories as their ground, women's spiritual quest and women's social quest would begin to coincide.[10]

And yet as suggestive as Carol Christ's approach appears to be, there seems to be at least one potential stumbling block to this whole 'storied' procedure. In our culture, the word 'story' has become practically synonymous with 'falsehood.' Thus when Christ writes that her work in *Diving Deep and Surfacing* is intended as a "description of a view of reality which emerges through women's spiritual quest [and] not a philosophical justification of it,"[11] the appeal to narrative might appear as a special pleading which seeks to evade questions of truth in theology. But if narrative is indeed the proper setting for displaying "the grammar of religious convictions," both we and Christ have no choice but to ask how the truth—or falsity—of such convictions is to be determined.

Consequently, in turning to James Cone, a natural question for us to ask might be, Is *your* work concerned with this issue of truth as it applies to narrative and theology? And Cone's answer to our question would be an unqualified *yes*. Cone sees one specific set of narratives as normative—those of the Bible—and one particular group of storied experiences as illuminatory—those of black people—and he argues that both Bible stories and stories about blacks serve as reciprocally interpretative keys for gaining a true understanding of God at work in the world. While the biblical narratives of the Exodus and of Jesus

Christ provide the fundamentals for comprehending God's way of liberating the oppressed, the stories of blacks, as for example, their history, their life stories, their folk stories, afford the means of discerning God's revelation and redemptive activity today. Cone maintains that both sets of stories are required for a true perception of reality. He writes:

> It is this affirmation of transcendence that prevents Black Theology from being reduced merely to the cultural history of black people. For black people the transcendent reality is none other than Jesus Christ, of whom Scripture speaks. The Bible is the witness to God's self-disclosure in Jesus Christ. Thus the black experience requires that Scripture be a source of Black Theology. For it was Scripture that enabled slaves to affirm a view of God that differed radically from that of the slave masters.
>
> To know Jesus is to know him as revealed in the struggle of the oppressed for freedom. Their struggle is Jesus' struggle, and he is thus revealed in the particularity of their cultural history—their hopes and dreams of freedom.[12]

For Cone, the stories of the Bible combine with the stories of 'the black experience' to offer an alternative vision to the ultimately distorted and distorting view of reality reflected in the tales told by whites.[13]

Indeed within that false picture of the world, Cone includes much of the theology done by whites. He claims that from Athanasius to Barth, such theology has shown a marked inclination toward a kind of Docetism which abandons the biblical narratives that tell of the life of a human, historical Jesus in favor of a spiritualized, timeless "idea-principle" that fits neatly into some philosophical system. In Cone's view, such a rendering of God's timely activity in our lives is absolutely faithless:

> We cannot have a human Christ unless we have a historical Christ, that is, unless we *know* his history. That is why the writers of the four Gospels tell the good news in the form of the story of Jesus' life. The events described are not intended as fiction but as God's way of changing the course of history in a human person.[14]

Cone equates the theology done by whites with mere ideology designed to preserve white interests and the status quo. He thinks that by spiritualizing and abstracting the gospel message, whites seek to blunt the cutting edge of a Scripture that promises liberation, freedom, and hope. True and truthful Christian theology, claims Cone, is not simply or even primarily a matter of reflection and theory; rather, it is a matter of telling certain stories and then appropriating them in one's own life story:

> If someone asks me, "Jim, how can *you* believe [the claims of Black Theology]? What is the *evidence* of [their] truth?" my reply is quite similar to the testimonies of the Fathers and Mothers of the Black Church: let me tell you a story about a man called Jesus who was born in a stable in Bethlehem. . . .[He] went throughout . . . Galilee preaching that the Kingdom is coming, repent and believe the gospel. The Kingdom is

the new creation where the hungry are fed, the sick
healed, and the oppressed liberated. It is the restoration
of humanity to its wholeness. This man Jesus was killed
because of his threat to the order of injustice. But he was
resurrected as Lord, thereby making good God's
promise to bring freedom to all who are weak and
helpless. . . .

I was told this story by my mother and father. . . .
They told this story as the truth of their lives, the
foundation of their struggle. I came to know this story as
the truth in my own struggle in situations of trouble.
Jesus is now my story, which sustains and holds me
together in struggle. I cannot and have no desire to
"prove" my story. All I can hope or wish to do is to bear
witness to it, as this story leads me to an openness to
other stories. Through this process, I hope to avoid
imprisonment in my own subjectivity and perhaps to
learn how to hear the truth when spoken by others and
to speak the truth when called to give an account of the
hope that is in me (I Pet. 3:15).[15]

But while Cone has at least taken up the issue of truth,
there are other problems which he has failed to confront,
much less resolve. For example, even granting that a
community's convictions presuppose some narrative
from which they have been derived, what ensures that
that derivation has been done using a proper hermeneutic? Some of Cone's own remarks provoke just this sort of
question in a particularly stark and intense way. Though
some theologians have argued that the Christian story
precludes any resort to violence,[16] Cone interprets the
story as leaving that option open:

I contend that every one is violent, and to ask, "Are you nonviolent?" is to accept the oppressors' values. . . .

We repeat: the question is not what Jesus *did*, as if his behavior in first century Palestine were the infallible ethical guide for our actions today. We must ask not what he did, but what he is *doing*—and what he did becomes important only insofar as it points to his activity today. . . . [The] gospel of Jesus means liberation; and one essential element of that liberation is the existential burden of making decisions about human liberation without being completely sure what Jesus did or would do. This is the risk of faith.[17]

Is Cone's interpretation of the story justified? What are the criteria constituting a valid hermeneutic? Almost instinctively, one wants to say that if narratives are to be justifiably employed as the ground and context of our religious convictions, there must be some guarantee that they serve as more than the mere homiletical or ideological 'icing' on our convictional 'cake,' and that furthermore, the ingredients in the batter do not simply depend on the selective taste in texts required by some individual's own particular theological recipe.

Lastly, but perhaps most importantly, there is one more question that we feel compelled to put to both Cone and Carol Christ immediately. If our differing convictional communities do indeed reflect different narrative traditions, are we then faced with the prospect of a vicious relativism which leaves us saying to one another, 'You have your story, and I have mine, and there is no way you can understand or judge mine, nor I yours'? Are we left with the grim possibility of a Carol Christ telling men that they cannot hope to appreciate or evaluate theologies based on women's stories? Or of a James Cone telling whites that a black theology stands impervious to all their challenges and critiques? Unless we can provide some answer to this sort of question as well as to the other questions that we have posed, then whatever promise narrative might hold for theology will prove in reality to be quite empty.

In one way or another, all these questions ask about the legitimacy of using narratives in theological enterprises. Of course, there is one sense in common usage in which to ask about legitimacy is to inquire about lineage and progenitors. While our inquiry into the justifiability of narrative for theology obviously cannot take that sense as primary, neither would we be wise, to dismiss it out of hand as being totally irrelevant to our interests here. Clearly, there is something about the work of Cone and Christ that strikes one as vital and important. But the importance of that something is not simply the result of contemporary political and social movements involving blacks and women. Rather, it's also a reflection of some recent happenings in theology. In trying to answer the critical questions we raised about the proposals put forth by Cone and Christ, we might do well to begin by seeking the roots—the theological ancestors—of those proposals.

In at least one respect, Cone and Christ might be considered the theological heirs to a position taken up a decade earlier by Joseph Fletcher in his book *Situation Ethics*. In that book, Fletcher indirectly appealed to a notion of 'story' by emphasizing that theology and ethics must not be done without first trying to get 'the full story' about the situation confronting us. Like Cone and Christ, Fletcher felt that contemporary ways of doing theology were seriously misguided and that theological systems consisting only of discrete doctrines, principles, and rules radically falsified human experience and robbed religious ethics of their vitality. Since the time of its initial publication, *Situation Ethics* has been analyzed and critiqued several times.[18] Nevertheless, I believe that our reviewing that work once more will prove quite beneficial to our purpose here, for such a review will help us understand more clearly the ground and thrust of the claims set forth by Cone and Christ as well as several writers like them yet to be discussed in this volume, that is, writers who stake out a central place for narrative in the doing of theology. Moreover, if we can trace some of the force behind these recent theological currents to some common theoretical wellsprings such as those found in Fletcher's book, might we not also begin to find that some of the problems in them stem from similar kinds of sources? To consider such problems, however, is to begin to address the larger problem of the justifiability of employing narrative in theology. And *that* is precisely the problem this book intends to confront.

There are many things in Fletcher's work that strike one as basically right. Writing in the mid-1960s, Fletcher was trying to strike a balance between the polarizing slogans of 'Law and order!' and 'If it feels good, do it!'

> A third approach, in between legalism and antinomian unprincipledness, is situation ethics. . . . The situationist enters into every decision-making situation fully

armed with the ethical maxims of his community and its heritage, and he treats them with respect as illuminators of his problems. Just the same he is prepared in any situation to compromise them or set them aside *in the situation* if [some other, more ultimate concern] seems better served by doing so.[19]

Fletcher fights against the idea that doing theology or ethics is solely confined to following rules. At his best, Fletcher is trying to make clear the distinction between being rule-responsible (taking rules as illuminators or general guides for behavior) and being rule-dependent (taking rules as absolute determinants of what *counts* as moral behavior). He is trying to throw in sharp perspective the difference between ethical norms and, e.g., the rules of baseball. John Searle has called rules of these latter sort "constitutive rules." Such rules constitute, create, or define certain practices. Typically, they have the form of "X counts as Y in context C." Hence, for example, a constitutive rule of baseball is: 'Three strikes are an out.' Searle points out that such rules are almost tautological in character.[20] Let us suppose that a batter with two strikes on him takes a big swing at another pitch and misses it. The umpire then cries out, "Strike three! Yer out!" For the batter to turn around at that point and ask the umpire, "Why?" shows in some basic way his failure to understand the practice of striking out (and perhaps of the rest of baseball) as being constituted by these rules. In that event, all the umpire can do—if he is a patient man—is repeat the rule regarding what constitutes a strikeout within the context of the game of baseball. If the batter persists in repeating his question, the umpire may be forced to throw him out of the game because the batter—and his logic—make the playing of the game impossible. At this point, the umpire is like the adult of whom a child keeps asking, "But *why* is a circle round?" The adult generally takes one of two approaches. He keeps answering, "Because that's just the way it *is*." Or, if his patience runs out, he follows the umpire's example, sending the bothersome child away, either to his room or down to the store on an errand.

By contrast, Fletcher argues that no ethical rule is ever so 'self-contained' that it makes no sense to ask of it, "But why?" For Fletcher, the rules of ethics tend to 'point to' values and ideals beyond themselves from which they draw their rationale. Situation ethics, says Fletcher, is "nominalistic":

> In Christian situation ethics nothing is worth anything in and of itself. . . . Persons—God, self, neighbor—are both the subjects and the objects of value; *they* determine it to be of value, and they determine it to be of value for some person's sake. It is a value because somebody decided it was worth something.[21]

Fletcher argues that something has gone wrong when moral rules cease to point beyond themselves but rest content to point only to themselves. Situations entailing moral dilemmas can set things right, can put these rules back in their proper place, for it is precisely within the context of these situations that such rules are shown to be nonabsolute, more open-ended, and hence ultimately *context-dependent*. Only when the rule is made to fit the situation—instead of the other way around—can our moral vision get the facts straight and so present a truthful, realistic picture of the way we do exist and the way we ought to live.

Importantly, Fletcher specifically notes that not everyone comes to the situation alike. One comes not as a 'person-in-general,' empty-headed and empty-handed in terms of his or her identity, but as previously stated, "armed with the ethical maxims of [one's] community and its heritage." Fletcher spends most of his book trying to show what it means to approach a situation from a Christian heritage, from within the Christian community. For a Christian situation ethic to be realized, agape must infuse both one's perspective on the situation as well as the obligations one takes up in that situation. Fletcher justifies this dependence on a love-ethic by arguing that for the Christian, his faith 'colors' his understanding of the situation and what response is most appropriate in it: *"The faith comes first. . . .* The Christian does not understand God in terms of love; he understands love in terms of God as seen in Christ."[22] Whether or not this justification is fully justifiable is not my present concern. What is important to notice, however, is that Fletcher tries to offer a detailed explanation of how a theological approach to a problematic situation might make a difference in resolving it. Thus, he writes:

> Christian situationism is a method that proceeds, so to speak, from (1) its one and only law, *agape* (love), to (2)

the *sophia* (wisdom) of the church and culture, containing many "general rules" of more or less reliability, to (3) the *kairos* (moment of decision, the fullness of time) in which the *responsible self in the situation* decides whether the *sophia* can serve love there, or not.[23]

In summary, Fletcher's position is that theologians must stop looking at doctrines and maxims in the abstract; they must instead try to 'get behind' them; they must try to 'get the full story' of what is happening in the situation in order to apply such doctrines and maxims with any degree of intelligence and significance.

And yet, after getting so much right, Fletcher ends up getting a great deal wrong. He seems unable to follow through on the insightful implications of what he has said, even leaning at times toward a reductionist account.

In the first place, Fletcher implies that the 'true nature' of 'the situation' is the same for everyone—Christian and non-Christian alike. He too readily assumes that 'the facts of the matter' speak for themselves and are simply 'there' waiting to be acted upon. "What is right is revealed in the facts: *Ex factis oritur jus*." Rather gratuitously in passing, Fletcher observes that "if it is true that one's opinions are no better than his facts, then situation ethics puts a high premium on our knowing what's what when we act."[24]

But surely 'what's what' is not just a matter of the facts themselves. Might not one reasonably maintain that an adequate description of the situation requires both 'the facts' as well as an appropriate interpretation of the significance of such facts? An example given by G.E.M. Anscombe[25] will help answer that question:

> A man is pumping water in the cistern which supplies the drinking water of a house. Someone has found a way of systematically contaminating the source with a deadly cumulative poison whose effects are unnoticeable until he can no longer be cured. The house is regularly inhabited by a small group of party chiefs, with their immediate families, who are in control of a great state; they are engaged in exterminating the Jews and perhaps plan a world war. The man who contaminated the source has calculated that if these people are destroyed some good men will get into power who will govern well, or even institute the Kingdom of Heaven on earth and secure a good life for all the people; and he has revealed the calculation, together with the fact about the poison, to the man who is pumping.

Let us ask the following questions about the man who is working the pump: What is this man doing? What is *the* description of his act? Quite rightly, Anscombe responds that *any* description of what is going on which has the man as its subject will in fact be true—e.g., "he is pumping," "he is moving his arms," "he is sweating." But there is another description that is somehow more complete than any of the others. This description of the man's action comes as an answer to the question, *Why* is the man pumping poisoned water into the house? To that question, the man himself might reply, "I'm pumping the water because it's my job, and I get paid for it." Or he might say, "I'm pumping the water out of friendship for

the fellow who hatched this plot; he saved my life once."
Or he might answer, "I'm pumping the water in order to
kill all those fascists inside." Such answers tell us not only
that the man is moving the pump handle up and down,
and thus pumping the water, but more importantly, they
tell us of the significance of the man's action, i.e., the
intention and meaning with which the act was done. And
it's precisely on the basis of such interpretation of the
facts—on the basis of such description—that one comes to
see the background context in the light of which action is
taken. Such interpretation is what enables us to take the
random, isolated bits of data and fit them together so as to
give us the possibility of talking about 'the situation
before us' in the first place. Surely, we would expect
Fletcher to be among the last to deny the importance of
the way that facts are interpreted in any description of a
situation; clearly, the description of a situation can
radically affect our response to it.

Yet surprisingly, Fletcher fails to grasp this notion in
certain crucial ways. When confronted with the question,
"Is adultery wrong?" he can only reply, "I don't know.
Maybe. Give me a case. . . . You are using words,
abstractions."[26] But that's exactly the point! The words *do*
matter; the ways in which we use our language to describe
what is happening is critically decisive. Those who have
substituted the words 'open marriage' for 'adultery' have
understood that point far better than Fletcher. In fact,
the kinds of extraordinary and dilemma-laden situations
which Fletcher exploits only arise because we do have
and use words like 'adulterer.' As Stanley Hauerwas has
perceptively seen,

It is one thing to attempt to limit the applicability of certain of our moral notions, but it is another thing entirely to try to say that a moral notion is rendered meaningless in the light of the unique situation. Rather it is apparent that examples of extraordinary situations can be delineated only within the context of moral notions. This is not to say that the way in which the situation is understood necessarily dictates the decision that the agent must make, it still must be his decision. However, the significance of our moral notions is not denied by such situations, for without such notions it is impossible to think of the situation as being extraordinary.[27]

Because of his assumption that 'the facts speak for themselves,' Fletcher cannot and does not take seriously the differences between persons caught in such extraordinary situations. Given his remarks about the important role that agape has to play in Christian situation ethics, Fletcher should have been able to avoid this problem. In the same sentence, we find Fletcher asserting that the actions of "a Father Damien on Molokai, a kamikaze pilot, a patriot hiding in a Boston attic in 1775, or a Viet Cong terriorist walking into a Saigon officers' mess as he pulls the pin of a bomb hidden under his coat" are all examples of agape.[28] Apparently, Fletcher would have us believe that all of these different actions reflect a self-sacrificing love for the other. But is that a true and faithful description of, for example, the kamikaze pilot's action? Fletcher has previously stated that the notion of *agape* has its paradigmatic locus and gets its moral significance *in the context of the story* of the life, death, and resurrection of Christ. But is that the story of the kamikaze pilot? More likely, the pilot's moral notions gain their significance from within the context of the story of the samurai warrior whose duty is defending both his liege lord and his own honor and 'face' even at the cost of his own life. Thus, to use the word 'agape' to refer to the pilot's actions might be to misuse the word, and worse, to falsify the actions and moral justifications of those actions as the pilot himself might understand and describe them. Ironically, Fletcher, for all his raillery against a rule-governed deontological ethic that fails to take seriously the differences between persons, nevertheless ends up doing much the same thing himself.

Moreover, not only does Fletcher fail to take seriously the differences between 'the Christian story' and the stories of other people, in the last analysis, he doesn't take the Christian story very seriously either. His way of acting on and acting out the Christian story with its 'agapeic ethic' finds its origin in the utilitarianism of Bentham and Mill; he merely substitutes an 'agapeic calculus' for their calculus of hedonism:

> Justice is love coping with situations where distribution is called for. On this basis it becomes plain that as the love ethic searches seriously for a social policy it must form a coalition with utilitarianism. It takes over from Bentham and Mill the strategic principle of "the greatest good for the greatest number.". . .
>
> Observe that this is a genuine coalition, even though it reshapes the "good" of the utilitarians, replacing their pleasure principle with *agape*. In the coalition the hedonistic calculus becomes the agapeic calculus, the

> greatest amount of neighbor welfare for the largest
> number of neighbors possible.[29]

The 'new math' of Fletcher's agapeic calculus works like
this:

> Self-concern is obligated to cancel neighbor-good
> whenever *more* neighbor-good will be served through
> serving the self. The self is to be served rather than any
> neighbor if *many* neighbors are served through serving
> the self. . . . We do not prefer one neighbor to another,
> but we *do* prefer the neighbor whose need is greater,
> and we prefer to serve *more* neighbors rather than
> fewer.[30]

Yet it is utterly mystifying how this kind of 'calculation'
comes out of or even reflects love understood as "God
seen in Christ." Instead, this method seems to be the
antithesis of such a vision! Hence, while in regard to its
refusal to take the differences between persons seriously,
situation ethics seems like a version of deontological
ethics, in regard to its emphasis on the importance of
counting heads, situation ethics curiously appears to be a
variation of utilitarianism.

I suspect that situation ethics, deontological ethics, and
utilitarian ethics share so much in common because they
ultimately share the same focus of ethical attention: the
decision that is to be made. Fletcher writes:

> The focus of this "new morality" . . . is clearly focused
> upon *decision*. . . .
>   Life itself, in fact, is decision. . . .

> Existence not only demands decisions, it *is* decision.
> Staying alive demands a decision, and committing
> suicide demands a decision.[31]

While the first claim of this trio is true, the last two are surely false. Although it may be true that *at times* we choose to stay alive, none of us ever chose to be made alive, to be born in the first place, and most of us go through life without ever choosing, but simply living. The point here is not merely biological; it is also logical— being is logically prior to deciding, choosing, and acting. The problem that runs through all decisionist versions of ethics, be they deontological, utilitarian, or situationist, is that they all tend to falsify the reality of our lives as moral agents by breaking up that ongoing, historical existence into discrete, unrelated parcels of dramatic moments called 'The Great Quandary That Must Be Solved!' For as Edmund Pincoffs has made clear, there is something pathological about the kind of person who would make everything in life into some kind of dilemma.[32] Additionally, we tend to show ourselves as the people we characteristically are either in those moments when we feel compelled to act in a certain way ("I *had* to do it—I had no choice; here I stand, I can do no other"), or as we display our character through the life story that we develop through time.

The notion of self is central to any theory of ethics, but it is exactly that notion which Fletcher, like other decisionists, leaves unexamined. He says that "[the] very first question in all ethics is, *What* do I want?"[33] But again, as Pincoffs has observed, there are other questions more basic than that one, questions which that one presupposes.[34] What does it mean to be an 'I,' a self existing in and over time? What is it that makes me the 'I' who I distinctively am, the 'I' who no one else can be? The answers to questions such as these go into what makes up 'the situation.' The 'I' who I am is part of 'the situation.' As even Hume realized, the self does not exist as a mere bundle of atomistic experiences. It is the integration of these experiences through time which enables us to talk about the development of a person with his own distinct moral character. He comes to every situation with a past; in turn, each new situation may help shape his moral vision and action in the future. Certainly, it is this very type of idea that is at the heart of the theories of Cone and Christ, namely, that some story is needed to give a person's life experiences coherence and continuity over time—else there can be only the experience of nothingness.

Now Fletcher later does admit that before the question, What ought I do? can be rightly asked, other questions must be appropriately answered. He writes that for the Christian, "before we ask the ethical question, 'What shall I do?' comes the *pre*ethical questions, 'What has God done?' "[35] In a sense, by asking this question, Fletcher is touching on something very important, for implicit within that question is the recognition that before one responds to any situation, one must first understand how the situation is set up, what options the situation really holds out to one.

For Fletcher to appeal to what God has done is

implicitly to invoke some notion about the way the world is as a result of God's action, the way that a human being is in such a world as this, together with some idea about what world and human being can and cannot become. Here, clearly, we are talking about the situation writ large. How is life set up? What are the options that reality holds out? Different answers to these questions reflect different visions of reality and life and thus serve as the impetus to the different ways of life embodied by, e.g., the committed Christian or the secular humanist. By contrast, Fletcher, due to his concentration on disconnected and isolated situations and decisions, is unable to provide any adequate account of what it means to be a human self living in the world, developing through time, displaying a distinct moral character.[36]

To state matters more succinctly, Fletcher's work stumbles because it lacks any explicit category of narrative which can generate and tie together such diverse elements as these, crucial to both theology and ethics. Although situation ethics does show the importance of attending to the background contexts against which theology and theological ethics are done, it stops short of realizing the full implications of its method. While it is always helpful to ask about *the* situation currently before one, religious traditions (as well as other types of traditions, e.g., political ones) have typically not been content to stop with that particular question alone. Instead, they have tended to ask the larger question, a question which they see this more particular question as presupposing, namely, What is the situation of being a human being in this world? The thinkers whose work we will examine in this study make the central claim that some sort of narrative is required to answer just that sort of question.

In conclusion, one might say of *Situation Ethics* that though it is 'on the way' to showing the importance of narrative for theology, it fails to go far enough on the path demonstrating the justifiability of employing narrative for theological purposes. It is that path which I intend to pursue throughout the remainder of this book.

Earlier I said that the shared central contention among those who claim a necessary relationship between theology and narrative is that the religious convictions which are at the heart of theological reflection depend on narrative for their intelligibility and significance. Now after seeing how the work of Fletcher, Cone, and Christ in one way or another reflects that claim, it is time to analyze that assertion more closely. How is it to be understood? But then, what is meant by conviction? By theology? By narrative? As a starting point, we might, following James Wm. McClendon, Jr., and James M. Smith in their book *Understanding Religious Convictions*, not unreasonably characterize convictions as being those kinds of persistent beliefs that a person or community holding them cannot easily relinquish without becoming a significantly different person or community.[37] Consequently, though there are many ways of describing theology,[38] a sufficiently broad (and non-persuasive) working definition might characterize that discipline as the elucidation, examination, and transformation of the religious convictions of some given community.[39] Similarly, as there are many ways of describing narrative, generally speaking, we might say that a narrative is the telling of a story[40] whose meaning unfolds through the interplay of characters and actions over time. Therefore, drawing each of these elements into a single statement, we can now declare that the primary claim of a 'narrative theologian' is that in order justifiably to elucidate, examine, and transform those deeply held religious beliefs that make a community what it is, one must necessarily show regard for and give heed to those linguistic structures which, through their portrayal of the contingent interaction between persons and events, constitute the source and ground of such beliefs. In short, the fundamental contention is that an adequate theology must attend to narrative.

There are, however, a number of ways that contention can be misunderstood. It is not, for instance, the assertion that the systematic theological task must itself be done in story form, as though discursive reasoning and expository writing were now to be abandoned. Rather, it is the claim that a theologian, regardless of the propositional statements he or she may have to make about a community's convictions, must consciously and continuously strive to keep those statements in intimate contact with the narratives which gave rise to those convictions, within which they gain their sense and meaning, and *from which they have been abstracted*.[41]

Nor is the contention of those who argue for the primacy of narrative for theology simply that since as Jews and Christians, for example, we learn about God through stories, we must therefore remain attentive to narrative forms if we are to maintain our credentials as 'theolo-

gians-in-good-standing.' Instead, it is the much stronger
view that virtually all of our convictions, nonreligious as
well as religious, are rooted in some narrative, and that
frequently, our more serious disputes with one another
reflect rival narrative accounts.[42] A theology to which this
kind of idea is central I shall call a 'narrative theology.'

But as we saw above, several questions come
immediately to mind. In an age which tends to think of
stories as prescientific (and unscientific) ways of accounting for our experience, how can anyone hope to base the
truth of his or her convictions on such apparently shaky
ground? Additionally, in a culture in which hermeneutics
have been conditioned by both historical and literary
criticism, how can anyone be so seemingly naive as to
found his or her theological proposals on *the* meaning' of
some particular story or group of stories? Finally, at a
time when we find ourselves increasingly beset by rapidly
multiplying and frequently conflicting ideologies,
theories, and schools, how can anyone in good conscience
invoke the notion of story, a notion which at least initially
might suggest the theological *bête noire* of subjectivism,
relativism, and perspectivism? Obviously then, at the
very outset of our work here, we have no choice but to ask
the question, How can a narrative theology be justified?

This book attempts to map out a strategy for answering
that question by coherently and critically exploring the
different ways that different types of narrative have
recently been used in theology.[43] This chapter began the
discussion with an examination of the 'contextualist'
Joseph Fletcher who, though justifiably stressing the
importance of looking at the wider background within

which theology occurs and against which theological
ethics takes place, nevertheless fails to focus adequately
on the narrative settings which give our theological and
moral notions their meaning and significance. In chapter
2, I will point out the need to distinguish carefully among
the different genres of narrative (e.g., fable, myth,
history) if these are to be properly employed theologically. Through an analysis of the work of R. B.
Braithwaite, John Dunne, and W. Taylor Stevenson, the
chapter will show what sorts of mistakes a theologian can
make by failing to pay sufficient attention to these various
narrative kinds—and to the type of claim and meaning
that each one bears. The third and fourth chapters take up
an investigation of the truth of narratives by looking at two
genres of narrative which distinctly and distinctively
make claims to being true: biography and autobiography.
Chapter 3 presents and appraises the theses of such
authors as James McClendon and James Fowler, who
consider the implications of life stories for theology.
Chapter 4 goes on to discuss the autobiographical
writings of Will Campbell and Elie Wiesel to illuminate
the ways that the truth—and truthfulness—of stories
such as these might be challenged and assessed.
Moreover, it also describes the ways the stories of such
individuals can in turn provide challenges and assessments of the stories of the larger religious communities
from which both the individuals and their stories spring.
The fifth chapter analyzes the views of several writers
who have expressly appropriated biblical narratives as the
basis for their theological proposals. Stories such as these
I term "paradigmatic narratives," for they claim not only

to *be true* accounts of what has happened in the past, but they also claim the capacity to *ring true* to common aspects of human experience, thus being paradigms of our existence which can sustain and transform that existence now and in the future. In some basic sense, paradigmatic stories say to us, 'This is what has happened so far, and hence, this is how you ought go on from here.' In that regard, these paradigmatic narratives have both a descriptive and a prescriptive dimension. Yet this is but to raise anew the issues of meaning, truth, and rationality which any narrative theology must address if it is to have any hope of being justified. Therefore, speaking to these issues becomes the explicit task of chapter 6. The study ends with chapter 7 which reviews and summarizes its findings.

Without doubt, this procedural map may appear to set us on a long, arduous, and somewhat twisted path. But if we are to reach an understanding of how a narrative theology can be justified, it is a path we have to follow just as there are stories whose twists and turns we have to follow if we are to come to appreciate what they have to say. To be sure, there are some stories—and studies—where a person is justified in saying, "Skip all that! Just get to the point!" However, there are other stories and studies in which a justifiable response to that demand is, "Sorry, but there is no way 'the point' can be extracted from the work; it *is* the work. Hence, you must read through and work through this piece for yourself."

And so it is for our work here.

II

'TELL ME A STORY':
FABLE AND MYTH

Nowadays, for many, the word 'story' connotes something fictitious, something not to be taken seriously, something which serves as an aid to the intellectually unsophisticated, who, had they sufficient powers of discursive reasoning, could simply dispense with these figurative ways of presenting abstract ideas. We are all familiar with phrases like 'the point of the story' and 'just a story' which seem to reflect such attitudes as these.[1]

Not surprisingly, religious narratives in particular are viewed in this light. Typically, such narratives have been taken to be fables or myths. As such, these stories supposedly have the function of making some point or of providing some moral, or of offering some prescientific or some pseudoscientific explanation of some state of affairs. In any event, these stories *as* stories have no valid meaning in and of and by themselves. As fables, once they have made their 'point,' they can be discarded; as myths, once they have been shown to be wrong by science, they must be discarded.

However, in this chapter, I intend to show that such an understanding of the nature and meaning of religious narratives is at best superficial and misleading. A study of the work of a number of writers will demonstrate that such an understanding—or rather, misunderstanding—comes from paying insufficient attention to the many different kinds of religious narrative as well as from a failure to use certain key terms such as 'myth' with any degree of precision. Moreover, this chapter will begin to take a look at the claims of other writers who contend that there are certain kinds of religious narratives whose meaning lies in the story itself, whose meaning cannot be gotten any other way than in and through the story, and whose ultimate meaning depends on whether or not the story is true. What kinds of stories these might be, and in what sense such stories can be said to be true are questions that will continue to demand attention in the chapters yet to come.

FABLE

A paradigmatic use of religious narrative as fable is displayed by Richard Bevan Braithwaite in his Eddington Lecture published as *An Empiricist's View of the Nature of Religious Belief*. For Braithwaite, "the meaning of a religious assertion is given by its use in expressing the asserter's intention to follow a specified policy of behaviour." Thus, the assertion by a Christian that "God is love" is not to be understood as referring to the Deity or to be making any claim about the nature of the Deity; rather, that statement refers to the intention of the person uttering it to live "agapeistically." But if a moral assertion also indicates an intention to follow a certain policy of behavior, what then distinguishes a religious assertion from a purely moral one? The answer, says Braithwaite, lies in the fact that religious assertions "refer to a story as well as to an intention."[2] And ultimately, these stories are the things which distinguish the adherents of one religious tradition from those of another. For Braithwaite, the really important difference between an agapeistically policied Christian and an agapeistically policied Jew is that although each is committed to the same behavior policy, such a policy is nevertheless associated with the "thinking of different stories":

> On the assumption that the ways of life advocated by Christianity and Buddhism are essentially the same, it will be the fact that the intention to follow this way of life is associated in the mind of a Christian with thinking of one set of stories (the Christian stories) while it is associated in the mind of a Buddhist with thinking of another set of stories (the Buddhist stories) which enables a Chrisian assertion to be distinguished from a Buddhist one.[3]

Now these stories do not justify the religious man's assertions, either logically or empirically. Instead, theirs is a psychological and causal connection. The only empirical claim that can be made about such stories is that "many people find it easier to resolve upon and to carry through a course of actions which is contrary to their natural inclinations if this policy is associated in their minds with certain stories."[4] Thus, in Braithwaite's view, were people made of 'sterner stuff,' the need for such stories as psychological supports would disappear. According to Braithwaite, in the last analysis, asking about the truth of a religious story involves no more than inquring about the sincerity of the intention of the one who 'entertains' such a story to follow some prescribed course of action.

Braithwaite's account of religious narrative in particular and of religious language in general is a reductionist account if there ever was one, and the reductionism operates on several different levels. First, as several of his critics have pointed out,[5] Braithwaite 'proves' his theory of religious language by taking one example of a religious utterance particularly well-suited to his purpose: "God is love." He claims that a Christian's utterance of this statement is correctly understood as being an expression of that Christian's intention to act in a loving manner. The utterance has no meaning other than this expression of intention, which Braithwaite calls the "conative" force of the utterance. Yet by focusing exclusively on the conative element, Braithwaite fails to account for a great many of the other kinds of utterances that religious speakers make, utterances whose conative force is not so clear. When the Buddhist mystic asserts, "There is nothing," one wonders what kind of intention such an assertion indicates. Or alternatively, when the children of Israel, after having crossed the Sea of Reeds, are described as exclaiming, "The Lord will reign forever and ever," one feels compelled to ask Braithwaite if they, too, were declaring their intent to reign forever. Certainly, the narrative context within which that exclamation occurs gives no support for such an interpretation. Yet Braithwaite takes no notice of the differing contexts within which texts like this occur. Consequently, he is caught in a vicious circle. Failing to take different contexts into consideration, he fails to take account of the different kinds of religious language; failing to take account of the different kinds of religious utterance, he is led to say that every religious utterance, made by any religious speaker, does the same work—i.e., declaring intentions—regardless of the context in which it is made.

Second, Braithwaite shows himself to be the reductionist that he is in his previously cited remarks about the Jew, the Christian, and the Buddhist, namely, that although each may tell a different story, all the stories, in the end, reinforce a single way of life. When Braithwaite comes to that conclusion "on the assumption that the ways of life advocated by Christianity and by Buddhism are essentially the same," one wants to know what justifies his assuming this. Moreover while Braithwaite may glibly remark that an "agapeistically policed Jew" is one who thinks of some Jewish (as opposed to Christian) story of agape, interestingly and importantly, he never gives an example of such a story. In fact, one might reasonably argue that for a Jew to act according to an agapeistic ethic, as that ethic is most *paradigmatically displayed through the Christian story*, would be for a Jew, practically speaking, to cease to be a Jew and to become a Christian instead.

Braithwaite does not and indeed cannot respond to

such a challenge because of the secondary, tangential role he gives to religious stories. If the stories are just so much excess baggage to be thrown off once one's train of thought and action properly gets rolling, then so, too, one's religious convictions ought to be left behind at the first available moment, for after all, the only thing that distinguishes a religious conviction from a purely moral one is some super-added—and ultimately superfluous—story. In Braithwaite's theory, both religious stories and religious convictions end up being nonessential elements of one's identity and one's sense of self as a moral agent. The logical conclusion of that theory is that in the end, Jews and Christians should give up those unessential stories that they tell, and instead become just plain old 'human beings' who follow the same basic *moral* way of life that all human beings ought to follow, a way of life that can be generally characterized as an "agapeistically policed" one. And after all, this is precisely what happens with a fable: one hears it, gets the moral, then throws the story away.

Now even if admittedly some religious stories can be characterized as fables (e.g., Nathan's story to David in II Sam. 12), one would be wrong to describe all religious stories as fables. In part, this is why there is something very odd about a statement like the following one by John Dunne: "The moral of the life of Jesus . . . would be 'Love one another as I have loved you.' "[6] We do not usually refer to or think of life stories as having a moral. Furthermore, one might say with Stanley Hauerwas that the story of Jesus does not 'have' a moral or a social ethic, but that instead "the story of Jesus *is* a social ethic."[7] That ethic is embodied in and exhibited through the story of Jesus and cannot be understood or acted out apart from that story. According to this theory of the role of religious narrative, there is simply no getting around the story; instead, in terms of the story's meaning for one's 'behavior policy,' one must go through the story and hope that the story goes through oneself in kind.

Similarly, the case could be made that a uniquely Jewish ethic is displayed most authentically in and through the narrative of the Exodus. That story reaches its climax at Sinai when the People enters into a covenant with God and assumes certain covenantal obligations as a result. What is important to notice here (and what accounts like Braithwaite's cannot even begin to notice) is that the assumption of such obligations, the adoption of a "covenantally policied" life, occurs within the context of a particular narrative. And it is this particular narrative that gives many of these obligations as well as the people who assumes them their own particularity and distinctive character. Indeed, the reason that so many "rationalist" or "universalist" commentators (both Jewish and non-Jewish) have had such difficulty in making sense out of a number of the 'ritual'—as opposed to 'moral'—commandments (their distinction; not the Bible's), lies in their not taking the story seriously and treating it as some kind of superfable which can be tossed aside as transcended once one has gotten its 'point.' Contrary to what reductionism like Braithwaite's may have to say on the matter, different religious stories can and often do themselves entail differences in policies or in ways of life that simply cannot be glossed over.

Lastly, Braithwaite shows himself to be a reductionist in his indifference to the many different genres displayed in religious narratives:

> What I am calling a *story* Matthew Arnold called a *parable* and a *fairy-tale*. Other terms which might be used are *allegory, fable, tale, myth*. I have chosen the word "story" as being the most neutral term, implying neither that the story is believed nor that it is disbelieved.[8]

But to use the word 'story' in such an uncritical, generalized, and all-encompassing way to embrace all the various types of narrative found within religious traditions is surely to render the term virtually useless for the purpose of making important, indeed vital, distinctions. Although all the terms that Braithwaite uses in the passage above may fall into the category of story, nevertheless, both logically and literarily speaking, there is still a good deal of dissimilarity among them. For example, Sallie McFague offers an important distinction between parable and allegory: "A parable is an extended metaphor. A parable is not an allegory, where the meaning is extrinsic to the story. . . . Rather, as an extended metaphor, the meaning is found only *within* the story itself although it is not exhausted *by* that story."[9] Furthermore, for certain religious narratives, despite what Braithwaite would have one believe, these logical and literary distinctions are critical. For instance, part of the reason from a literary point of view that the story of the Exodus and the story of Jesus have historically gotten such a hold on people rests in those stories' *not* being fables or allegories. They are not the kinds of stories to which one can rightly say, "Hurry up. Just get to the point." To say it may be an indication that one missed the point, missed the meaning of these stories, and mistook them for poorly constructed and simpleminded stories whose meaning is incidental and extrinsic to them, stories which one need not hear to the end in order to catch the meaning. But surely, one misses the meaning of the story of Christ if one fails to hear it through to the end, and for a Jew, where is the end of the story of the Exodus?

The logical difference between those two stories and other kinds of stories such as fables or allegories owes something to this literary difference. Although Braith-waite contends that "it is not necessary . . . for the asserter of a religious assertion to believe in the truth of the story involved in the assertions,"[10] the Exodus story and the story of Christ carry with them the claim that they are in some basic way essentially true. This truth claim is what partially justifies these stories' putting a claim in turn on those who hear them, for these stories say, "Live your life according to me. Base your life policy—your life story—on this story, for insofar as this story is a true one, it offers a credible basis for the adoption of such a policy and story in your life." Historically, Jews and Christians have adopted certain policies of behavior, certain ways of life, because they have staked their lives on the truth of their respective stories, of their respective stories *and no other*. Braithwaite's analysis simply ignores this fact, and given his reductionist tendencies, it is not hard to see why.

MYTH

While Braithwaite is among those who have mistakenly thought of all religious narratives as being mere fables, there are many other people today, who in one way or another, have classified them all together under the rubric of 'myth.' While Braithwaite maintained that the truth of such stories could be believed or disbelieved, many of those who categorize the stories as myths want to say that the stories are false *by definition*. At best, as myths, the stories can only reflect some kind of preconscious understanding of reality. Thus, they can be said to 'ring true' to something basic and primitive in each human being. But in no way can they be said to *be* true. They are, in the end, *only* stories.

But such an analysis is itself untrue. Like Braithwaite's analysis, this one, too, fails to take into account the many kinds of religious narrative and the important differences among them. In particular, however, this kind of analysis shows a profound misunderstanding of the nature of myth, and to the extent that it misunderstands that, it is also unable to keep clear about the essential differences between the myths of archaic lore and other stories such as the narratives of the Bible.

Here again, showing how a reductionist account goes wrong may offer the best way to begin to bring home this point. As mentioned, some writers are willing to grant to myths some kind of validity. They do not say that myths are merely fanciful or fictitious tales with absolutely no basis in reality. Instead, they claim that myths do refer to a reality of sorts—the reality of the structure of the human psyche and its way of ordering experience. The work of John Dunne, which in turn relies heavily on the work of C. G. Jung, provides a good example of this line of thought. Dunne believes that one's ablty to see correctly the relationship between himself and the world depends on his ablty to "pass over" to a different standpoint; he is then in a position to come back "enriched to [his] own standpoint and to a new understanding of [his] own life, . . . an understanding of [his] own life which can guide [him] into the future."[11] Dunne attributes the theoretical justification of his notion of "passing over" to Jung:

> The reason it just might work is the process of what Jung called "individuation." According to his idea there is a natural process of development which takes place as a man goes from childhood to youth to manhood to old age, a process which goes on independently of whether or not the man himself understands what is taking place.[12]

Dunne calls this story of a man's development within the world, this story of a man's relationship to the world, a man's "myth."[13] Because of the commonality of all human development experience, Dunne claims that not only is there the possibility of passing over, but also that that possibility entails the idea that "each man is somehow all men, that each life is somehow all lives." In coming to understand this idea, a man comes to see that it is as though he "had passed over to all lives and all times."[14]

The implications of Dunne's theory for religious narratives are enormous:

> El, Yahweh, Abba, ar-Rahman, Allah, and the like are
> names which in their context signify what God is or was
> to a given epoch or people, and . . . it would be
> fallacious to single out one of these names and the
> relationship it signifies as the only true one to the
> exclusion of the others. . . . *As it stands therefore, it is
> possible to speak of El, Yahweh, Abba, ar-Rahman,
> Allah and the like as though they were all names for one
> and the same God.* . . . What we are getting at here is a
> way of understanding *the convergence of the religions
> which is taking place or may be taking place in our
> time.*[15]

Now on a more skeptical view of things, one might say
that the events taking place in our time seem to be
showing just the opposite! They seem to be pointing to a
divergence rather than to a convergence of religious
belief. For example, the resurgence of a militant Islam
which is ready to take on Western culture together with
its Jewish and Christian underpinnings certainly must
count against Dunne's contention. As for Dunne's other
assertion, namely that El, Yahweh, Abba, ar-Rahman and
Allah are "all names for one and the same God," although
each of these names may be in some way linked to the
others from the perspective of the history of religion, it is
by no means clear that each successive religious tradition
maintained an identical or even similar conception of the
deity as the tradition that preceded it. That was precisely
the point at issue between Judaism and Christianity in the
first century. While the church claimed that the God of
Israel had manifested himself in Jesus, Judaism saw that
claim—that conception—as a radical distortion of its own

understanding of the Lord. More than that, it saw such a conception as being incommensurate with its own. But Dunne, like Braithwaite, cannot see that, cannot even take such differences into account, because being every bit as much a reductionist as Braithwaite (and perhaps being even more of a reductionist since his reductionism has an explicit theoretical basis), Dunne thinks of religious stories as being so much window dressing for the common human psyche which they frame.

Finally, even if we grant some degree of validity to the kind of psychological reductionism that the writing of Dunne and Jung (and even of Freud, though in a different way) seems to advocate we need not necessarily come to the same conclusions. For example, Mircea Eliade, whose work in the field of the meaning of myth and mythic structures has served as the bench mark for all others, observes: "For psychoanalysis . . . the truly primordial is the 'human primordial,' earliest childhood. The child lives in a mythical, paradisal time." In a footnote to this remark, Eliade explains that "[this] is why the unconscious displays the structure of a private mythology. We can go even further and say not only that the unconscious is 'mythological' but also that some of its contents carry cosmic values; in other words, that they reflect the modalities, processes, and destiny of life and living matter."[16] Yet after having said these things about the relationship between myth and the unconscious, and after having granted that psychoanalysis creates the possibility of an individual's returning to "the Time of the origin" (as compared with archaic societies which allow for only a collective return to that time), Eliade quickly adds the vital qualifier that not all myths and rites of return are on the same plane of meaning: "To be sure, the symbolism is the same; but the contexts differ, and it is the intention shown by the context that gives us the true meaning in each case."[17] But these contexts—the narratives which are told, heard, and spelled out in ritual acts—are exactly the things that the reductionist ignores, which indeed he must ignore for his theory to hold. While it may be true to say that the great myths and other great religious narratives ring true to life, it is quite another thing to say that every narrative rings true to every life. This very thing in part accounts for one's belonging to one religious tradition rather than to another, for committing one's life to one religious narrative rather than to another.

Eliade's research into the nature and meaning of myth has many other significant implications for our analysis. Although many people currently use the words 'myth' and 'fiction' as being virtually synonymous, Eliade makes it quite clear that things were not always so. In societies in which myths still lived and resonated with and in the lives of those who heard them and took them to heart, people were careful to distinguish *the myths*, which were considered to be *true stories*, from the *fables* and *tales*, which were thought of as *false stories*. While within any one archaic society such myths were considered to be absolutely true, between different societies, opposing views might be held regarding what could rightly be called 'a myth,' i.e., an unqualifiedly true story, and what ought to be properly regarded only as a 'tale,' i.e., a false story.[18]

At first glance, one might suppose that Eliade's comments about the truth-claims of myths could easily be utilized as a means of supporting the truth-claims of a great number of religious narratives, such as those basic ones of the Bible upon which Judaism and Christianity are primarily founded. Whereas before, some people might have been led to think of these stories as being myths, in the sense of being mere fictions and falsehoods, *post*-Eliade, a 'defender' of these stories could turn and say, "Myths these stories are indeed, and *as myths* they are absolutely true! What's more, you, who have used your scientific method and your historical critiques to dismiss such narratives as being 'mere myths,' must realize that such scientific and historical thinking is itself a reflection of a basically mythic mode of thought, for insofar as you have believed scientific and historical critical method to set the ultimate standards of truth, you have shown yourself to be participating in a great myth of your own!" Such is in fact and in short the twist given Eliade's research by W. Taylor Stevenson.

Indeed, Eliade's research into the formal qualities of myth provides Stevenson with his starting point. These formal criteria consist of: (1) the story's constituting the History of the acts of the Supernaturals, (2) this History's being considered to be absolutely true and sacred, (3) the story's being concerned with a paradigmatic instance of creation, (4) the fact that the story's being known enables one to know the origins of things and thus enables one to control them, and (5) the story's possessing the ability to 'seize' the hearer such that he becomes caught up in the power of the events recalled or reenacted in such a way as to be able to 'live' the myth.[19] Stevenson, after having noted this structural outline, concludes: "We believe that what is often called 'historical consciousness' conforms essentially to what Eliade calls 'myth,' and consequently we may assert that history is a mythic way of viewing reality." A little later on, he adds: "This formal definition of myth fits the Christian Kerygma perfectly."[20]

But Stevenson's conclusions are drawn from both a superficial and distorted reading of Eliade's work. Part of Stevenson's problem lies in his failure to pay close enough attention to Eliade's usage of the word 'history,' a usage that enables Eliade to make clear-cut and important distinctions between those religious narratives that can be characterized as myths and others that cannot be so classified. For instance, at the very outset of one of his seminal works, *The Myth of the Eternal Return*, he clearly contrasts mythic thinking with historical consciousness: "The chief difference between the man of the archaic and traditional societies and the man of the modern societies with their *strong imprint of Judaeo-Christianity* lies in the fact that the former feels himself indissolubly connected with the Cosmos and the cosmic rhythms, whereas the latter insists that he is connected only with history."[21] Of course, says Eliade, the "archaic man" believes that the Cosmos too has "a history," if for no other reason than that it has been created and organized by either supernatural deities or heroic ancestors. However, the crucial difference between this kind of "history," transmitted through the myths, and the

"History" spoken of by "Judaeo-Christianity" and modern man is that the history of the Cosmos

> is a "history" that can be repeated indefinitely, in the sense that the myths serve as models for ceremonies that periodically reactualize the tremendous events that occurred at the beginning of time. The myths preserve and transmit the paradigms, the exemplary models, for all the responsible activities in which men engage.[22]

Eliade concludes this passage by straightforwardly stating, "It is not difficult to understand why such an ideology makes it impossible that what we today call a 'historical consciousness' should develop." Mythic thinking which views reality in terms of infinitely repeatable cycles stands firmly opposed to historical consciousness which sees the truth of existence in the light of development, evolution, and change.

The differences between mythic thinking and historical consciousness are present according to Eliade on other levels as well. In myth, ordinary everyday profane time is without meaning; meaning can be found only in the repetition of archetypal gestures made originally by supernatural beings or heroic ancestors "before" time. The reality to which the myth appeals is one that stands in stark contrast to the "unrealities" of the profane world. "In the last analysis, the latter does not constitute a 'world,' properly speaking; it is the 'unreal' *par excellence*." However, in the case of historical consciousness, just the opposite is true. Historical consciousness is what it is precisely to the extent that it finds meaning in

the unique, the new, and the irreversible. As Eliade
points out, it is for this very reason that the gaining of a
historical consciousness is a fairly recent development in
the story of humankind, a development against which
"archaic humanity defended itself to the utmost of its
powers."[23]

Moreover, as historical consciousness initially manifests itself among the Israelite writers of the Bible, one
finds "for the first time . . . affirmed, and increasingly
accepted, the idea that historical events have a value in
themselves, insofar as they are determined by the will of
God. This God of the Jewish people is no longer an
Oriental divinity, creator of archetypal gestures, but
[one] who reveals his will through events."[24] For both
Judaism and Christianity, ordinary, profane time is real,
and it is real precisely because it—rather than some other
"Great Time" which transcends it—is the locus (and
focus) of redemption and meaning.[25] Whereas "the
primitive lives in a continual present," man, according to
the biblical narratives, is an historical being, whose
historical past and whose memory of that past both have
meaning.[26] In fact, these differing attitudes between
classical myth and biblical narrative regarding the
meaning of time are even reflected in differences of
literary style. Erich Auerbach remarks that while the
Homeric epic "takes place in the foreground—that is, in a
local and temporal present which is absolute," by
contrast, one finds that Abraham's actions, for example,
"are explained not only by what is happening to him at the
moment, nor yet only by [some characteristic] . . ., but
by his previous history."[27] Finally, as Eliade

so cogently observes, part of the reason that the word 'myth' carries such a negative connotation in the West, i.e., a connotation of spurious falsehood, lies in the fact that "Judaeo-Christianity" firmly and consistently opposed that particular kind of understanding which it rightly saw as being radically opposed to its own.[28] This opposition was so thoroughgoing that in Christian tradition in particular, and in Western civilization in general, the words 'myth' and 'falsehood' became synonymous. Hence, in the face of an attentive reading of Eliade's careful analysis of the differences between mythic thinking and historical consciousness, Stevenson's thesis appears hopelessly confused and completely untenable.

However, the source of Stevenson's confusion runs even deeper than this. Stevenson is quite correct in maintaining that although from within the framework of a historical consciousness a person may argue about the truth or 'objectivity' of certain views regarding matters that claim to be historical in nature, nevertheless, the truth of this historical view of reality *per se* "cannot [itself] be argued conclusively. . . . [there is, e.g.,] no conclusive demonstration of the rightness or superiority of the historical understanding of experience over the ultimately ahistorical understanding of experience subscribed to by the Buddhist."[29] As Wittgenstein has reminded us, there may come a point at which two parties representing different "pictures of reality," e.g., the Christian historical and the Buddhist ahistorical, reach an impasse in their discussion such that each must turn to the other and say, "I have reached bedrock, and my spade is turned. . . . I am inclined to say: 'This is simply what I do.' "[30] Of course, one hopes that such an impasse, if it does occur, takes place at the end of the discussion between parties with conflicting claims rather than being taken for granted at the outset. In any event, Stevenson has rightly taken up Wittgenstein's point that conflicting ultimate claims may in the end prove intractable to solution.[31]

But having gotten this point straight, Stevenson goes on to make other assertions which are the result of blurring basic lines of distinction between categories. He argues that the fact that people do maintain the historical view of reality as being the absolutely true story of the world "shows the continuing vitality of the myth."[32] Yet it is one thing to say that mythic thinking and historical consciousness both make appeals to ultimate truth-claims; it is quite another to say that historical consciousness *is* just one more form of mythic thinking. What might be more properly said is that mythic thinking and historical consciousness appeal to two different and *incommensurate* conceptions of time and the meaning of time. The one true thing that can be said about these two different modes of thought with their two different conceptions of time is that neither one can or does do without any conception of time whatsoever. Making a kind of Kantian point, Steven Crites has astutely observed that although various cultures, through the narratives they offer, may provide us with diverse conceptions of time, "there is only one absolute limit to that diversity: It is impossible that a culture could offer no interpretation of this temporality at all."[33]

Unless we keep clear about such things, we easily run the risk of misreading, misunderstanding, and ultimately falsifying the kinds of claims that biblical, historically oriented narratives make. To be sure, among the biblical narratives, one can find those which might be appropriately categorized as myths, e.g., the Creation stories or the story of Adam and Eve. And as Eliade himself admits, "It is beyond doubt that 'mythological elements' abound in the Gospels."[34] Examples such as these reflect some (but not all) of the qualities of mythic thinking to which we referred earlier. But again, it is one thing to admit the existence of certain mythic elements in the Bible or in certain biblical narratives and quite another to classify, for example, the Exodus narrative *as a whole* as being a myth. A biblical theologian like Rudolf Bultmann is quite correct in perceiving that certain mythological elements in the Gospels do not 'fit' within the larger context of both the biblical and modern understanding of reality. These mythological elements display an interpretation of reality and time that is basically at odds with the historical interpretation that characterizes most of Western thought. However, one can be equally at odds with the biblical understanding of reality by carrying this line of thought too far and by applying it too uncritically. G. E. Wright very aptly states that the result of such 'methodological hastiness' can well be that "history and historical research in the Bible are no longer important. All we need to do is to work with the 'mythology'; it makes no real difference whether the events really happened or not."[35] But this kind of claim is the antithesis to that made by the Bible, namely that God acts most decisively through particular historical events and persons. Very cogently, Wright argues that if biblical criticism moves from a concern with historical research to an interest in mythology, then the focus of biblical theology must likewise be shifted from history to some other subject such as "man's existential situation" or the "investigation of being."[36] But these two concerns are decidedly nonhistorical (and consequently, unbiblical)—the former because it focuses on "the existential present" to the exclusion of almost everything else, and the latter because its concern with "Being as such" takes its cue from a Platonic notion of timelessness. The biblical idea of history sees man as a being who has both a past which cannot be ignored and a future which has yet to be worked out.[37]

For biblical narratives like that of the Exodus or of Jesus' life, death, and resurrection, it is not enough that they should merely ring true to some common human experience. At that level, they could simply be great works of creative fiction, or among the best examples of skillfully crafted fables or allegories. Instead, their 'saving power' is inextricably tied to their *being true*—not in the way that myths are true, i.e., beyond and 'before' and outside of time—but rather in and through time and history.

Such narratives as these, and their implications for theology, are the kinds of stories that will be the focus of our attention for the rest of our study. However, before we attend further to these kinds of stories which make claims about the significance and truth of all human life, we would do well to take a close look at stories that center on the meaning and truth of individual human lives—biographies and autobiographies. Such stories draw what power they have from their ability to ring true and their claim to be true.

III

'LIFE STORIES I':
BIOGRAPHY

The importance of narrative is perhaps nowhere more evident and justified than in the portrayal of a life. Name, rank, and serial number—even job description—are not the same as self description. Such descriptions may be fine for the enemy interrogator or for the 'pickup' at the mixer or for others who have only a passing interest in us as the people who we really are. However, we take the time to tell our *life stories* to those to whom we feel close, to those whom we trust, to those whom we think it important that they come to know and understand us as the people we truly are. To be sure, one may abstract certain elements, details, and statements of 'fact' from the story which must remain, which does remain, basic. For, after all, it is the story from which these abstractions *are abstracted*, and it is the story that provides the context that gives the various elements their meaning and significance. As Steven Crites has so well put it:

> We state the matter backwards if we say that something called mind abstracts from experience to produce generality, or if we say that "the body" has feelings and sensations. It is the activity of abstracting from the narrative concreteness of experience that leads us to posit the idea of mind as a distinct faculty. And it is the concentration of consciousness into feeling and sensation that gives rise to the idea of the body. Both mind and body are reifications of particular functions that have been wrenched from the concrete temporality of the conscious self. The self is not a composite of mind and body. The self in its concreteness is indivisible, temporal, and whole, as it is revealed to be in the narrative quality of experience. Neither disembodied minds nor mindless bodies can appear in stories. There the self is given whole, as an activity in time.[1]

In this chapter and the next, I will examine the implications of the study of life stories for theology. In this chapter, I will focus on biography, and in the one to follow, I will turn my attention to autobiography. Whatever their differences, both biography and autobiography claim to be true—'true to life.' In great works of biography and autobiography, this claim is twofold: the claim that it is true to the life of the one whose story it is, and the claim that this life story holds out some truth about life that the one hearing or reading it can incorporate into or at least relate to his or her own life story. Thus biographical and autobiographical narratives claim both to *ring* true and to *be* true.

Religious narratives, such as the 'paradigmatic' scriptural stories of Judaism and Christianity, make a similar claim. They are stories intended to be truthful accounts of "the activity of a self in time"—God. They are also meant to portray the activities of other selves in time—e.g., Abraham, Moses, the apostles. In doing all this, in depicting the story of God and man, the religious narratives also claim to have something to say about the story of the one who hears or reads them. They claim to have something to say *about* and *for* the truth of his existence as well. For this reason, a number of thinkers have become interested in the significance of life stories for theology. These writers would claim that although propositional theology may abstract from and reflect on the 'data' provided by life stories in order to gain greater clarity or precision, propositional theology cannot become a substitute for such stories nor can it afford to ignore them altogether. Again, as Crites has rightly remarked, the narrative is prior to both abstraction from it and interpretation of it. James McClendon states the relationship between 'biographical theology' and propositional theology in the following way: "Biographical theology need not repudiate and should not ignore the propositional statement of theological doctrine. What it must insist is that this propositional statement be in continual and intimate contact with the lived experience which the propositional doctrine by turn collects, orders, and informs."[2]

My procedure in this chapter will be straightforward

and direct. I will begin by discussing two different methodological approaches to the question of the relationship of biography to theology: McClendon's *Biography as Theology* and a book written by James W. Fowler and several others entitled *Trajectories in Faith*. Afterward, I will use a concrete example of biography, Peter R. L. Brown's *Augustine of Hippo*, as a means of illuminating the strengths and weaknesses of each approach and as a way of suggesting modifications in each method.

Both the writers of *Biography as Theology* and *Trajectories in Faith* agree that the study of life stories is central to the study of theology; indeed, the phrase "life stories" appears in the subtitle of each work. Thus, McClendon contends:

> In or near the community there appear from time to time singular or striking lives, the lives of persons who embody the convictions of the community but in a new way. . . . Such lives, by their very attractiveness or beauty, may serve as data for the Christian thinker, enabling him more truly to reflect upon the tension between what is and what ought to be believed and lived by all. To engage in such reflection, however, is the proper task of Christian theology. . . . Theology must be at least biography.[3]

For their part, Fowler and his colleagues maintain that:

> Telling the stories of saints and heroes is a universal feature of religious life. Insights into the personality of a great teacher and a narrative that gives the full context

> of the teaching lend a note of authenticity to the records of instruction. . . . Always, however, the biographical details remind us that saints and heroes are real people whose teachings we repeat and whose lives we honor. . . . Their stories invite us to enter the structures of faith that supported their lives.[4]

However, though both books agree on the centrality of biography for theological reflection, they significantly disagree about the best way of portraying and of understanding—of giving coherence to—the random events and experiences of a life. In other words, they disagree about the way in which to shape these individual life experiences into a *biography*, i.e., into a life story, the depiction of the activity of a self through time. This disagreement in turn leads to another disagreement among the authors, namely, a disagreement about *what it is* in any life story that has significance for theology. For McClendon, the methodological key is that of "image"; for Fowler and his school, the primary conceptual tool is that of "structural development."

BIOGRAPHY AS THEOLOGY

McClendon's interest in biography is broader than the import of life stories for theology. His concern also extends to ethics, and he believes that the study of biography intersects with a crucial—and of late neglected—area of ethical inquiry: the role of character. McClendon believes that many of the problems facing contemporary ethics "lead to the problems of theology and back again"; thus, in his view, there is a vital need for "a way in theology which incorporates the study of character—biography as theology." Recently, the field of ethics has tended to focus attention on the morality of the individual act. Such attention has come at the expense of an investigation concerned with the nature—the character—of the person who does the act. McClendon makes this distinction quite clear:

> The characterless rubber-ball person may bounce until he kills, and that killing may be for a fleeting 'motive'—anger, or envy, or bloodlust. And that *act* may be truly bad. Yet we may be inclined to say of the rubber ball himself that he has not yet risen to the level of badness. We would say this, for example, of a child whose characteristic ways were not yet shaped, but also of a pitiable social psychopath.

As McClendon says, a person's character, the development of the self he is over time, is, for good or bad, "paradoxically both the cause and consequence of what [he does]."[5]

McClendon next looks at another area ignored by contemporary ethics: the importance of community. He asserts that "communities [too] have their own distinctive characters." The character of the community in which an individual is fostered and nurtured is part of the heritage—for better or worse—of his own character. Obviously, for his part, the individual may develop a character which may affect—for better or worse—the character of the community in which he lives. Thus, McClendon notes that in any event, the study of "an ethics of character" is in reality the study of an "ethics of character-in-community."[6]

For McClendon, the common strand that ties all these various notions of biography, theology, character, and community together is that of "image": "By images, I mean metaphors whose content has been enriched by a previous, prototypical employment so that their application causes the object to which they are applied to be seen in multiply-reflected light; they are traditional or canonical metaphors, and as such, they bear the content of faith itself."[7] The images of which McClendon speaks, those which are in some way "prototypical" or "traditional" or "canonical," are those which reflect the vision—the character—of a community. In turn, such images converge in an individual's life to shape "the way he sees things," *his* character. That is, these images help form the context within which a man sees his life and within which he makes his life's commitments. In living out his life under the vision of these dominant images (and according to McClendon, this is what is meant by 'religion'), a man's life becomes the image of that vision for others. He comes to embody that vision and so display it to others. So, for example, the dominant image of Dag Hammarskjöld's life was that of the Servant and the Cross; for Martin Luther King, Jr., it was the set of images related to the vision shaped by the Sermon on the Mount and by the biblical account of the Exodus; for Clarence Jordan, it was the image of *koinonia*. For their part in turn, these lives become the embodiment—striking, 'compelling' images—of the Christian doctrine of atonement and reconciliation.[8]

At this point, one might be tempted to think that the import of such lives, the import of biography for theology, is merely the claim that certain lives may be regarded as 'useful,' i.e., as 'instructively illustrative.' But McClendon persuasively answers that such a view is wrong-headed, arguing that if we *could* show that such lives are useful, then:

> We could presumably also say what they were useful for; that is, we could have discovered features or aims of Christian faith and life which were *logically* prior to the lives which so usefully exhibit these features or expedite these aims. In this case biographical theology would necessarily depend on this prior knowledge.[9]

But again, narrative is prior to abstraction; the stories of Christian lives are prior to the formulation of Christian propositional and doctrinal theology: "Christianity turns upon the character of Christ." "Jesus compels, St. Francis compels, I think Clarence Jordan compels; the doctrine we may draw from their life stories, if it is compelling, is so just because it had prior embodiment in them and may be embodied again."[10] In calling attention to the "compelling" quality of such lives, McClendon is not saying that we must or ought to 'like' those whose lives they are; we may be 'struck' in fact by the repulsiveness of certain lives. Rather, what McClendon *is* saying is that doctrine is not only formed, but validated—to the extent it can be validated—in light of the evidence provided by lives such as these: "If there were no such lives we should be imperiously urged to acknowledge that this doctrine had lost its power; if in the future there should be no more such lives, we should then have to make that concession."[11]

McClendon further cautions against the temptation of thinking that the character of either an individual or a community can be fully understood by the examination of images alone. He writes: "Images are a clue to character, just as metaphors are illuminators of speech. But to treat speech as if it were all metaphor is a stultifying strategy, and so is it folly to treat character as if it were only a bundle of images."[12] Images may help shape and form the way we see; they may cause a shift in our vision and perspective so that we come to see more clearly things that we had overlooked or ignored before; like models in science, they may provide the best way of speaking about phenomena not directly observable: God and self in the world. In doing all this, however, images must ultimately serve to shed light on convictions, those "rock-ribbed beliefs which, if a man is something or stands for something, show us more precisely what he stands for and what or who he is."[13] The task of a propositional theology is to study these convictions, not, according to McClendon, as so many simple propositions, "but as the propositions by which men live."[14] In the last analysis, the goal and orientation of theology must be "towards a theology of life"—as the last part of the analysis and the orientation of *Biography as Theology* make clear.

TRAJECTORIES IN FAITH

While McClendon stresses the importance of dominant images which shape the character and in-form the content of the lives which embody and reflect them, Fowler and his associates emphasize the primacy of certain formal developmental structures instead: "The Research Project on Faith and Moral Development has attempted to understand faith as a human universal by identifying basic *structures* of faith that all human beings seem to share. A structure of faith is a formal description of the way faith functions in life."[15] The writers believe that their approach of structural development is particularly well-suited to the task of exploring the nature of faith. For them, faith is the "liminal awareness" that all of the various diverse experiences and encounters in life are yet tied to a "unifying center of meaning and value." Thus, a focus on "faith development" is a focus on the changes "not so much in *what* we believe as in *how* we believe, how we 'construe' the whole of our experience." Such a focus, claim the 'structural-developmentalists,' calls attention to "faith as a lifelong process in which the structures of faith emerge, evolve, and are transformed."[16] This process is what gives coherency to a life and what forms the basis for the relationship between life stories and theology, such that life stories can be the subject of significant theological investigation and reflection.

The authors take the theoretical basis for their concept of structural-development from the work of Piaget and Kohlberg. That work argues that both a person's cognitive and moral development depend on his ability to pass from his present "stage,"—i.e., his current level of maturity and his present way of employing an integrated set of operations to face and tackle problems—to a new stage in which he will be called upon to utilize a new set of operational patterns in order to master difficulties for which the methods of the earlier stage are inappropriate. Hence, "a stage transition means a revolution in the [individual's] *way* of knowing and understanding." A person subsequently comes to "construe" his experience and the whole of his life in a way different from the way he had viewed them before. In moving from one stage to the next, in incorporating the skills and structures learned during one period of his life into a later period, the individual is able to give his life increasing degrees of coherency and integrity. Without such mastery and incorporation of these earlier skill-operations, transition from stage to stage is impossible, for the *possibility of even recognizing new problems and challenges as such* depends on this prior mastery and incorporation of the techniques of previous stages. Therefore, conclude the authors, "Progress through the structural-developmental stages is not inevitable." However, the authors do insist that the structural-developmental approach of Piaget, Kohlberg, and others like them does in fact provide a "predictable sequence" of stages which enables the researcher to discover a pattern of coherence among the manifold experiences contained in any individual life. And since for the writers, "faith is a way of giving coherence to our world," the structural-developmental approach offers, in their view, a valuable way of following the development and character of faith through all the twists and turns of an individual life story.[17]

The schema which the authors adopt has six distinctive stages of faith development.[18] During stage 1, "Intuitive-Projective Faith," the child largely imitates the examples of faith visibly set by "primal adults." In the second stage, that of "Mythic-Literal Faith," individuals appropriate for themselves the stories, symbols, beliefs, and practices of their community, showing thereby that they, too, belong to that community. In this stage, stories, symbols, beliefs, and practices tend to be accepted without question. During the third stage, "Synthetic-Conventional Faith," the individual, as he moves beyond the immediate world of his family into a larger world of more complex and diverse involvements, attempts a synthesis of various values and data in order to achieve a basis for a coherent identity.[19]

The transition to the fourth stage—"Individuative-Reflective Faith"—is particularly critical in terms of the person's overall faith development:

> It is in this transition that the late adolescent or adult must begin to take seriously the burden of responsibility for his or her own commitments, life-style, beliefs, and attitudes. Where genuine movement toward stage 4 is underway the person must face certain unavoidable tensions: individuality versus being defined by a group or group membership; subjectivity and the power of one's strongly felt but unexamined feelings of critical reflection; self-fulfillment or self-actualization as a primary concern versus service to and being for others; the question of being committed to the relative versus struggle with the possibility of an absolute.[20]

If "self-certainty" characterizes stage 4, then "self-criticism" typifies stage 5. In this stage, one must try to get beyond the *conscious* attitudes and outlooks which made up the earlier stage and instead attempt to come to a recognition of "one's *social* unconscious: the myths, ideal images, and prejudices built deeply into the self-system by virtue of one's nurture within a particular social class, religious tradition, ethnic group, or the like.[21] The attainment of the sixth and final stage of faith development, "Universalizing Faith," is, according to the authors, "exceedingly rare." Persons who reach this level both embody and make possible "the spirit of a fulfilled human community." The lives of such persons display the kind of comprehensiveness that is faith's "by definition":

> The rare persons who may be described by this stage have a special grace that makes them seem more lucid, more simple, and yet somehow more fully human than the rest of us. Their community is universal in extent. Particularities are cherished because they are vessels of the universal and thereby valuable apart from any utilitarian considerations. Life is both loved and held to loosely. Such persons are ready for fellowship with persons at any of the other stages and from any other faith tradition.[22]

In addition, this developmental sequence formula has other advantages besides its enabling the "psycho-historian" to "tie the story of a life together." It also provides a "heuristic tool" for the psychohistorian's reconstructing, interpolating, and/or extrapolating any of the various stage-transitions for some particular subject for whom other forms of 'evidence' are not readily accessible:

Beginning from a clearly established structure at one stage of development we can proceed backward through time to marshal the evidence characterizing earlier faith stages, and we have a general description of the sorts of changes later in life that would be indicative of further faith development. The stages of faith development, in short, allow us to plot a trajectory in faith.[23]

For example, Katherine Ann Herzog takes as her subject of study Anne Hutchinson. Although Hutchinson's life was brought to an abrupt and tragic end by an Indian attack in 1643, Herzog can nevertheless go on to theorize that had Anne lived, given her level of faith development at the time of her death, she may have been well on her way to stage 5. Herzog writes:

> We have no documentation of Anne Hutchinson's thoughts and beliefs during this time; however, we can hypothesize that Anne's faith changed. There was no longer a need to relate to a large community and affirm her faith through them. . . . We do know that she welcomed Indians into her home with kindness and that she was settling into a new, more peaceful way of life. . . . For the first time, the external tensions were gone, and Anne moved into a more accepting, though more withdrawing, time of her life. . . . It was in the last year of her life that Anne may have made a transition to paradoxical-consolidative faith, stage 5. . . . There was a letting go that was at the same time an acceptance of others.[24]

Like McClendon, Fowler and his associates present a number of life stories to test and illustrate the theoretical model: Malcolm X, Blaise Pascal, Ludwig Wittgenstein, Dietrich Bonhoeffer, and, of course, Anne Hutchinson. The structural-developmentalists, however, do set an explicit limit to the extent to which their method may so far be applied to other life stories. They state that the method works most successfully when used to investigate the lives of Western figures, born after 1500, and no longer living. These limitations arise due to three factors. First, say the authors, reliable biographical and documentary material in sufficient quantity to afford a valid reconstruction of faith development seldom exists for subjects born before the sixteenth century. Second, the authors find that in the case of persons still living, their "work is often in transition," and their past, in ways similar to that of some distant historical personage, "often cannot be fully known." Finally, the authors' restriction of their research to Western subjects arises from the current lack of any cross-cultural comparisons in faith development.[25]

Yet at least two of these three limiting factors seem rather odd. For whereas earlier, the structural-developmentalists had claimed that one of the major assets of their method was its ability to provide an understanding of faith "as a human *universal* by identifying basic structures of faith that *all human beings seem to share*,"[26] the school now issues a disclaimer about the method's applicability (or rather its non-applicability) to non-Western subjects. Or again, whereas previously the writers had maintained that the method's "predictable sequences" enabled them to plot "trajectories" of faith development forward or backward from any particular developmental stage, they now back off from that claim in the case of living subjects, after observing that their "work is often in transition and [their] past . . . often cannot be fully known." Such disclaimers raise questions about the status of the theoretical model used by the structural-developmentalists. Is that model, as the earlier claims for it would seem to suggest, meant as a universal normative standard by and against which to compare, measure, and predict the faith development of any and all human lives? Or is it, as the later statements limiting its applicability would seem to indicate, meant rather as a hypothetical construct which itself must still be tested and validated in the light of the data provided by a variety of life stories yet to be examined? The structural-developmentalists never seem to get very clear about this matter, and the ambiguity here may be the first sign of other, more serious weaknesses in their approach. For ultimately, the developmentalists must determine whether their approach may not be applied to some figures (e.g., non-Western subjects) because it has *not yet* been so applied, due to the lack of sufficient data, or whether it *cannot* be so applied, due to the lack—the impossibility—of some totally neutral, nonperspectival, vantage point from which to judge the character of all human life.

AUGUSTINE OF HIPPO

However, that determination will have to wait until the structural-developmental approach, as well as the dominant-image approach put forward by McClendon, are each subjected to critical analysis. That analysis will ask the question of whether and to what extent either approach may be applied to other cases to yield coherent and theologically significant life stories. Of course, answering *that* question could itself become an endless, and ultimately, inconclusive process, as first one life, then another, is taken and examined in turn. The biographical account of one life, however, that of Augustine by Peter R. L. Brown, may prove helpful for our purposes. Although Brown's biography will not enable us to prove, strictly speaking, the validity or invalidity of either method, it will nevertheless provide us with a useful way of illuminating the strengths and weaknesses of both methods, thus allowing us to make some suggestions regarding how each method might be refined.

Before the analysis proper begins, a few methodological points ought to be made clear. Although the structural-developmentalists might object that Augustine is a pre-1500 figure, such an objection in this instance will have to be 'overruled.' For if one of the criteria of the psychobiographer is that a life-to-be-studied provide the researcher with a "data base not only of extant literary works by the subject but also of reasonably reliable biographical studies assembled by other traditional methods,"[27] then Augustine's life certainly passes muster. Given Augustine's own writings, including his revolutionary, autobiographical self-study, the *Confessions,* coupled with the vast number of traditional biographies that have been written about him, his life clearly provides a sufficiently ample data base for the investigator. Moreover, although both McClendon and the developmentalists claim that their respective methods could be used to examine lives which are not explicitly 'religious,' a life like Augustine's which was deeply religious, avowedly Christian, and obviously influential theologically, must be considered at least an ostensibly fair and valid 'test case' for either method. Furthermore, Brown, in *his* approach, is not committed to either McClendon's approach or to that of Fowler and his co-writers, nor does he write out of any explicit or specific theological interest. Rather, his point in his scholarly treatment of Augustine's life story is

> to convey something of the course and quality of Augustine's life. Not only did Augustine live in an age of rapid and dramatic change; he himself was constantly changing. . . . Augustine will have to meet the challenges of new environments. . . . By writing, by acting, by influencing an ever-increasing body of men, he will help to precipitate changes in the world around him, that were no less headlong than his own inner transformations. I shall be more than satisfied if I have given some impressions of the subtle overlapping of these [different] levels of change.[28]

There are several places in *Augustine of Hippo* where, if one did not know that Peter Brown was the author, one might assume that the biographical account presented had been written by the structural-developmentalists instead. For example, the description of Augustine's move from Manichaeism and Neo-Platonism to a Christian position, which incorporated, yet transcended, both, sounds very much like a prime instance of a move from stage 4 to stage 5. Originally, Augustine had been a committed and strident follower of the dualist Mani, believing, says Brown, that through a sheer act of the intellect alone, he could protect whatever good and godly part he had within him from the onslaughts of evil in the world about him. At age thirty, however, Augustine began a shift to Neo-Platonism, and his involvement with that philosophical movement

> did nothing less than shift the centre of gravity of Augustine's spiritual life. He was no longer identified with his God: this God was utterly transcendent—His separateness had to be accepted. . . . Just as Augustine could no longer identify himself with the good, so he could no longer reject all that did not measure up to his ideals as an absolute, aggressive force of evil. . . . [The] Platonic books [offered] a view in which evil was only one, small aspect of a universe far greater, far more differentiated, its purposes more mysterious and its God far more resilient, than that of Mani.[29]

But the total transition into the stage of "Paradoxical-Consolidated Faith,"—the stage during which the absolute certainties of the fourth stage are critically reviewed—had yet to be accomplished. Augustine would need to come to see the limitations and flaws of Neo-Platonism as well as those already perceived in Manichaeism. As he moved toward forty years of age, he realized that "he would never impose a victory of mind over body in himself; he would never achieve the wrapt contemplation of the ideal philosopher."[30] In fact, Augustine's involvement with Manichaeism provided him with the basis for his critique of Neo-Platonist thought. If Neo-Platonism had challenged the Manichaen doctrine of determinism, Manichaeism had, for its part, raised serious questions in Augustine's mind about the actuality of the freedom of the will and about the will's true ability to overcome deeply entrenched evil and perversity.

Brown claims that out of the clash between these two paradoxical philosophical positions came the consolidation of faith represented by the *Confessions*. For in moving toward *confessio*, toward both "accusation of oneself" and "praise of God," Augustine came to recognize that "if the denial of guilt was the first enemy [i.e., Manichaeism], self-reliance [Neo-Platonism] was the last." Brown writes: "to reduce such a change, as some neat scholars have done, to a sloughing-off of 'Neo-Platonism' and the discovery of some 'authentic' Christianity is to trivialize it."[31] This is the kind of statement with which the structural-developmentalists would wholeheartedly agree. They write: "It is sometimes necessary to conceive the dilemmas of experience in sharp unequivocal contrasts (faith stage 4) before it is possible to reappropriate the truths of both sides in a paradoxical relationship (faith stage 5)."[32]

If faith development is predicated on the successful passage through and appropriation of previous stages into the current level of development, then certainly, Augustine's *Confessions* are a testimony to the validity of that sequential scheme, for in that work, "Augustine is led to see man bound by the continuity of his inner life."[33]

Brown argues against the idea that the book can be understood "in terms of a single, external provocation, or of a single, philosophical *idée fixe*"; he claims instead that it is best understood as the attempt of a man to find himself through a 'therapeutic' examination of his past in which "every single fibre in Augustine's middle age grew together with every other, to make the *Confessions* what it is."[34] Indeed, Brown stresses that one of the things that differentiates and distinguishes the *Confessions* from other ancient (and even medieval) autobiographies is its insistence upon the importance of a man's past, rather than some focus on certain "essential, ideal qualities."[35] Moreover, not only did Augustine's life story differ from others written by contemporaries in its emphasis on the past as the basis for the understanding of the present, but it also differed from other 'conversion-tales' in its understanding of the *meaning* of conversion, i.e., of the implications of conversion for the present and the future. Brown notes that in the ancient world, conversion had been the central theme of religious autobiography. "Such a conversion was often thought of as being as dramatic and as simple as the 'sobering up' of an alcoholic."[36] By contrast, Augustine did not view his conversion in such terms; he did not see his life as the result of such a conversion as being something now finished once and for all. Brown observes that the "amazing Book Ten of the *Confessions* is not the affirmation of a cured man: it is the self-portrait of a convalescent."[37] One need only compare Brown's remarks here with some by the structural-developmentalists concerning the ongoing nature of faith

development to see the affinity that the group might feel
for Brown's account of this transitional period in
Augustine's life:

> Perhaps the most insistent claim of faith-development
> theory is that faith is a continuous process. . . . The
> continuity of faith. . . . is not the persistence of a
> finished set of beliefs. It is the continual testing and
> reformulation that keeps beliefs alive precisely by
> ensuring that they do *not* become reduced to fixed
> ideas.[38]

And yet, it would be wrong to conclude that
Augustine's life simply went on to follow the developmental sequence laid out by the Fowler group. In terms
of developmentalist theory, Augustine's life story never
moved on to stage 6, to "Universalizing Faith." Now the
developmentalists themselves have readily admitted
previously that progress from stage to stage is not
inevitable, and that in particular, the attainment of the
sixth stage is "exceedingly rare." But is it the case that
Augustine's development came to an end with the writing
of the *Confessions?* Or rather did his development
continue, but in a far more rich and complex way than the
structuralist account can show? In answering these
questions, an expanded employment of McClendon's
'methodology of images' will offer us a good deal of help.

At the outset, one must note that in some ways,
Augustine's story does seem to exhibit some 'classic' stage
6 characteristics: "The persons best described by this
stage have generated faith compositions in which their
felt sense of an ultimate environment is inclusive of all

being. They become incarnators and actualizers of the spirit of a fulfilled human community."[39] As Bishop of Hippo, Augustine, passing from his middle years into old age, does display this kind of "universalist" sense and "activist" spirit. But what dominates and leads him on as he writes the *City of God* is the *image* of the *peregrinus,* the resident stranger—a personality quite familiar to the ancient world. Typically, such a person might feel homesick for his native land, some far distant country, while at the same time accepting with gratitude the favorable conditions that his current place of residence affords him. In that spirit, he might well work with others in this host environment "to achieve some 'good' that he is glad to share with them, to improve some situation, to avoid some greater evil." For Augustine, to be a Christian is to be the *peregrinus par excellence,* and thus, the *City of God* "is a book about being otherworldly in this world"—in order to transform the world. It is the image of the *peregrinus*—rather than some abstract theory of developmental stages—that explains Augustine's move into a wider circle of involvements, to seek out others in community. Brown comments on the increasing importance of such relationships for Augustine's latter years:

> Augustine the young convert could not have written such a book [as the *City of God*]. Indeed . . . we can see how much the harshness of the young man had mellowed. He has become far more open to the reality of the bonds that unite men to the world around them. He

had, for instance, once said that the wise man could "live alone with his mind"; now he will pray to have friends.[40]

Augustine's reaching out to others is an expression not only of his *self*-image as *peregrinus,* but also a reflection of the image he has of himself as the bishop-as-*nourisher;* indeed, as can be seen from John 21:15-19, that image is also a *canonical image* in McClendon's sense of the term. As Brown points out, Augustine spent his middle age giving; during a fifteen-year period between 395 and 410, he wrote some thirty-three books and rather lengthy epistles. As Bishop of Hippo, seeing human weakness constantly, Augustine "will turn his creativity into a form of giving food: he will always present it as 'feeding' men as much in need of nourishment as he now felt himself to be."[41] Hence, the canonical images of *peregrinus* and *nourisher,* rather than some predetermined stage sequence, seem to have been the crucial factors explaining Augustine's coming to a "sense of an ultimate environment" and becoming an "actualizer of the spirit of a fulfilled human community."

But additionally, there are other dominant images in this part of Augustine's life which not only shape and inform this part of his developmental process, but also shape it in a way that is far out of line with the course of faith-trajectory which the developmentalists would have charted. Although the developmentalists characterize a universalizing faith as one which cherishes particularities "because they are vessels of the universal" and as one which is "ready for fellowship with persons at any of the other stages and from any other faith tradition,"[42] the dominant images of Augustine's later life give his vision of universalism and of community quite a different color and texture than that envisaged by the developmentalists. Augustine's understanding of universalism is formed in the light of his understanding of the image of the *catholic* church; his notion of community is molded by the images of *disciplina* (discipline) and *saluberrima consilia* (literally: "the most healthy advice").

During the latter part of his life, Augustine saw his world beset by the discord of heresy and by the breakdown of Roman law and order in the face of advancing barbarian attacks and incursions. Brown says that increasingly, "the image of the Division of Tongues at the Tower of Babel came to dominate his thought." For a man of Augustine's position—community leader, bishop, theologian—the primary question became, What ought to be the role of the church in a world such as this one? While his adversaries, the Donatists, might think of the church as an "ark," i.e., a place of refuge from the storm, Augustine conceived of the catholic church as an instrument for the reunification of the human race; "it might absorb, transform, and perfect, the existing bonds of human relations."[43] Augustine believed, however, that the church, in its efforts to perform such a service, could legitimately call to its aid two 'acolytes': 'discipline' and 'medical treatment.'

Augustine derived the image of discipline from an age which "thought, only too readily, in terms of military discipline and uniformity." Likening the sacraments to the tattoos which the Emperor had branded onto the

backs of his soldiers' hands in order to facilitate the
punishment of deserters, Augustine argued that Christ
the King was similarly justified in recalling to *his* ranks,
by force if necessary, those who had received his mark
and who had yet been unfaithful to their charge.[44]
Moreover, as God had disciplined the children of Israel in
a way that a loving father uses corrective punishment to
bring his wayward offspring back into line, so, too, the
church, in Augustine's eyes, was correct in using the
power of the Christian Emperors to chastise opposing
sects such as the Donatists and the Pelagians in order that
these groups might be restored to the right path and so
that unity and harmony might once again prevail within a
truly catholic church.[45]

Along similar lines, the image of *saluberrima consilia,*
i.e., "the most healthy advice," helped crystallize
Augustine's concept of ecclesiastical authority. The image
had first struck Augustine during a period of his youth
when he had found it necessary to withdraw and study in
order to apply " 'medicine' to his soul."[46] In old age,
however, it became a 'remedy' for dissent. Writing of
Augustine's encounter in his later years with a young
Donatist by the name of Victor, Brown remarks that to
Augustine, "a bishop's duties were not only 'pastoral';
they had also become 'medicinal.' Laymen who
pontificated to the clergy would be well to remember this
'tonic' of authority. Augustine intended to 'correct'
Victor, not to follow him."[47]

Thus one finds that the older Augustine became, the
more his office and his thought were marked by greater
degrees of intolerance and by increasing levels of

repression—and all in the name of the development of a universal Catholic Church. In some sense, Augustine succeeded at his task, for he provided the uncertain world in which he lived (as well as the world of the Dark Ages that would follow) a Catholic Church which was "an oasis of absolute certainty." Near the end of his account of Augustine's story, Brown looks back over the course of the man's life and concludes that the chronicle of that life "could be regarded as a steady progression towards 'the ecclesiastical norm' of Catholic orthodoxy."[48] One suspects that this is hardly the kind of development of "universalizing faith" that the structural-developmentalists have in mind!

Obviously the developmentalists could respond here by saying that Augustine simply failed to progress fully into the sixth stage. But herein may lie part of the weakness of their theory: it is a bit *too* theoretical. That is, the parameters of development appear a bit too rigid and fixed, almost *a priori* in nature, as though any and every life must fall within their boundaries if it is truly to have 'progressed' and 'developed.' But such a view hardly seems plausible. As the developmentalists themselves admit, the theory does not seem to work too well when applied to certain kinds of lives. Such 'non-applicability" may be due to the fact that the theory is neither broad enough nor artful enough to account for the vast yet sometimes subtle differences of radically diverse lives. Or is it more basically the case that the theory offered by the structural developmentalists needs (and lacks) theological candor? Indeed, their theory seems to have a distinctly Christian and decidedly liberal bent to it. Their characterization of the sixth (and highest) stage of development in particular reflects just such an orientation and bias:

> [Stage 6 persons] are "contagious" in the sense that they create zones of *liberation from the social, political, economic and ideological shackles* we place and endure on human futurity. . . . [Universalizers] are often experienced as subversive of the structures (including religious structures) by which we sustain our individual and corporate survival, security, and significance. *Many persons in this stage die at the hands of those whom they hope to change. Universalizers are often more honored and revered after death than during their lives.* . . . Life is both loved and held to loosely.[49]

Although at times the structural-developmentalists forthrightly state that "our faith is marked in important ways because we are Jewish, Catholic, or Presbyterian,"[50] and then go on to assert that "the focus on structural changes in faith does not minimize questions of content,"[51] their mode of approach tends to militate against one's believing that the writers have taken their own remarks to heart. Besides their relying perhaps too heavily and uncritically on the work of Piaget, Kohlberg (and Erikson), the writers may have flawed their work by not paying sufficient attention to the *content* of faith as that content is formed by various religious traditions. It is simply not enough to say that "faith is a way of giving coherence to our world."[52] Different religious traditions may have different conceptions about what it is that gives the world such coherence. Certainly, Augustine's concept of coherence and universality differed greatly from that of Fowler and his co-authors, and if there is something 'wrong' about Augustine's conception, the structural-developmentalists must show how and why that is the case, rather than simply *asserting* that their own conception is the proper one. After all, Augustine is the one called by many "Saint" and "Father of the Church."

Thus, the developmentalist theory is found wanting in ways that are somewhat paradoxically opposed. Its understanding of the nature of faith is too 'open-ended,' while its scenario of developmental stages is not open enough. Perhaps the problem is simply a case of focusing too much attention on form and not enough on content. Clearly, the very possibility of referring to 'a life' and not simply to some random bunch of 'experiences' or 'events' requires that some sort of structure be found in or given to those experiences and events. But in the case of a story, and particularly of a life story, the structure must have the kind of flexibility that allows the story to be told in all of its ins and outs, twists and turns; failing this, the story will be rightly regarded as artificial and untruthful—not 'true to life.' Perhaps the most telling criticism of the writers of *Trajectories in Faith,* a book putatively about the importance of life stories for theology, is that the method they develop is so 'story-less'—or so the authors would have us believe. It is as though somehow they themselves stand outside and above any and all stories, investigating the lives of others from some pure and privileged nonperspectival and story-free standpoint which thus enables them to issue universally true criteria about what

counts—what *must* count—and what does not count—
what *cannot* count—as progress in faith development.
Surely the life of Augustine, must, at the very last, cast
some doubt on both the method's explicit claims as well as
on its implicit assumptions.

By contrast, one of the strengths of McClendon's work
is that it seems to be willing to let diverse lives—through
their own diverse images—'tell their own stories.' This
willingness may in part be due to McClendon's vision of
his own project, a vision somewhat different from that of
the structural-developmentalists: "I have repeatedly
noted that the point of these biographical investigations is
not to discover the beliefs of these examined subjects with
a view to recommending the beliefs when discovered as
beliefs for all."[53] McClendon's task in *Biography as
Theology* is the discovery of religious convictions through
an examination of life stories lived under the influence of
dominant images; the process of justification of these
deeply held beliefs is a subject McClendon reserves for a
later book, *Understanding Religious Convictions*, and a
subject to which I will turn in a later chapter. At any rate,
because McClendon is not committed to any prior
overarching and 'normative' theoretical framework in the
way that the developmentalists are, his method allows for
the fruitful and open exploration of the life story of an
Augustine as well as of a Hammarskjöld or a Hutchinson.

And yet, the work of the developmentalists and
Brown's biography of Augustine suggest for their part
ways in which McClendon's method might itself be
corrected and revised. If part of the problem with the

structuralists' theory is that it provides too much structure, one of the flaws in McClendon's approach is that there is virtually no methodological structure to it. McClendon is never very explicit or expansive on the question of how a "dominant" image comes to be recognized and regarded as such by the investigator. Must the image be something explicitly referred to by the subject in his writings or in his public pronouncements, or is it something which the investigator may validly be able to infer from other sources? Although in his work McClendon seems to opt for the former position, he never spells out the matter to any great degree. Moreover, even when the investigator can pick out a certain image and see that in the subject's life the image has been particularly influential, what assurance is there that the subject's understanding and use of that image and the researcher's understanding and use of the image are one and the same? If the researcher comes from a different religious or cultural background from that of his subject, or if the subject is using that image in a way which is radically different from the way it has been traditionally used by his own community, then the chance for such misunderstanding increases. While McClendon certainly *does* admit that "theology is not only from a perspective but to and for a community" and *does* go on to say that his work is meant to address those "who have inherited the Bible as focal for tradition or for life,"[54] he still needs to set forth some more explicit indicators to show how misunderstandings across communal and traditional lines might be avoided.

Lastly, as Augustine's life story makes clear, there is

rarely only one static "dominant image" in a person's life; earlier images are often absorbed, modified, or abandoned in the light of later ones, and as one might expect, the development of these subsequent images will have an effect on the development of vision and character over time. But McClendon's account, with its talk of a "convergence of images" combining to give a life its "characteristic vision or outlook,"[55] leads one to think of human life in rather static terms, as though the image, the vision, and the self come to rest at some fixed point of equilibrium.[56] But whatever else a biography may be, it is the story of development of the self through time. If it ignores the factor of time, it may end up being little more than a philosophical portrait; if it fails to pay attention to some notion of development and change, it may come to resemble an ancient royal chronicle which tells in great detail how the king did this and how the king did that, but which never really shows what kind of person, what kind of *self*, the monarch really was. And indeed, the ancient chronicle was usually not intended to provide this kind of information. Perhaps a more helpful notion than McClendon's "convergence of images" is one borrowed from Crites, namely that of "image-stream."[57] As we go through life we may come to see our life experiences in the light of certain images, but in turn, these experiences may also come to shape our vision, bringing us to an awareness of new images as well as to a new self-image. Our images may train our vision to regard our lives in certain ways, but the character of our lives over time may come to shape what we regard as worth attending to. It is this dynamic, reciprocal, and evolving process to which *Biography as Theology* ought perhaps to attend more closely.

Thus, in some sense, *Biography as Theology* and *Trajectories in Faith* each serve to illuminate and broaden the perspective of the other. While the former provides the developmentalists with a means of getting at the content of a life which makes it the uniquely individual life it is, the latter serves to remind those who would stress the importance of images, vision, and character of the significance of the development of all these things through time so that the story of a life might truly be portrayed. In any event, whatever their differences, both studies agree on the importance of life stories for theological reflection, for they both contend that it is the business of theology to make us reflect on life. First, there is McClendon who writes:

> Of course any theologian has his bias; this will be true whether he does biographical theology or some other kind. If, however, he thinks his way into the Christian lives he seeks to know, their participation in the redemptive life of Christ becomes a redeeming element of the investigation and in the investigator. . . . In this sense, we return from the lives we have examined to our own lives; the examiners become the examined, and our claim on our "saints" becomes their many-sided claim upon us.[58]

Next, the faith developmentalists say:

> A faith development biography is not only an investigation of the subject; it is at the same time an exploration of

the investigator and the investigative model. Faith development theory may tell us much about Malcolm X, but as James Fowler notes, Malcolm in his turn tells us something about the theory and its limits, and about who we are ourselves.[59]

Last comes Possidius, Bishop of Calama, and the earliest biographer of Augustine: "Yet I think that those who gained most from him were those who had been able actually to see and hear him as he spoke in Church, and, most of all, those who had some contact with the quality of his life among men."[60] Though a propositional theology may have its place, that place is limited by life itself, for as its propositions are abstracted and drawn from life, so too, in the end, they must return to life and have meaning for life in order to be theologically significant.

In this chapter, I have been primarily concerned with examining the implications of biographical life stories for theology. In following this relationship through, I have not paid particular attention to the question of evaluating the truth of life stories. Part of the answer to that question involves the notion of an "angle of vision." After all, changes in standpoint and changes in perspective lead to the constant revising and rewriting of biographies. In autobiography, matters of standpoint, perspective, and angle of vision become crucial in answering questions of truth—and truthfulness—and it is to a discussion of these issues that I will now proceed.

IV

'LIFE STORIES II':
AUTOBIOGRAPHY

Autobiographies, like biographies, may sometimes strike us with the kind of compelling quality that starts us reflecting on our own lives; by providing us with the self-images of others, they may present us with a kind of mirror with which to see our own images and lives more clearly. Like biographies, autobiographies, too, gain part of this compelling quality by claiming to be 'true to life,' that is, by both ringing true to some common ground of human experience and by being true to the facts of the individual lives of which they speak. However, the truth of autobiography comes from another feature as well: the truthfulness of the self who writes the story of the self who is. That is, such truthfulness—or lack of it—by the autobiographer may provide the truest disclosure of the person he or she really is. In large part, truthfulness and disclosure are matters of standpoint and intention. To be sure, being faithful to 'the facts' is as important to the autobiographer as it is to the biographer, and obviously, chronology does impose some sort of order on those facts. But whereas the omission of certain facts may seriously undermine the veracity of the biographer, the deletion of some facts and the inclusion of others may not ultimately discredit the autobiographer's account of *who he is*. If through faulty memory, or narrowness of vision (or even conscious intent to deceive), the autobiographer imposes a new and different pattern and configuration on the facts, such novel re-collection and re-presentation by the self-who-writes may nevertheless truly reveal a good deal about the self-who-is.[1] Sallie McFague notes the importance of this distinctive characteristic of autobiography for theological reflection: "Autobiographies give practical wisdom because they are the story of the engagement of a personality in a task, not of the task alone. It is this peculiar meshing of life and thought that is the heart of the matter with autobiographies and which is, I believe, their importance for religious reflection."[2] McFague's phrase, "the engagement of a personality in a task," is the key to unlocking the question of truthfulness in autobiography and a clue to getting at the justifiability of the use of narrative in theology. For it is in the writer's "spelling out"[3] of his engagements that truth and falsehood appear in ways peculiar to autobiography—as self-acceptance or as self-deception. In turn, the degree to which a writer in telling his life story displays self-acceptance or as self-deception by his ability or inability to face 'the realities' of his life and so include them in his story is, at the same time, the degree to which any claims that he might make about 'life and its meaning' will be either attested or belied. In this chapter, as in the last, I will begin with a conceptual overview of the issues involved, and then I will conclude by looking at concrete examples of autobiographical writing—Will D. Campbell's *Brother to a Dragonfly* and a number of works by Elie Wiesel.

In part, the spelling out of one's engagements, the author's telling of the events of a story which is *his* story, is a matter of the writer's standpoint. Autobiography is not merely a matter of memory; it is more a matter of recollection. As Crites, recalling Augustine, has observed: "All the sophisticated activities of consciousness literally re-collect the images lodged in memory into new configurations, reordering past experience."[4] In large measure this act of recollecting the images of memory into patterns and configurations of significance—of turning *chronos* into *kairos*—depends on and reflects the author's present standpoint. Which past events will be included, which will be left out, which given significance, which dismissed as trivial, are issues that reveal the author's current angle of vision and current perspective on his past. It is a matter of how he or she views the facts of the past "in the light of all his [or her] experiences and knowledge since the facts recorded took place."[5] The standpoint, the determination of what will be recalled and how, gives a life its unity, its coherence, its shape—in short, its story. Moreover, not only do such things form the character of the story, but additionally, what is revealed and what remains hidden may say and reveal a good deal about the character of the person writing. In fact, it is this very sense of the shaping of the narrative by the writer's perspective on things—and not merely the incorrect reporting of certain facts—that awakens the reader's critical judgment of the story, the storyteller, and the credibility of both. The following passage by Roy Pascal neatly delineates this relationship between standpoint, story, and character:

> All autobiographies must . . . have a story-structure. . . . It is their mode of presenting truth. They are . . . cumulative structures, and we experience them as wholes, so that at any moment the earlier parts, the earlier experiences, are present in the reader's mind. The reverberations from past experiences do not need to be explicitly recalled afresh at every moment, nor does each new situation need endless dissection. In all new events, the author's past experience is recalled objectively in the shape of formed behaviour, feeling, thought. Thus events build on events to construct the achieved personality.[6]

For the biographer, the structure of his account of a life story—its beginning, its middle, and its end—may be framed by the biological structure of life—birth, maturation, and death. However, for the autobiographer, for the one who writes as he lives and who lives as he writes, that kind of structure is not readily available. Although he knows he is past the starting point of birth, he is not likely to know where in the middle of life he is nor when the end of life will come. The 'end' around which the autobiographer thus shapes his story (and his life) is not the end signified by his death, but rather the end signified by his intentions. In *Thought and Action,* Stuart Hampshire has argued that our having intentions is essential to our being human. Furthermore, Hampshire makes the even stronger assertion that it is precisely in our ability to act intentionally, in our ability to be engaged in trying to bring about certain effects as we follow "what is happening now as leading into what is to happen next" that we come to have a notion of temporal order in the first place. Hampshire says that behavior, to be counted as human, intentional action must have some minimum degree of consistency and regularity and *continuity* about it. Such continuity and connectedness carry with them "a trajectory of intention that fits a sequence of behaviour into an intelligible whole, intelligible as having a direction, the direction of means toward an end." Inherent in this "trajectory of intention" is a sense of a "relation of before and after," which, in Hampshire's view, gives the assurance of the continued existence of the self through time and thus meaning to a statement such as, *"I did* it." If someone were to give a purely 'external' description of the behavior of another, he might be able to do so without falsifying any one piece or part of that overt behavior. And yet, he *might* still end up presenting a distorted and unfaithful account of the other's 'life activity' by failing to take into account the way the other, the *agent,* himself would characterize, describe, and account what he had been doing in his life. In doing all this, of course, the agent would be saying something about the meaning of his life—about the way he intends and means his life to be and to be understood.[7]

Obviously, the autobiographer is the one who is, *prima facie*, the person most in position to be able to give this kind of description of his life, a description given from 'the inside looking out.' An autobiography is at the same time both a 'life work' and the reflection of a life work. As Barrett J. Mandel has put the matter, "The 'point' of [the autobiographer's] life becomes the point of the book, just as, simultaneously, writing the book gives meaning to his life."[8]

If telling one's story is partly a matter of standpoint and intention, it is also partly a matter of style, and here, too, the manner in which the story is presented can be just as revelatory of the character of the author, of the author himself, as the events related. In fact, Roy Pascal claims that "style in general is the most revealing element in any autobiography."[9] The style with which a story is told may be indicative of the *teller's* characteristic style, of his or her individually unique way of doing things. But more importantly, the style in which the story is cast may reflect on the story's truth and on the teller's truthfulness, and again as with the element of standpoint, this element of style may be that which most gains the reader's trust or which puts him on his guard. For example, Augustine, by writing his autobiography in the form of a *confession*, honestly and sincerely means to encourage the reader's belief in the veracity of his account, for after all, the primary addressee of the work is not the reader, but God the All-Knowing, whom no man dare try to deceive. But, of course, the work is also addressed to the reader, who, knowing that this address to the Lord is the ultimate guarantor of the truthfulness of Augustine's writing, can now take his autobiography to heart as a life story which presents a credible and trustworthy basis for hope, comfort, and conversion for his or her own life as well.[10] By contrast, the *Autobiography* of Charles Darwin, written in another form and style, offers quite a different story of the self-who-writes, a story which ultimately leaves the reader unconvinced about its claims. James Olney, in his book, *Metaphors of Self,* shows that Darwin's autobiography, his 'metaphor of self,' reflects the way the man saw the world and his own life in it. Darwin saw the universe as "a closed mechanical system of cause and effect," and he saw his own role in it as that of the detached and neutral scientific observer; consequently he wrote an autobiography which according to Olney is a kind of "mechanical metaphor": "Always conscious of the significance of external phenomena, Darwin was almost equally and oppositely unself-conscious; for the self does not present collectible and classifiable facts. Hence the brevity of the *Autobiography*."[11] Darwin's life story reads not so much like an autobiography as it does a lab manual for conducting an experiment. Thus, while it presents the results of Darwin's 'observations on life,' it has relatively little to say about Darwin's own life. Because Darwin failed to see that he "as the observer and the experimenter stood at the very center of the process and so had to be taken into account with the result," he also failed as an autobiographer.[12] And because Darwin could not even give an adequate account of his own life, whatever claims he had to make either about the meaning of that life in particular or about 'life in general' seem equally unconvincing.

Obviously, autobiography, in portraying a life story, is not life, but art, and in some sense therefore imposes an artificial structure on the life depicted. For example, life itself is not divided into nice, neat chapters and periods.[13] However, there are far more serious ways in which an autobiography can falsify life; there are ways in which an individual in viewing and relating his or her life story can create an artifice that not only fails to portray the self truthfully, but which in some sense is destructive of the self, for it makes it virtually impossible to talk about the self as it truly exists in all of its complexity. If, from the point of view of literary analysis, "the original sin of autobiography is first one of logical coherence and rationalization,"[14] from the perspective of psychoanalysis, the same phenomenon lies at the heart of self-deception. In the end, both problems have the same root: the desire to achieve a high degree of consistency and coherence in one's life story at the expense of comprehensiveness of vision. Roy Pascal writes: "The autobiographer must rigorously select from his life, and perhaps the chief danger is to make the line linking past and present far too exactly continuous and logical."[15] Similarly, Herbert Fingarette remarks in his book *Self-Deception*, that the person engaged in self-deceptive practices will try to develop an elaborate "cover-story" to protect him from having to "spell out" what he has in fact been doing, of having to face up to life: "He will try to do this in a way which renders the 'story' as internally consistent and natural as possible. . . . [Whenever] new inconsistencies between actual engagements and cover-story arise, the individual is moved to ever continuing effort and ingenuity to elaborate his story and to protect its plausibility." Both the deceptive autobiography (which may be, but need not necessarily be, a self-deceptive story as well) and the self-deceptive cover story arise out of a desire to achieve and display an integrated story—a story showing integrity—no matter what the cost, or rather, even at the cost of having to shut out other parts of one's life and oneself from one's vision. With great sensitivity to the drives at work in the self-deceptive individual, Fingarette observes that "the less integrity, the less is there motive to enter into self-deception. The greater the integrity of the person, and the more powerful the contrary inclination, the greater is the temptation to self-deception."[16] The flawed autobiography, the flawed account of who a person is and what that person has been doing in and with his or her life, is a reflection of a flawed, too-narrow vision, a vision not broad enough in scope to include the wider range of the self's engagements.

For Fingarette, this notion of the self's "engagements" plays a central role in understanding the formation of a self's story. By "engagement" Fingarette means a person's "conduct, aims, hopes, fears, perceptions, memories, etc.," and moreover, someone's "engagement" refers both to "what someone does [and] what he undergoes as a human subject."[17] To speak, therefore, of one's engagements is to speak of how one construes the world and how one construes oneself and one's activity in that world as well.

But as Fingarette makes clear, we are not usually conscious of our engagements, nor do we generally need to be until and unless we are called upon to make them explicit. Fingarette calls this becoming explicitly conscious of an engagement the "spelling-out" of that engagement.[18] He prefers this term over the often-used metaphor of 'vision,' for whereas this latter notion carries a passive connotation which is in some ways discontinuous with the concept of consiousness, the idea of spelling out something suggests the active use of an operational skill.[19] Thus, on this understanding of things, becoming explicitly conscious of one's engagements is not so much a matter of seeing as a matter of saying. However, the mere *capacity to perform* "spelling-out" is not enough. Since one does not usually spell-out one's engagements (e.g., driving, going to the market, eating) unless one has reason to do so, the total *skill* of "spelling-out" involves not only the capacity to use it, but also the knowledge of when and for what reason to use it:

> Skill in driving a car is not merely the ability to perform certain movements; it is also the ability to assess the possibly conflicting considerations in a situation in order to settle which movements to perform, when to do so, and precisely how. Skill in speech calls for assessing just when to speak, when not to speak, how to speak, what to say. Skill in spelling-out requires analogous assessments.[20]

The characteristic mark of the person engaged in self-deception, the thing most revelatory of his character as a self-deceptive human being, is "that even when normally appropriate, he persistently avoids spelling-out some feature of his engagement in the world." The word, "persistently," emphasizes the fact that self-deception is not merely a matter of a single, isolated decision or act; rather, it is a matter of *policy*, a policy adopted to preserve and protect a person's current way of conceiving and maintaining the integrity of the self. Having to spell out some engagement, having to become explicitly conscious of it as being one's own, presents too great a threat to this present conception of selfhood, and, therefore, such spelling-out is habitually avoided: "What the self-deceiver specifically lacks is not concern or integrity but some combination of courage and a way of seeing how to approach his dilemma without probable disaster to himself."[21] The self-deceiver and the deceptive autobiographer both lack a story which is expansive and comprehensive enough to allow them to acknowledge and incorporate disharmonious and unflattering elements into their lives. In short, they lack a story that can sustain them in the face of those engagements that seriously challenge the current stories they give of themselves.

As a consequence of his desire for consistency and integrity (integratedness) of character, the self-deceiver increasingly finds himself forced to hold certain potentially disruptive engagements in static isolation from the rest of his own perceived life activity. Fingarette calls this tactic "disavowal." Disavowal tends to be characterized by three things: (1) the rigidity with which the engagement is held in isolation, (2) the denial of responsibility for the engagement, and (3) the incapacity to spell out the engagement. Simply put the self-deceiver refuses to avow these engagements as *his*. And the thing that qualifies this phenomenon as self-deception rather than mere deceptiveness, deceit, or deception is that it is sincere.[22] The self-deceiver wants us to believe these things about him because he believes them about himself. And here, a sharp line of demarcation can be drawn between the self-deceiver and the consciously evasive autobiographer. Some autobiographers, such as retired politicians, may quite self-consciously omit certain political failures or gaffes from their memoirs in order to cast their careers in a better light 'for posterity.' We have the feeling, however, that if we could just speak to these figures 'off the record,' that in a relaxed moment, they just might 'own up' to these blunders and mistakes. However, with the self-deceiver, things are decidedly different. Self-deception is, as the word implies, *reflexive*. In this way, it throws up a double barrier to truthfulness. Not only does the self-deceiver avoid becoming explicitly conscious of some engagement, he also skillfully and sincerely creates a cover story which permits him to avoid becoming explicitly conscious that he is, in fact, avoiding becoming explicitly conscious of the original engagement. For this very reason, no amount of preaching or moralizing to the self-deceived person will get him to 'open up' and be more truthful about the nature of his engagements. Instead, "direct appeal to integrity and moral concern, by evoking the motives of self-deception, strengthen the inclination to it and are self-defeating."[23] The skill of spelling-out, which involves both assessment and capacity, is the basis of other skills such as the skill of sophisticated planning and the skill of rational estimation in complex situations. Thus, disavowal, the inability to spell-out, also spells a loss of self-control and a subversion of both personal and moral agency. As a result, therefore, disavowal is in some basic way truly self-destructive; it is not insignificant that we sometimes describe the inability of the self to spell-out its engagements and thus achieve wholeness by using another word instead of the word "disavowal": *breakdown*. Avowal, by contrast, is the ability to spell out some engagement and thus integrate it "into that *achieved synthesis* which is the personal self."[24]

But how does a person go from disavowal to avowal, from a self-deceptive cover story to a truthful life story? In another of his books, *The Self in Transformation*, Fingarette outlines the process. There he writes that he views the ego as "the organizing or synthetic function, [which] represents an autonomous drive toward meaning." By contrast, anxiety "is the other face of the ego"; it is ego-disintegration; "anxiety is meaninglessness." The neurotic, in ways similar to the self-deceiver, holds onto a meaning-scheme, i.e., "a pattern of behavior and experience," which is "arbitrary, partisan, fragmented," an engagement in the world characterized by "partial-ity in [the] relating of facts one to another in meaningful ways." Once again, comprehensiveness is sacrificed for the sake of consistency. Once more, fragmented, unintegrated, and erratic behavior results from inadequate meaning-schemes and untruthful stories. Patches of meaninglessness occur.[25] Because the neurotic's story is not comprehensive enough in its vision, some of life's experiences become for the neurotic incomprehensible in turn.

Hence, the therapist's task is to introduce an alternative meaning-scheme to the neurotic as a way of reconstruing and reorganizing present experience. Fingarette claims that "insight therapy [is] the attempt to provide integrating meanings where before we had the 'disconnected and unintelligible.'" In suggesting an alternative meaning-scheme to the one the neurotic currently holds, the therapist does not reveal some "hidden reality" or "the truth about some hidden past." He does not, therefore, offer the patient new information about the past. Rather, he offers a new way of construing the past, and with it, a new orientation toward the present and future as well.[26] Fingarette provides an excellent illustration of this point, and I will quote it in full:

> Suppose that I remember preventing my little brother from getting on his tricycle and telling him that he would hurt himself. I remember getting on it myself and saying that I would show him how to ride. I remember feelings of satisfaction when doing this and feelings of annoyance when he cried. The annoyance is accompanied by verbalized thoughts to the effect that "he does not realize that I'm trying to help him; he is a crybaby." Now these are the kinds of things that I *remember*. Nowhere do I remember feeling hatred and jealousy of him. (I could not truly *recall* such feelings, for I *felt* no such feelings at the time.) I may have forgotten but now suddenly I remember that I also used to drag him off my

mother's lap while crying out fearfully that he might fall. Suddenly (because of the analytic setting and work, therapeutic interventions, the fact that I am now an adult, etc.) everything hangs together in a new way—and a much more unified, meaningful way. These very events are perceived and re-experienced in terms of the meaning-scheme "jealous aggression toward brother" rather than the scheme "well-meaning help of brother." I do not discover unfelt feelings; I reinterpret the feelings I felt (and this may lead me to have new feelings and responses now). I reinterpret the known events, reinterpret them not intellectually and as an observer but existentially, as experiencing subject and responsible agent.[27]

The validation of a therapeutic insight such as the one described above lies in its ability to tie together previously disparate and unconnected feelings and behavior into some sort of meaningful pattern. Furthermore, the preference of one meaning-scheme over another rests precisely in its degree of comprehensiveness, i.e., in the ability of one meaning-scheme rather than some other to give comprehensibility and intelligibility to experiences and behavior previously regarded as random and erratic. Yet ultimately, the test of whether or not an alternative meaning-scheme 'works' is not theoretical, but practical. The therapist's job is not simply to construct skillful and ingenious linguistic models; in the last analysis, the patient must not only be able to 'talk the game,' but also be able to play the game for and by himself—with autonomy, with intention, and with spontaneity:

> When all is said and done, the practical test is not in *a priori* claims or philosophical name-throwing, but in practice—sustained, serious, constantly critical, and sensitive practice. The most general criterion in the context of our inquiry is this: What kind of meaning-scheme *does* finally bring control and order along with spontaneity into our experience?[28]

In a sense, then, by reconstructing my world, I can come to reconstruct my world along with the self I am in that world. However, this reconstruction effort is just that: it is not the creation or formation of a self and world *ex nihilo*. Instead, it is the *transformation* of the self that is already in the world. As such, this transformed self is "one of a limited but not exhaustively specifiable range of possible selves." The transformation depends on an act of self-acceptance, on the self's willingness to acknowledge and avow previous engagements on its own. The transformed self sees these previous engagements as part of the self (selves) it was before, as part of its past, as part of its heritage which is "neither rejected as unfair nor considered as alien and repressed." Fingarette supplies an illuminating analogy comparing the relationship between the 'new' self and the 'old' to that of a child and his parents:

> The [child] comes to identify with the parents who bore him even though he had no choice in his being born their child or in the nature which they impart to him. So the psychic "offspring," the newly reorganized ego, must, if it is to maintain its own integrity, function as the

> continuation of the old ego. There must be not merely
> causal and temporal continuity; there must also be
> psychic identification.[29]

The possibility of the transformation of the old self into
the new (rather than the complete formation of a self *de
novo*) is what makes talk about the identity and
development of the self through time intelligible.

Now all of this—i.e., one's recognition of certain past
acts as *one's own,* one's *acceptance* of one's past, one's
acknowledgment of the self one has been heretofore—is
what we have previously termed "avowal." Avowal as
acceptance of the past is, in Fingarette's view, the
necessary condition of moral responsibility, of the
willingness to respond to the present and go on from
there toward the future.[30] From this perspective, the
taking of responsibility is not so much a matter of
accepting blame for something in the past as it is the
occasion for determining "to face the world as it is *now*
and to proceed to do what we can to make it the world we
would like it to be." Thus, for Fingarette, responsibility is
primarily a matter of commitment. Therapy, in seeking to
provide a new meaning-scheme, generates a "new vision
which shall serve as the context of new commitment."[31]

The basis for new vision and new commitment is
nothing other than a shift in standpoint and perspective.
In coming to see one's life from 'another point of view,'
one comes to formulate a new version, a re-vision, of one's
life story. Because this new story will likely be more
encompassing in scope than the older version, it may
therefore lack some of the older version's internal

consistency. Thus it may appear to be at points open-ended and in certain places to have loose ends about it. And yet for these very reasons, the new version may also have a credibility and truthfulness that the old story lacked. For again, although a life story may reflect the ends and purposes of the one who tells it, the way in which everything in a life will turn out in the end is something the teller of the story cannot know.

In this chapter, I have made use of the writing of a number of different thinkers to investigate the relationship between autobiography and truth. These writers have occupied a number of different perspectives in their approaches to the subject—psychological, philosophical, literary. But whatever their differences in approach, importantly, they all agree that a person's ability to give a truthful account of his life in order to assume moral responsibility for his actions is tied to his capacity to transcend his present standpoint and take a look at what he has been doing from another angle of vision. Fingarette contends that the possibility of the patient's arriving at significant choice through therapy depends on the willingness to "contemplate," "explore," and "savor" a variety of alternatives through the " 'free' production of thoughts, feelings, fantasies, and memories."[32] For Hampshire, too, a necessary condition of anyone's being free, rational, and moral, is the ability to "detach" oneself from one's current way of seeing things, to take up "the vantage point of other systems of thought," and so try to "see round" in order to attempt to redescribe one's present intentions and one's past conduct from another point of view, thus endeavoring to defend one's actions against charges of arbitrariness and *partial*-ity.[33] The same theme is struck by the literary analysts, Pascal and Olney. Pascal maintains that good autobiography represents a new stage in self-knowledge and a new formulation of responsiblity towards the self; it involves "a mental exploration and change of attitude."[34] Olney, for his part, makes a distinction between the autobiographers whom he labels "simplex" and those whom he calls "duplex" on much the same basis. In the writings of the autobiographers simplex, men like Darwin, J. S. Mill, and George Fox, Olney says that one finds "little or no self-awareness, little or no criticism of the assumed point of view"; there is only one way of seeing things and "there is the felt assumption in each case that this is the way the thing is said, that there is no other way."[35] By contrast, the autobiographers duplex have, according to Olney, the capacity for self-criticism. Men like Augustine and Montaigne exercise both awareness and self-awareness, consciousness and self-consciousness, thereby enabling them as they reflect on their lives not only to see life with their own eyes, but also to see themselves in the act of seeing life with those eyes. In the process, they are forced to transcend their present points of view and so gain a wider field of vision that makes their lives more fully comprehensive and comprehensible.[36]

All of these writers seem to be agreed that part of the justifiability of any life story lies in its potential for revision and reformulation. That is, a story must continually empower, perhaps even *force*, the one who tells it to be self-critical, to look at his current story from the perspective of stories other than his own. For

narratives this criterion is what the principle of
universalizability is to propositional systems. Unless our
story gives us the capability—the skill—to 'step back' and
look 'round' and spell out our engagements, then the
tendency toward fashioning a story which is deceptive
about the self and the world—and destructive of
both—will be difficult, if not impossible, to hold in check.

As the therapist holds out to the patient alternative
meaning-schemes, so, too, certain religious traditions,
through the narratives they offer, present different
visions of reality. At crucial moments, the meaning-
schemes that these religious narratives display, may, like
those of the therapist, break through to a person so that he
may reformulate his own life story in the light of the
meaning-scheme portrayed by that larger story. In
psychoanalytic terms, this process may be called 'insight';
in religious terms, it is called 'conversion.' In either case,
the result is a transformation of the self. And in this way,
the ultimate prescriptive claim that a religious tradition
makes *via* the story it relates is that the one who hears it
ought to *"become that story"* and thus so embody that
story in his own life that, through his life, he will go on to
relate it to others.[37] As a suggested meaning-scheme in
therapy is validated by its impact on the experience of the
patient,[38] the validity of a religious vision concerning the
meaning of life is attested to by its being taken up into a
life as a viable alternative.

Having now provided a theoretical framework within
which to explore the relationship between autobiography
and truth, I intend to look at some concrete examples of
autobiographical writing to illustrate the ways in which

the truthfulness and justifiability of life stories may be challenged, critiqued, and assessed. But in looking at the autobiography of Will Campbell, the Christian who is "Brother," and the autobiographical writings of Elie Wiesel, the Jew who is "survivor," the discussion will not be merely judging the truthfulness of these life stories; it will also be reflecting, if only indirectly, on the validity of the transcendent religious visions of which these lives are themselves reflections.

WILL D. CAMPBELL

On the frontispiece of Will Campbell's autobiography, *Brother to a Dragonfly*,[39] appears the first line of a Gerard Manley Hopkins poem:

> As kingfishers catch fire, dragonflies draw flame;
>   As tumbled over rim in roundy wells
>   Stones ring; like each tucked string tells,
>   each hung bell's
> Bow swung finds tongue to fling out broad its name;
> Each mortal thing does one thing and the same:
>   Deals out that being indoors each one dwells;
>   Selves—goes itself; *myself* it speaks and spells,
> Crying *What I do is me: for that I came*.
>
> I say more: the just man justices;
>   Keeps grace: that keeps all his goings graces;
> Acts in God's eye what in God's eye he is—
> Christ. For Christ plays in ten thousand places,
> Lovely in limbs, and lovely in eyes not his
> To the Father through the features of men's faces.

Campbell's life story is a spelling out of how he came to see himself and others clearly in a world beset by ambiguity and distortion. It is a story not only about the meaning of being "Brother" to Joe Campbell, "the dragonfly," but also about the meaning of each person's being that which he alone uniquely is while at the same time being that which every man is in common with every other, namely "what in God's eye he is—Christ."

Campbell's story begins with his childhood in the rural Mississippi of the Great Depression, a hard time for a Southern Baptist farm family already in or near poverty before the Depression began:

> And [Grandma Bettye] wore the flannel bathrobe to
> church
> the very first Sunday after Christmas.
> Because it was the prettiest thing she
> had ever seen,
> and the Lord deserved the best.
> And because it was 1933 and she didn't have a
> bathroom.[40]

Joe, Campbell's older brother by two years, was, in that childhood time, "leader," "worker," and "shield." Will Davis, called "Dave" as a boy, was "the sickly one" and "the one marked early to be the preacher." The word "marked" is crucial. Campbell tells us that in those days of his youth, designations of identity and role, though given by others, were accepted without question:

> By role, designation, category and assignment Joe was
> the worker. I was the sickly one and therefore

something of a drone. Sister was just that—Sister. Daughter with three brothers and thus special. Paul was the baby. We lived that way and if those categories and designations and roles seemed unfair to any of us we never discussed it. That's who each one was. One did not ponder identity. Everyone knew and understood, without being told. Without asking questions. *This* is who I am. *That* is who you are. The question. "Who am I?" need not, and did not, come up. That's the way we lived.[41]

Campbell's autobiography is essentially the development and working out of his answers to the questions "Who am I?" and "Who are you?" as he goes through life and finds need of such questions and answers.

However, those relationships, identities, and designated roles remained clearly marked and defined right into "Dave's" late adolescence. Ironically, even when Campbell announces, upon going off to college at age seventeen, that he no longer wants to be called "Dave," but "Will," Joe, the leader and protector, is the one who authorizes and legitimizes the change: "A man ought to be called what he wants to be called." Writing of that moment, Campbell acknowledges that "Joe was the first to declare me a man."[42]

The arrival of World War II and Joe's draft notice marks the beginning of a change in perspective on Will's part about his own identity as well as his brother's. Only then did the questions, "Who am I?" and "Who are you?" arrive. As he recalls Joe's words telling of his being drafted—"Well, Brother, they've called my number"—Will remembers that

Joe had not called me "Brother" since [childhood]. Now, as he embraced me, he called me "Brother." But we both knew it meant something different then. It was what he would call me from then on. It became the rule. It was violated only when there was some strain between us.[43]

As the beginning of the war had spelled the beginning of a change in relationship between the two, the end of the war carried in its wake an end to the roles that had once seemed so clearly defined. The roles of boyhood, so neatly and distinctly drawn, are reversed in manhood. Joe, having had his leg broken in a car wreck, is honorably discharged and comes home to recuperate; he lies on his mother's couch, insisting that he cannot get up. Suddenly, the "worker" becomes the one who is "sickly." And Will, who is both on the verge of going away to study for the ministry and on the eve of going off to get married, notices that "for the very first time, I began to feel a hesitation on Joe's part in being my leader." While before Joe had always been willing to reassure Will whenever he had been uncertain about something in his life, Joe now meets Will's uncertainties with uncertainties of his own. Instead of answering questions about what Will should do with his life, Joe keeps asking over and over again what Will thinks he should do with his. Will finds Joe, his "shield," no longer there, and consequently, finds himself left unprotected: "I began to be frightened at the sight of him lying day after day on the cot in our mama's house. And during those days I began to have the lonely feeling that my leader was gone from me."

However, this change in perception of the relationship between his brother and himself is not the only vision-shift which Will experiences; he has another one concerning those who are also his 'brothers.' During the war, Joe had written to him and had urged him to read Howard Fast's *Freedom Road,* a historical novel about the struggles and trials of an illiterate freed slave named Gideon Jackson. Looking back, Campbell writes that the book "turned my head around." "I knew that my life would never be the same. I knew that the tragedy of the South would occupy the remainder of my days. It was a conversion experience comparable to one I had never had, and I knew it would have to find expression."[44] Will, now ordained minister, also becomes worker, protector, and leader in the struggle of blacks for civil rights. Joe, now pharmacist, becomes addicted to a variety of tranquilizers and stimulants. Once again, roles and categories seemed so clearly marked and defined—the helper and the afflicted, the strong and the weak, the liberated and the enslaved. Only in retrospect, looking at those events from another angle of vision, can Campbell realize that the lines were not so sharply drawn; only in writing out and spelling out his life story, his *autobiography,* can Will fully and openly admit:

> Each of us did what we did for good reasons. And for questionable reasons. . . . Joe took his pills so he could help other people. And so he would feel good. I took on the University administration, the State Legislature, and the mores of the South to help other people. And to make me feel good. Joe took his pills because he wanted

to. And because he needed them. And, even at the time,
I suspected that my battle with bigotry might have to do
with my glands as well as my faith.[45]

In the time that followed, as Will's star rose, Joe's sunk
lower, until, after being continually thrown by drugs into
alternating moods of rage and depression, he finally hit
bottom and had to be placed in a mental hospital for
veterans. Will, "the one who is called to preach," is the
one now called to take Joe to the institution. Now Will is
firmly in charge as the brother who is leader and shield.
Nevertheless he feels somewhat strange and ambivalent
about these new roles:

> I . . . knew that he was not sick enough to be in a
> veterans mental hospital. But I thought it was a way to
> buy some time. And I was still playing God. Maybe the
> horror itself would be therapeutic. Maybe the thought
> of having to go through this again would restore him to
> the old brother I wanted so much for him to be.[46]

In the course of one of Will's visits to Joe in the hospital,
an exchange occurs between the two brothers that also
calls into question Will's roles as leader and shield in the
Civil Rights Movement. Will tries to justify his
commitment to civil rights as being part of his
commitment as a Christian. Furthermore, he extends his
argument to include a concern for the red-necks who
oppress the blacks "because anyone who is not as
concerned with the immortal soul of the dispossessor as
he is with the suffering of the dispossessed is being
something less than Christian." Finally, he concludes his

"remarks on the race problem" by making a point which
Joe had always agreed with in the past, namely that the
problem "did not have to do so much with the blacks as it
had to do with us."[47]

Now it is Joe's turn. He offers an "alternative
meaning-scheme" to Will's account of his engagement:

> Maybe you're the one who needs help. You think you're
> going to save the goddam South with integration, with
> putting niggers in every schoolhouse and on every
> five-and-dime lunch counter stool, and locking them up
> in the same nut hatch with white folks. Well, shit! What
> you're saying is that you're going to use the niggers to
> save yourself. What's so Christian about that? . . . Well,
> I thought, I was going to save myself with *pills* too. . . .
> Your niggers are like my pills. They prop you liberals up
> and make you feel good. . . . But when you crash![48]

Joe does not merely call into question the truthfulness of
Will's engagements as worker and leader and shield, but
more basically, he calls into question Will's calling as
preacher and his engagement as Christian. But Will isn't
ready yet to acknowledge the validity of the meaning-
scheme that Joe has "suggested." It would take more time
before the "liberal crash" which Joe had predicted would
come to pass. Some time would have to pass before Joe's
parting words that day would gain their full meaning:
"Anyway, Brother, you've got your hands full being
brother to me. Don't try to be brother to the whole damn
world."[49] Time was yet needed for Will to answer the
questions "Who am I?" and "Who are you?"

That time comes with the cold-blooded shooting of a

young black divinity student and civil-rights worker named Jonathan Daniel by a white southern deputy sheriff named Thomas Coleman. Will receives the news of the slaying from Joe as the two visit at the home of P. D. East, a kind of Mississippi Mencken, a man who was a gadfly, taking on the mores of the southern political, social, and religious establishments through his columns in his short-lived gazette, the *Petal Paper*. Once, he had challenged Will to sum up "the Christian Faith" in ten words or less. At the time, Will had responded, "We're all bastards but God loves us anyway." Now, after having watched Will respond to the news of Jonathan Daniel's murder by calling the man who did it a cracker, a red-neck, and a Kluxer, P. D. brings up this 'definition' once more:

> P. D. stalked me like a tiger . . . , "Was Jonathan a bastard?" . . . I knew that if I said no he would leave me alone and if I said yes he wouldn't. And I knew my definition would be blown if I said no. So I said, "Yes."
> "All right. Is Thomas Coleman a bastard?"
> That one was a lot easier. "Yes. Thomas Coleman is a bastard."[50]

Then, sitting there in the presence of "two of the most troubled men [he] had ever known," Will gets "the most enlightening theological lesson [he had] ever had in [his] life." Leaning forward, P. D. put the question squarely, "Which one of these two bastards does God love most? Does He love that little dead bastard Jonathan the most? Or does he love that living bastard Thomas the most?"[51]

In a very real sense, the 'moment of truth' had arrived

for Will. His own story stood challenged and judged from the perspective of another story, the story of what it means to be a Christian:

> Suddenly everything became clear. Everything. It was a revelation. . . . And I began to whimper. But the crying was interspersed with laughter. . . . I remember trying to sort out the sadness and the joy. Just what was I crying for and what was I laughing for. Then this too became clear. I was laughing at myself, at twenty years of a ministry which had become, without my realizing it, a ministry of liberal sophistication.[52]

The Christian story gives Will the ability to see through the self-deceptive cover story he had been acting out. But more than that, it gives him the skill and courage to face up to what it means to one who ministers, "one called to preach." For when P. D. disagrees that God does in fact love both bastards, saying of Thomas Coleman that "they ought to fry the son of a bitch" for killing "a good man," Will finds that he has no choice but to admit, acknowledge, and confess that

> The notion that a man could go to a store where a group of unarmed human beings are drinking soda pop and eating moon pies, fire a shotgun blast at one of them, tearing his lungs and heart and bowels from his body, turn on another and send lead pellets ripping through his flesh and bones, and God would set him free is almost more than I could stand. But unless that is precisely the case there is no Gospel, there is no Good News.[53]

This transformed vision of the meaning of his life becomes for Will the context for transformed commitments in his life. His moral commitments could no longer be only on behalf of the black and merely in opposition to the Klansman, as though the world were neatly—and irreconcilably—divided into two nice, simple categories of good and evil. From now on, Will would minister to the Klansman too, knowing that though "kingfishers catch fire" and "dragonflies draw flame," nevertheless, each individual creature—including the Klansman—is yet in the end "what in God's eye he is—Christ." For Will, the Christian story was a story of reconciliation, and such a story ruled out the possibility of his "denying . . . my history and my people"—the reconciled. Devoting his life to ministering to the Klan became a way for him of embodying his devotion to that story. In that Christian ministry, Will learns (and re-learns) important things ". . . from and about people who were our people—mine and Joe's. Whatever they stood for. Whatever they did. In a strange sequence of crosscurrents we were of them and they were of us. Blood of our blood. Our people. And God's people."[54] The questions "Who am I?" and "Who are you?" had been answered.

Those answers made it possible for Will not only to come "to terms with [his] own history, whatever that history might be,"[55] but they also enabled him to become reconciled to the history of his relationship with the one who was literally "blood of his blood"—Joe. As the title of Campbell's book suggests, if the book is a telling of any story, it is a telling of that story, and in that sense, the book itself is testimony to such reconciliation. The dragonfly metaphor does not allude solely to the Hopkins poem; it also refers to a significant childhood experience that Will and Joe shared. Will had gone on a trip, and upon his return home, Joe took him out to a clearing in the woods and started digging in a tiny mound of clay. He produced a Bayer aspirin box, and told Will that on the previous Sunday, he had captured a dragonfly, a "skeeterhawk," and had buried it alive in the box. Since dragonflies were believed to have "something to do with luck," Joe intended that this one should serve as an omen of sorts. He would dig it up on Wednesday, and if it were still alive, that would show that on Wednesday, Will would be returning home; if it were dead, it would mean that he would be gone for a long time. Now Joe stood and opened the lid of the box slowly and gently, and "two brothers stood as close as two brothers could stand, beholding the proof of one brother's experiment." The wings fluttered briefly. Joe snapped the lid shut. And the thought never occurred to Will that the dragonfly was dead, that the flutter of the wings had been caused by the wind. All that mattered was that Joe had buried the "skeeterhawk" on Sunday, saying that if it were still alive on Wednesday, Will would be back home, and the wings *had* fluttered, and the two brothers were back together once more. Recalling how they raced home afterward, Campbell writes: "And two brothers tried to outrun each other, and tried harder not to outrun each other, back to the yard. For there was no thought of ascendancy."[56]

Not until a long time later, not until after Joe's self-destructiveness leads to a massive and fatal coronary could Will begin to see and admit that the desire to outrun, to gain ascendancy, might in fact have been at the heart of their relationship. Sister's remark before the funeral that Joe "loved us all, but he worshipped you" sets Will thinking:

> Was it somehow all wrapped up in that Bayer aspirin box and the wings of the dragonfly, fluttering in a hot summer breeze forty years earlier? Had he been such an idol to me that I had unwittingly, unconsciously set out to turn it round and become his idol? . . . An idol who reached idol stature by courting and even flaunting success in the face of the worshiper who had never known success such as he had known? Not success epitomized by the evil of the world's goods. . . . Epitomized rather by the evility of this world's *goodness*.[57]

As the moral distinctions between black and red-neck which had once seemed so clear had come to be seen as being not so clear, as being not so morally unambiguous, Will's simple categories for describing his relationship with Joe—"leader," "shield," "sickly one"—undergo a similar transformation involving greater depth and complexity. The resulting recognition of the reality of the relationship is not the occasion for guilt or for blame, but for acceptance. Campbell reflects on his feelings at Joe's funeral:

> I knew I had to be the leader in the sad task of laying him down, knew in fact that I had been his leader for a long time, and wondered in those moments if the root of his problem might have been as simple as the leadership.

But that kind of self-doubt and pity had to be a fleeting
thing.[58]

"Oh, Will, he just never had a chance." And it was
true. He didn't have a chance. But I don't know why. I
don't know when along the way it happened. Something
to smash whatever chance there was. Whatever it was,
elusive, consumptive, and portentous, here was its
codicil.[59]

Campbell's undertaking to write his autobiography, to
spell out as truthfully as possible the story he understands
as his, is evidence of both his acceptance of what has
happened in the past as well as of his willingness to
respond to it as best he can and so go on from there:

Ah, Brother "Skeeterhawk." I remember. . . . I remember all the things you taught me and all the love you
gave. O, Dragonfly, why did you fly so fast? And so high?
Where did it all begin? I still don't know. But I
remember. I remember you. I remember us. Some day
I'll write it all down, I'll write that book you were always
going to write. But never did. It'll be your story,
Brother—the story of Joe. . . . I'll write it down the way
it happened. I'll be tempted to write it down the way I
wished it. I'll be tempted to write it the way you wished
it too. The way you wished it before it was too late.
Before the world took you. But I won't do it that way,
Brother. . . . You used to joke on birthdays and
Christmas and anniversaries, "All I want is a few kind
words." They'll be there too. A few kind words will be
there. Kind words for the dragonfly. I'll make them as
pretty as I can. . . . You were never ashamed to weep.
And I'll cry too, later, when they have all gone away. But

not yet. Not now. For I'm the preacher here, the
technician practicing his trade. And technicans don't
cry. Technicians don't have kinfolk. . . . I remember it,
Brother. I remember it all.[60]

In childhood, Joe had caught a dragonfly on Sunday
and had said if it were alive on Wednesday, Will would be
coming home and they would be together again. Joe was
buried on Tuesday—St. Valentine's day. The only words
Will can remember speaking at his brother's funeral were
those of the benediction:

> We have gathered, O Lord, to say good-bye to our
> brother. Our Campbell brother. Our East Fork
> brother. Our Christian brother of all humanity.[61]

In moving from acknowledgment of what he has been in
the past, to self-acceptance of what he is in the present, to
willingness to take responsibility for what he shall
become in the future, Will Campbell's story moves along
the lines of the classic Christian story—from confession to
reconciliation to transformation. And in moving thus, his
story may move others who hear it.

ELIE WIESEL

Although in certain basic ways the 'objective circumstances' confronting two men may appear similar, such as,
for example, the presence of evil and suffering in the
world, their responses to such circumstances may differ
vastly—perhaps even incommensurately—due to the
differing visions of reality they have as reflected in the

differing paradigmatic or 'transcendent' stories which they hold. To no small degree, the lifework of Elie Wiesel, Jewish survivor of the Holocaust, differs from that of Will Campbell for this very reason. Wiesel's story, told through autobiographical novels and expository essays rather than through autobiography *per se*,[62] holds out a distinctly Jewish vision of reality; it reflects a different paradigmatic story from that of Campbell. It is a story which offers a different meaning-scheme, an alternative background context in the light of which commitments are made. This Jewish transcendent story thus simultaneously provides the context within which to understand the thematic content of Wiesel's work and against which to analyze the development of his thought. For though Wiesel's recurring literary motifs and images—survivor, witness, storyteller—are given by that context, the moral vision of his later work at times seems to signal a departure from it. From the point of view of the Jewish paradigmatic story, that departure is a double act of faithlessness: it plays false to the story itself and at the same time displays an untrue picture of the reality of human existence in the world.

At one point in his novel, *The Town Beyond the Wall*, Wiesel writes: "If all the nations, in the long course of history, have taken bitter pains to trample on the Jews, it is perhaps because they wished to know that strange people who, more than any other, possess the secret of survival, the key to the mystery of time, the formula for endurance."[63] Elie Wiesel is Jew and survivor; he is also storyteller. For him, these three personae are inextricably connected. As Jew, he is the eternal survivor whose story history tells. As survivor, he is the one who assures that the Jewish story still lives. As storyteller, he is the one who narrates the meaning of Jewish survival:

> Whoever survives a test, whatever it may be, must tell the story, that is his duty. . . .
> For whoever lives through a trial, or takes part in an event that weighs on man's destiny or frees him, is duty-bound to transmit what he has seen, felt and feared. The Jew has always been obsessed by this obligation. He has always known that to live an experience or create a vision, and not transform it into link and promise, is to turn it into a gift to death.[64]

Ultimately, therefore, the role of the Jew is that of witness, the one whose survival testifies to the meaning of life: "A Jew fulfills his role as man only from inside his Jewishness. . . . That is why, in my writings, the Jewish theme predominates. It helps me approach the theme of man. . . . To be a Jew today, therefore, means: to testify. To bear witness to what is, and to what is no longer."[65]

This motif of the Jew as survivor and his story as witness to a true and valid portrayal of reality and its meaning has deep roots in Jewish theology. The surviving presence of the Jewish people in the world has been traditionally seen as evidence of God's continuing presence in the world. Certainly, one of the main themes of the Jewish story, traditionally understood, is that the redemption of the people Israel from the "house of bondage" in Egypt serves as testimony to Israel, to Egypt, and to all mankind of the existence of a God who cares and saves.[66] The later

Rabbinic *midrash* (exegesis) on Isaiah 43:12 makes the matter explicitly clear: "When you are my witnesses, I am God, and when you are not my witnesses, I am, as it were, not God."[67] The contention, starkly put, is this: were the Jewish people to disappear from the face of the earth (e.g., through annihilation or assimilation), then the claims of that people about God, world, and man would be discredited. Wiesel's writing, in asking again and again how it is possible to speak of God's presence in the presence of the destruction of six million Jews, reflects this traditional theme. It is within the context of the traditional story that Wiesel's story of the hanging of a child in a concentration camp gains its full measure of intelligibility and poignancy. As Wiesel sets the scene in his earliest autobiographical work, *Night*, he relates that two adults were hanged alongside the child, but because the child's weight was considerably less than theirs, his death was longer and more agonizing in coming:

> For more than half an hour he stayed there, struggling between life and death. . . . And we had to look him full in the face. . . . His tongue was still red, his eyes not yet glazed. Behind me, I heard [a] man asking: "Where is God now?" And I heard a voice within me answer him: "Where is He? Here He is—He is hanging here on this gallows."[68]

Hence, the survival of the Jew, the oppressed victim, *as Jew* in the face of the oppressor is a highly significant act. The Jew's act of survival is an ongoing avowal of the Jewish story. Wiesel writes: "Rejected by mankind, the condemned do not go so far as to reject it in turn. Their faith in history remains unshaken, and one may well wonder why. They do not despair. The proof: they persist in surviving—not only to survive, but to testify. The victims elect to become witnesses."[69]

At the same time, the survival of the Jew is also a continuing disavowal of the oppressor's story. The persistence of the Jew in telling his story, in spelling-out with his life and even at the cost of his life what human life is all about according to a Jewish conception of it, is simultaneously an act of testifying against the truth-claims of stories told by others—be they those of the Egyptian or of the Nazi.[70] Recalling the days in the camps, Wiesel says: "In those days, more than ever, to be Jewish signified *refusal*. Above all, it was a refusal to see reality and life through the enemy's eyes—a refusal to resemble him, to grant him that victory, too." And herein lies the root of the difference between the respective visions of Campbell and Wiesel. Campbell looks at the Klansman and sees his brother, "blood of our blood"; Wiesel looks at the Nazi and sees his enemy, 'the shedder of our blood.' And that is precisely as it should be, given the different paradigmatic stories of the two men. The story of the Christian is the story of a world reconciled; the story of the Jew is the story of the world in need of and waiting for reconciliation. In the Christian story, the basis for salvation and new life is the death of Jesus—the self-sacrifice of God, done for the sins of all; in the Exodus story, the prelude to redemption and a new life is the death of sinners, the Egyptians—the enemies—at the hand of God. While Campbell's justification of his ministry to the Klan lies in his claim that "we are all bastards but God loves us anyway," Wiesel's rationale for his lifework as witness to the story of survival flows from his contention that "not to remember [is] equivalent to becoming the enemy's accomplice."[71]

Yet it is finally on the shoals of the complexities of the relationship between enemy and survivor that Wiesel's own story and vision seem at times to break apart. Is it only by committing the act of forgetfulness that the survivor can become "the enemy's accomplice"? Or are there other ways that the oppressed can become the oppressor's partner? Wiesel's later work at certain points seemingly lacks the ability to sustain an investigation of these questions and their implications. At these very points in fact, the story Wiesel renders tends to break away from the traditional Jewish story and appears simultaneously to break up into a fragmented, distorted moral vision. Indeed, it is against the backdrop of Wiesel's own earlier writing that this moral fragmentation, so apparent at times in his later work, stands in starkest contrast.

In his early writings, however, Wiesel is consistently sensitive to the thinness of the line between victim and victimizer. The narrator of *Night* (1958) recalls with guilt and anguish how concentration camp life had turned him as a child against his own father, had turned an 'innocent' into one devoid of innocence. He remembers his reaction to the sight of his father being beaten by a half-crazed Kapo (camp trustee):

> I had watched the whole scene without moving. I kept quiet. In fact I was thinking of how to get farther away so

that I would not be hit myself. What is more, any anger I felt at this moment was directed not against the Kapo, but against my father. I was angry with him, for not knowing how to avoid [the Kapo's] outbreak.[72]

Nor is this only one isolated moral 'lapse.' Later, after having watched the son of a Rabbi Eliahou try to abandon his old and feeble father in order to increase his own chances for remaining alive, the child prays to God to give him the strength to remain faithful to his own father if he himself is ever put to a similar test. But being subsequently separated from his father, he thinks to himself, even as he goes out in search of him, "Don't let me find him! If only I could get rid of this dead weight, so that I could use all my strength to struggle for my own survival, and only worry about myself." Although he immediately feels ashamed of himself, "ashamed for-ever," he nevertheless only reluctantly gives up his soup ration to his father when he finally does find him: "No better than Rabbi Eliahou's son had I withstood the test." And when the father does die, after having first made repeated cries for water, only to be met with repeated blows from a Nazi guard and with his son's repeated failures to respond, the only thing the boy can even remotely feel is a sense of relief:

His last word was my name. A summons, to which I did not respond. I did not weep, and it pained me that I could not weep. But I had no more tears. And, in the depths of my being, in the recesses of my weakened conscience, could I have searched it, I might have found something like—free at last![73]

Such a confession, an admission in effect that perhaps life really is for the strong who must not be burdened in their struggle to survive by the weak and the unfit, is essentially an espousal of the Nazi story and a granting of its truth-claims about existence. Such an admission shows the ease with which the victim can take up the story of the oppressor and make it his own.

In the novel *Dawn* (1960), the theme of the potential transformation of the survivor of attempted murder into murderer himself is taken up once more. The narrator, Elisha, is a survivor of the death camps in Europe who has come to Palestine to fight with the Jewish underground against the British and thus join the effort to create a Jewish state, a place where Jews can enjoy the "right to the light of day, to joy, to the laughter of children."[74] The underground has given him the task of executing a captured British officer, Captain John Dawson, whose life the underground has vowed to take in retaliation for the British hanging of one of the organization's own men. As Elisha struggles with himself about whether or not to carry out his orders, the images of his past, the 'ghosts' of his murdered relatives and his own lost childhood, loom up before him. When he retorts by asking them of what concern the killing of John Dawson could be to them, they answer: "You are the sum total of all that we have been. . . . In a way we are the ones to execute John Dawson. Because you can't do it without us. Now do you see?"

In 'the presence of his past,' Elisha begins to understand the meaning of such an act: "An act so absolute as that of killing involves not only the killer but, as well, those who have formed him. In murdering a man I was making them murderers."[75] Finally, Elisha goes down to the room where Dawson is being held. Although it is not yet time for the scheduled execution, Elisha reasons that he has a responsibility to be there in advance because it would be "cowardly to kill a complete stranger." He even has hopes that the condemned man will tell him a funny story, thus showing that there are no hard feelings on his part, that he, too, realizes that Elisha, a soldier, is just doing his duty. Yet strangely, as Dawson begins to tell Elisha about himself, Elisha recoils: "I mustn't listen to him. . . . He's my enemy, and the enemy has no story." As Dawson calls out his name (in a scene reminiscent of the dying father's call in *Night*), Elisha shoots and kills him: "That's it. . . . It's done. I've killed. I've killed Elisha."[76] In killing an innocent man, in failing to distinguish that man from those who are truly 'enemy,' Elisha, the Jew, has killed the Jew he is by turning the history and heritage of his Jewish past into a legacy of murder.

The Town Beyond the Wall (1964) stands as Wiesel's most creative exploration of the relationship between good and evil—and man's response to both. The story is told from the perspective of a man named Michael as he sits with his thoughts, memories, and hallucinations inside a prison in Eastern Europe. He had returned home to the town of his childhood to take care of some 'unfinished business.' The trip had been made possible through the agency and 'connections' of a certain Pedro, a smuggler who befriended him. Along the way, something went awry, and the police arrested Michael, imprisoned

him, and throughout the course of the story, keep
torturing him to make him reveal his rendezvous point
with the illusive and mysterious one named Pedro. As the
plot unfolds, we come to see that Michael's torments
represent the torment of post-Holocaust humanity, and
that questions about the identity and whereabouts of
Pedro represent questions about the nature and place of
God in a post-Holocaust world. We also learn the nature
of Michael's unfinished business. Twenty years earlier,
he saw a man watch indifferently from his window as
Michael and his family were carted away to the camps.
Thus, Michael's search for the man is not only a search for
an answer to the question of how such indifference is
possible, but also of how talk of humanity and God is
possible in a world of such indifference. Speaking in
prison to Pedro as if he were there beside him, Michael
confides his reasons for returning home:

> *Are you listening, Pedro?"*
> *"I'm listening, little brother. . . . ."*
> *"Do you understand that I need to understand? To
> understand the others—the Other—those who watched
> us depart for the unknown; those who observed us,
> without emotion, while we became objects—living sticks
> of wood—and carefully numbered victims?"* Pedro
> *bowed his head still lower, as if repentant and asking
> forgiveness. . . .*
>
> This was the thing I had wanted to understand ever
> since the war. Nothing else. How a human being can
> remain indifferent. The executioners I understood; also
> the victims, though with more difficulty. But the others,
> all the others, those who were neither for nor against

. . . those who were permanently and merely specta-
tors—all those were closed to me, incomprehensible. . . .

  *It's because of him that I risked my life—and yours,
too, Pedro, I know—to come back.*[77]

The real enemy of both God and man is not the Gestapo
guard, but the one who is uncommitted, who is spectator,
who "acts as if the rest of us were not." Eventually,
Michael does search out and confront the man seen long
ago in the window, and he delivers his message of
contempt—not hate. The man cannot accept such a
message: better the hate than the contempt, for at least
hate is at some level a recognition of the human. So in one
last effort to gain Michael's hate and to regain his own
humanity, the man denounces Michael to the police. As
the police drive Michael off to prison, the man yells out,
"I feel sure you'll hate me." Only now does Michael see
that: "He had become human again. Down deep, I
thought, man is not only an executioner, not only a
victim, not only a spectator: he is all three at once."[78]
Michael now realizes that the preservation of humanity,
the preservation of God's presence in the world, the
preservation of sanity in and for human existence, are all
dependent on having "someone across from me." In
Michael's case, that "someone" is a silent boy sharing the
same prison cell. By reaching out to him and by trying to
bring him back to sanity, Michael engages in the attempt
to recreate the world and man out of the chaos which has
engulfed them: "To be indifferent—for whatever reason—is to deny not only the validity of existence, but also

its beauty. Betray, and you are a man; torture your neighbor, you're still a man. Evil is human, weakness is human; indifference is not."[79] If the ultimate enemy of God, man, and world is indifference, then the ultimate role of the survivor is to be the witness who testifies against it. His life may offer devastating evidence of the evil and the weakness that the human can engender, but his presence stands as indicting testimony against the inhumanity of indifference.

And here a problem arises. Given the sensitivity of Wiesel's moral vision and the forcefulness of his art in the early writings, how is it that at times in the later writings his perspective seems to harden while his powers of perception appear to weaken? For sometimes in this later work, another Wiesel seems to appear. This Wiesel is not the novelist/storyteller whose art lets him explore reality from a variety of angles. Instead, this Wiesel resembles the essayist/polemicist whose writing comes 'to make a point.' And it is this Wiesel whom a sympathetic reader captivated by the earlier work may find both troubled and troubling. Wiesel's comprehension of the complexities, ambiguities, and nuances of the relationship between good and evil, his awareness of the victim's potential to become oppressor, so evident in his earlier work, are seemingly left behind in certain parts of his work stemming from the late sixties and seventies, i.e., from the traumatic period following the Six Day War in 1967 and the Yom Kippur War in 1973. In writings which at times border on the moralistic, Wiesel gives his victims—simply because they are victims—a protective aura and halo which makes moral criticism of them all but impossible. For example, in a piece written in 1975, "A Plea for the Survivors," Wiesel pointedly asserts: "You will tell me that they are not saints, that there were among them, as among you, men and women who are less than perfect. That they are not all messengers. . . . Perhaps. . . . and . . . who gives you the right to judge them? They owe you no accounting; they owe you nothing."[80]

Morally, this is a dangerous claim to make, and it apparently provides the basis for a dangerous kind of moral argument that Wiesel seems to have fallen victim to himself. The logic of that argument runs like this: since the survivors have been victims, and since they have thereby become persons whom no one else may legitimately morally criticize, it thus follows that they should be—must be—morally incapable of victimizing others. In a letter "To a Concerned Friend" (late sixties-early seventies) reflecting that kind of reasoning, Wiesel writes:

> The Jew in victory will not disappoint you: he remains unchanged, even under changing conditions. He may no longer be victim, yet he will never be tormentor. He will not try to break the will of enemies in his power by means of gallows and/or humiliation. . . . Walk about the Western Bank and you will feel neither the horror nor the pity inevitably inspired by the European ghettos. . . . Also, people here are free. Free to go wherever they wish, see whomever they wish. The local dignitaries will speak overtly of their opposition to Israel: they know they won't be punished.[81]

The increase in the levels of tension and violence between Jew and Arab in the West Bank in the late seventies, however, would seem to belie the veracity and validity of such claims as these. But what seems to belie these claims of the later Wiesel even more is the moral vision displayed in the writing of the earlier Wiesel. What kind of claim is Wiesel making in *Night* and *Dawn* if not the one that even a victim can become a victimizer? What is Wiesel's message in *The Town Beyond the Wall* if not that "man is not only an executioner, not only a victim, not only a spectator," but "all three at once"? In the last analysis, the answers to these questions are not ones that Wiesel must merely provide for us. Ultimately, they are ones he must provide for himself.

Indeed, on those occasions when Wiesel appears to lose sight of the moral vision displayed in his earlier work, he also appears ready to take the short step from being above even the *possibility* of moral criticism and reproach to being in position to criticize and reproach others self-righteously for their alleged moral shortcomings. For instance, although he grants that keeping a 'moral scoreboard' of victimization is "out of place and odious," he nevertheless goes on to chastise Solzhenitsyn in a diary excerpt of 1975 for failing to give the suffering of the Jews adequate attention in his writing about the oppressiveness of the Soviet regime:

> He tells at length about the persecution of the priests—but not about the persecution of the rabbis, Talmudists, and scholars, the mainstays of the yeshivoth. He describes the measures against the church—

but not those against the synagogue. He dwells on the often heroic torments of believing Christians—but says nothing about the pain and resistance of the believing Jew.[82]

Hence, when Wiesel's moral vision becomes transfixed by—and fixated on—the thought that the victim can never become the victimizer, and so stands as moral judge above all moral judgment, his style tends to become moralistic while his tone sounds increasingly preachy. Whereas part of the power of Campbell's story lies in the way in which the author artfully allows the images of "brother" and "dragonfly" to develop and move through time, Wiesel's images of "victim and "survivor" seem stuck in time—frozen, fixed, static—and thus cripple both his powers of storytelling and the story he would tell.

Importantly, in those instances that Wiesel moves to this narrowed perspective of some of his later work, he leaves behind not only the wider moral vision of his earlier stories, but also the paradigmatic Jewish story as well: if there is one thing that both the biblical and rabbinic traditions see and say clearly, it is the conviction that even Israel, the formerly oppressed-but-now-redeemed, may yet sin, and the Torah makes explicit that even those who were sinners and oppressors may yet be reconciled.[83] These elements of that paradigmatic Jewish story stress the importance of the capacity for self-criticism and the ability to move from blame for injustices committed in the past to moral responsibility for what shall be done in the future. These central parts of the

Jewish story count against the truthfulness and the justifiability of the kind of story that Wiesel at times seems inclined to convey. But the relationship is reciprocal. The story put forward by Wiesel on such occasions counts against the justifiability of the Jewish story, too. The inability of the Jewish story to provide Wiesel with a story that can consistently sustain his moral vision and protect him from false and destructive stories, undermines the credibility that Wiesel or anyone else would claim for the Jewish story. For at some point, one must ask, If a paradigmatic story cannot even provide the one who espouses it with the skill to see and live life truthfully, why ought anyone else take that story seriously? Why ought anyone else consider that story as a possible 'live option' for his own life? If only on this level alone, the Jewish story as testified to by Wiesel's own story appears at times somehow less credible, convincing, and compelling—less justified—than the Christian vision of reality reflected in and witnessed by Will Campbell's life story and life's work.

Throughout this chapter, and the ones preceding it, I have referred repeatedly to the notion of paradigmatic stories, e.g., 'the Christian story,' 'the Jewish story,' and I have even on occasion talked about the criteria of assessment such stories involve. However, by and large, the discussion of these stories and their justifiability has been conducted in a rather indirect and secondary way in order first to begin to show some of the ways in which particular kinds of stories are necessary—as the background contexts in and against which our moral and religious convictions gain their meaning and significance—and second, to sort out some of the various kinds of stories these paradigmatic stories are *not*—e.g., fables and allegories—and lastly, to give some indication of the ways in which certain kinds of stories—life stories such as biographies and autobiographies—may be shown to have important implications for theology and may provide at least part of the basis for both raising and answering the questions of truth and justifiability in narrative. These tasks now completed, the time has come to investigate the character and claims of some of these paradigmatic stories themselves, and it is to these topics that the next chapter turns.

V

'THE STORY OF OUR LIFE':
BIBLICAL NARRATIVE

The title of this chapter alludes to a phrase found in the work of the great American theologian, H. Richard Niebuhr. Forty years ago he reminded his colleagues that the early teachers of the church, when asked what they meant by 'God,' 'salvation,' 'revelation'—by a 'Christian' understanding of experience—were frequently compelled to turn at last "to the story of their life, saying, 'What we mean is this event [i.e., the life, death, and resurrection of Christ] which happened among us and to us.'"[1]

Niebuhr's observation may seem to some a statement of the obvious. Yet at times, there are things so obvious that we fail to notice them. In his day, Niebuhr was trying to redirect theological attention to something, which though plainly evident, had nevertheless been consistently overlooked: the fact that the most basic Christian

convictions had their fundamental source and setting
within a framework constituted by biblical narrative. In
our day, other religious thinkers are once again
reasserting the necessity of attending seriously to biblical
narrative for an adequate understanding and justification
of those convictions which are at the heart of a Christian
or Jewish theology. This chapter will attend closely to the
work of these contemporary figures as well as to that of
two of their intellectual forebearers, i.e., Niebuhr and
G. E. Wright, in order to explore both the major themes
stressed and the critical issues raised in the employment
of biblical narrative for theology.

With the rise of neoorthodoxy in the first part of this
century came a call for theology to break out of its
bewitchment with various philosophical and secular
movements (e.g., Hegelianism, naturalism, romanti-
cism, liberalism) and pay heed instead to the Bible's
'message.' But short of reverting to an untenable
fundamentalism, how could that demand be met? In their
own distinctive ways, H. Richard Niebuhr[2] and G. E.
Wright[3] represent attempts at answering that question.

Although many religious thinkers had noticed that
much of what the Bible has to say is cast in story form,[4]
Niebuhr was among the first explicitly to address the
significance of that feature for theology. In the first place,
Niebuhr believed that the great religions in general, and
Christianity in particular "make their impact on us by
calling into question our whole conception of what is
fitting—that is, of what really fits in—by questioning our
picture of the context into which we now fit our actions."[5]
In Niebuhr's view, these religious traditions, through

the stories they present, both ask and respond to the question, "What is going on?"[6]

The Meaning of Revelation (1941) gives Niebuhr's account of Christianity's response. The book's claim is that for Christians, understanding "what is going on" is a matter of following a special kind of story: history. Quite pointedly, Niebuhr reminds us that

> The preaching of the early Christian church was not an argument for the existence of God nor an admonition to follow the dictates of some common human conscience, unhistorical and super-social in character. It was primarily a simple recital of the great events connected with the historical appearance of Jesus Christ and a confession of what had happened to the community of disciples. Whatever it was that the church meant to say, whatever was revealed or manifested to it could be indicated only in connection with an historical person and events in the life of his community. The confession referred to history and was consciously made in history.[7]

In short, Christian storytelling is history-telling.

Niebuhr realized, however, that the notion of 'history' is ambiguous. Out of all the contingent events in the world, what justifies our singling out some of them and tying them together in a single story? More basically, what originally enables us to claim that *a story* is there at all? He likens revelation to an illuminatory passage in an otherwise opaque book. Such a passage sheds light on what has come before and on what will follow so that we can gain some understanding of the work as a whole. In terms of history, revelation is the "intelligible event which makes all other events intelligible." In Christian terms, revelation "is called Jesus Christ, in whom we see the righteousness of God, his power and wisdom. But from [this] we also derive the concepts which make possible the elucidation of all the events in our history."[8]

At this point, Niebuhr makes his now famous distinction between "internal" and "external" history. As his remarks about revelation make clear, he does not naively believe that 'history' is just 'there' waiting to be read off the surface of events. He is fully aware that many histor*ies*, many stories, are abroad in the world, each claiming to provide a way of making sense of the world. What criteria are there for choosing among these rival narrative accounts? The theory of internal versus external history represents Niebuhr's attempted solution.

The discussion is reminiscent of Buber. Thus, while 'I-It' best expresses one's relationship to the events of external history, 'I-Thou' characterizes the relationships of internal history. The concerns of external history "are all impersonal; they are ideas, interests, movements among things." By contrast, the stuff of internal history is essentially personal in nature. External history describes "what is going on" from the point of view of a detached spectator; internal history narrates the course of events from the perspective of the engaged participant. For Niebuhr, neither can be reduced to the other:

> If we begin with the spectator's knowledge of events we cannot proceed to the participant's apprehension. There is no continuous movement from an objective inquiry into the life of Jesus to a knowledge of him as the Christist

who is our Lord. Only a decision of the self, a leap of faith, a *metanoia* or revolution of the mind can lead from observation to participation and from observed to lived history. And this is true of all other events in sacred history.[9]

To be sure, there is a point at which internal and external history may converge—the revelatory experience in which "the truth is transformed and the search for continuous relations in the world which contemplative reason views is expedited and liberated."[10] Through such transformation, the purely 'neutral' and descriptive becomes normative and prescriptive. History becomes not just any story, but *our* story. In Niebuhr's view, a justifiable theology ultimately does not merely *read* biblical narrative: it *confesses* it.

Most certainly, that theme resonates through the work of G.E. Wright, who saw a biblically based theology as "first and foremost a theology of recital, in which Biblical man confesses his faith by reciting the formative events of history as the redemptive handiwork of God."[11] At a very basic level, Wright's book, *God Who Acts* (1952), is an extended critique of those who would do theology on purely propositional, speculative—i.e., non-narrative— grounds.[12] By contrast, Wright contends that a truly biblical theology must be a confessional theology whose business is "to tell a story and then to expound its meaning."[13]

For Wright, as it had been for Niebuhr, that story is an essentially historical account whose meaning extends to all of history. Thus, the historical narratives found in the

Bible offer an interpretative context in which "individual events are set and ultimately receive their meaning." Such events for Wright represent the acts of God and the human responses to them, and biblical faith, rather than being a projection on them, instead arises from them. Through the biblical portrayals of such historical events as the Exodus and the life, work, and death of Christ, we come to understand the character of God and the destiny of man. Wright therefore concludes that any justifiable biblical theology must constantly keep in mind that

> Israel's doctrine of God . . . was not derived from systematic or speculative thought, but rather in the first instance from the attempt to explain the events which led to the establishment of the nation. . . . The knowledge of God was an inference from what . . . had happened in human history. . . .
>
> For Israel the covenant, by which the meaning and implications of election were concretely stated, was not faith projected on history, but a real event of history which illumined the meaning of subsequent history.[14]

Wright believes that in the last analysis, the justifiability of both faith and theology depends on the justifiability of the interpretative context displayed by historical biblical narratives.[15]

At this juncture, we must be very careful. Neither Wright nor any of the other figures in this chapter would claim that a biblically faithful narrative theology can simply dispense with theology's traditionally more abstract, propositional formulations. What they would and do claim is that the basis of theology must not be those formulations *alone*. Although theology must involve critical reflection, it must not forget the narratives from which such reflection draws its significance and force. Wright puts the matter this way:

> Biblical theology cannot be completely unsystematic—indeed it must constantly and critically observe its own discrepancies and paradoxes—but it is not primarily concerned with an abstract "system of thought." It is rather a reflective discipline which seeks to portray the peculiar Biblical concern with man's involvement in a God-directed history and with God's activity relative to man's historical problem, need and hope.[16]

Hence, a justifiable theology must grasp both poles—narrative and systematic reflection on it. If Wright himself at times seems rather heavy-handed in his emphasis of the former over the latter, perhaps he may be excused in light of the theological circumstances in which he wrote. On the one hand, for instance, there was Tillich's investigation of the Unconditioned (and so unhistorical) Being; on the other, there was Bultmann's call for the demythologization (and, as Wright saw it, the subsequent abandonment) of biblical narrative in favor of some more 'authentic' existential stance.[17] Even so, however, the basic thrust of Wright's thesis cannot be ignored. Whatever else a theological account of biblical faith may be, it must at least be faithful to the biblical narrative in which it has its source and from which it derives its meaning: "In other words, the fundamental requirement of a Biblical theology is that the historical movement and interaction of the Bible be retained while the faith is being set forth in summary statements *true to its own nature*."[18] In the end, for both Wright and Niebuhr, understanding 'the Bible's message' depends on grasping the fact that biblical narrative unfolds not merely biblical history, but essentially all history.

However, as attractive and powerful as the views of Wright and Niebuhr seemed to be, they were not without problems of their own, problems which, left unresolved, eventually undermined the credibility of their claims. Although there may be valid warrant for linking the biblical message to revelation in history, Niebuhr and Wright never really made it clear whether that message resided in the biblical text itself, in a phenomenon 'behind' the text, or in some combination of text plus event.[19] Due to their lack of clarity on this point, Wright and Niebuhr are thus left open to the even more damning criticism of James Barr, who claims that while they may have succeeded in taking history seriously, they nevertheless have failed to take *the biblical text* seriously:

> The "historical" acts of God make sense only because they are set within a framework of conceptions, stories, and conversations which cannot be expressed by any normal use of the term "history." Even in the prime example, the Exodus, the idea that God intervenes is intelligible only because this God identifies himself in dialogue with Moses as the God of the Fathers, and thus relates himself to the preceding narrative. The Exodus story cannot be interpreted as a story having its point of origin in the Exodus "event"; for that "event" itself depends both in the form of the story itself and in any

> historical actuality which may have taken place on what
> was already thought and said and known before the
> event took place.[20]

By uncritically allowing the category of biblical narrative
to collapse into a vague notion of 'revelation-in-history,'
Niebuhr and Wright had set the stage for the collapse of
much of the theoretical foundation used to support their
claims. While a good deal of biblical narrative does
display certain historical elements and features, a truly
narrative theology must not forget that what has primacy
is *the narrative* and *not* the various component parts
which the narrative contains.

Indeed, in the seventies, a whole new generation of
theologians began to appear whose work constantly
returns to just this point, for part of the point of their work
is to restore biblical narrative to a position of central
importance for the doing of theology. While not unaware
of the earlier criticism directed against thinkers such as
Niebuhr and Wright, these contemporary theologians
were dissatisfied with the apparent theological alternatives provided by, e.g., the New Hermeneutic and the
New Quest. According to one of these current narrative
theologians, Hans Frei, theology guided by such
alternatives had become "a matter of fitting the biblical
story into another world with another story rather than
incorporating the world into the biblical story."[21] For
thinkers such as Frei, recent theological trends, instead
of casting biblical narrative into obscurity, had merely
underscored its relevancy all the more.

The rest of this chapter will be devoted to the work of

this new breed of narrative theologian. A survey of that work will enable us to raise certain critical questions at the end of the chapter, which in turn will let us embark on the next chapter's analysis of the overall justifiability of a narrative theology. The present discussion will follow a rough and ready typology. The first type consists of those figures who take the structure and form of biblical narrative as being the best guide for understanding the structure of reality. I shall therefore discuss them under the heading, "Structuring the Story." By contrast, those figures of the second type focus on the content of the Bible's stories, on what is unfolded and developed in and through the narrative. Their interests revolve around two interrelated topics: what a story means, and what it means to understand and *follow* a story. Consequently, I will examine them under the heading, "Following the Story." The third type embraces those theologians whose primary concern is the ethic expressed through biblical narrative. These I have classified under the rubric, "Enacting the Story." Obviously, several writers could be classified under either or both of the other headings as well. For example, one would expect that those who fall under "Enacting the Story" would surely have something to say about the importance of the way a story is structured and the manner it is followed. However, as I said before, this present means of proceeding will not only let us see some of the dominant themes of narrative theology; it will also let us begin to appreciate more fully some of the critical issues involved in using narrative for theology.

I. STRUCTURING THE STORY

As I stated above, the writers in this group attend to the structure and 'shape' of biblical narrative. Although they are also concerned with *what* is expressed in the stories, their more basic interest is *how* such things are expressed. For them at least, how things are presented in a story determines much of what is represented by the story.

In this section, as in the others to follow, I will begin with the work of a theologian whose thought I take to be somewhat theoretical and abstract and then go on to examine another writer whose suggestions are relatively more concrete and substantive. Thus, I hope to indicate some of the conceptual underpinnings of this biblically based narrative theology as well as some of the ways biblical narratives have actually been theologically employed. To repeat, I believe that one of the strengths of this procedure lies in its capacity to illuminate the crucial critical questions involved for justifying a narrative theology.

1. *Hans Frei* (1922-   ) is a German-born scholar, whose academic career, both as student and as teacher, has largely been spent at Yale, where his interests have centered on the relationship between religious thought and Western culture. In his book, *The Eclipse of Biblical Narrative* (1974), Frei describes what he believes to be the mistake responsible for crippling biblical criticism and theology over the past two hundred years: the separation of a biblical narrative's meaning from its truth and the disjunction between the story and 'reality.'[22]

Frei asserts that although most of the significant Bible commentators of the 1700s agreed that several of the biblical stories had certain "realistic" or "history-like" aspects, these features eventually were ignored and even denied outright simply because the commentators lacked a method for isolating them and accounting for their presence.[23] However, prior to that time, three factors played key roles in supporting a "traditional" or "pre-critical realistic reading" of the Bible; ironically, these same three factors would later help undermine that very kind of reading. First, because biblical narratives were read literally, "it followed automatically that they referred to and described actual historical events." Second, for the traditional reading to work, it had to assume that "if the real historical world described by the several biblical stories is a single world of one temporal sequence, there must in principle be one cumulative story to depict it." That assumption in turn quite naturally led to a theory of "figuration"—the belief that earlier Old Testament stories prefigured a New Testament fulfillment. However, the third and most crucial leg supporting the precritical realistic reading was the notion that "since the world truly rendered by combining biblical narratives into one was indeed the one and only real world, it must in principle embrace the experience of any present age and reader. . . . He was to see his disposition, his actions and passions, the shape of his own life as well as that of his era's events as figures of that storied world.[24] In other words, extra-biblical thought, experience, and reality were made accessible through the biblical story—and not the reverse.

However, in Frei's view, that relationship has gradually become reversed during the course of the last two centuries. Frei contends that during that time, theology lost sight of both the primacy and character of biblical narrative. He notes that beginning as early as the seventeenth century, critics and commentators increasingly ceased regarding the Bible's stories as being in any sense 'historical,' tending instead to treat them as primitive, prescientific formulations of realia better accounted for through other kinds of descriptive formats, e.g., scientific historical research. Consequently, the biblical narrative was no longer the *sine qua non* which rendered accessible the structure and substance of all human existence. On the contrary, it had been reduced to a secondary and rather inessential source which might happily at times 'chime in' with results derived from other theological (and non-theological) settings.[25] In any event, the connection between narrative and reality had been severed. Those who still wished to *save* the story now had to show that it somehow linked up with the world 'out there.'

In a very thorough historical analysis, Frei shows that the strategy involved in trying to save the story was based on a tragic error in judgment—the mistaken attempt to detach the story's meaning from its truth. What resulted were two new—and irreconcilable—disciplines: biblical theology and historical criticism. Historical criticism abandoned the idea that the biblical narratives presented one cumulative story that displayed the whole movement of human history toward an end. Instead, it argued that the real reference of the text lay *outside the text*. That

reference was twofold: (1) to the original meaning of the
text to its original audience, and (2) to the way in which
the text's account of things either fit or failed to fit "what
really happened." Consequently, there was no attempt to
unify the canon; a unified view of reality reflecting an
overarching biblical narrative became an impossibility.
The only remaining source for such unification was
biblical theology, and its role was to "establish the unity of
religious meaning across the gap of historical and cultural
differences."[26] By and large, trying to bridge that gap took
the form of attempts to show the unity of biblical ideas,
concepts, and beliefs from some timeless perspective. In
any case, the damage had been done. The question of the
biblical story's truth (historical criticism) had been
separated from the question of the story's meaning
(biblical theology), and the answers to both questions
were thought to lie outside the story itself.

In Frei's judgment, this flawed theological strategy,
begun in the late seventeenth century, has continued
down to the middle of the twentieth. He claims that for all
their differences, such diverse figures as Locke, Butler,
Semler, Schleiermacher, Ritschl, Brunner, Bultmann,
Rahner, Ebeling, Pannenberg, and Moltmann have all
adopted the strategy of separating truth from meaning
and narrative from 'reality': "They have all been agreed
that one way or another the religious *meaningfulness* (as
distinct from demonstration of the truth [of the claim of
biblical narrative]) could, indeed must, be perspicuous
through its relation to other accounts of general human
experience."[27] Frei concludes that theologians, in leaving

behind biblical narrative, have been forced to move to some other framework of meaning such as "radical hope, radical faith, radical obedience, or radically authentic being." He claims, however, that each of these new conceptual frameworks entails an "ethicizing, existentializing, privatizing stance," offering only a

> tenuous apprehension of a genuine, public, determinate and real world which is capable of significant depiction and of significant impact on the identity and destiny of the individuals engulfed in it. Lacking is the sense of a depictively rendered coordination of historical forces, specific circumstances and individuals, which would allow the last to be at once specific selves and yet identifiably rooted in a determinate, societal type.[28]

And here Frei makes the kind of observation with which the other figures in this chapter would most likely wholeheartedly agree. He cogently points out that biblical narrative was not abandoned for some more directly available world or reality; instead, the biblical story was exchanged *for another story* thought to depict reality in some truer and more meaningful way. As Frei sees it, modern theology has reflectd a clash between stories:

> The alternative to this dismissal of Jesus from the context of any and every real world seems to be to turn his life, teaching, and destiny into a figural representation. . . . *By something like figuration in reverse, he is now entered into another story.* . . . It may be the "progressive" world rendered by Karl Marx's dialectical

depiction, or a world of which the real substance is "salvation history." In any event, the reinterpretation means that the reversal which started in the late seventeenth century has been fully effected. The elements of the story that figural interpretation had originally woven into one single narrative have now been transposed into another framework. Their meaning, detached from their narrative setting, is now their reference to some other story, some other world, some other context of interpretation.[29]

The reversal to end all reversals had taken place.

Frei obviously believes that that reversal resulted from a consistent failure to attend sufficiently to the structure of biblical narrative. His own suggestion for setting things straight once again is to (re)consider the biblical stories as "realistic" or "history-like" narratives and thus pay more serious attention to their "narrative shape." That kind of realistic, history-like quality, says Frei, arises from the sort of depiction that "constitutes and does not merely illustrate or point to the meaning of the narrative and theme it cumulatively renders; and simultaneously it depicts and renders the reality . . . it talks about." Quite perceptively, Frei notes that in history-like writing, as in history writing, "the story is the meaning." In both types of writing, the meaning emerges in and through that particular story form. Realistic narratives, such as those in the Bible for example, display the kind of narrative structure in which the "descriptive shape and meaning cohere" through the "direct interaction of character, descriptively communicative words, social context and circumstance, whether miraculous or not."[30] In Frei's view, the difference between realistic narratives and truly historical accounts is that of "reference or . . . lack of reference"; it is not, however, that "a different kind of account [is] appropriate in each case."[31] In any event, Frei stands by his basic claim: to take the structural shape of biblical narrative seriously is to take it as the shape of reality.[32]

2. *Sallie McFague* (1933-   )is the Methodist, Yale-educated, former dean of the Vanderbilt Divinity School, who was previously married to fellow-theologian Eugene TeSelle,[33] and who has consistently been interested in the implications of literature for theology. Her book *Speaking in Parables* (1975), provides one of the most thoroughgoing analyses of the way in which the structure of some particular story may shape a particular under-standing of reality. In it she claims that the structure displayed by parables furnishes the basis for all Christian—and indeed all human—understanding of God, self, and world.

McFague argues for this thesis on both anthropological and Christological grounds. By 'parable,' she means an "extended metaphor," and she claims that our need for metaphor lies in the fact that "metaphor follows the way the human mind *works*. Metaphor is not only a poetic device for the creation of new meaning, metaphor is as ultimate as thought. It is and can be *the* source for new insight because all human discovery is by metaphor." Metaphor shows human beings to be the kind of creatures we uniquely are—"the only creatures in the universe . . .

who can *envision* a future and consciously work toward achieving it. The process is a dialectic of imaging new frames and contexts for our ordinary worlds, of seeing a new world which is also the old world."[34] In sum, the structure of both metaphor and parable reflect the structure of human thought and thus the structure of humanly perceived reality as well.

For their part, McFague's Christological claims are just as bold. Rather than simply allude to the well-known fact that many of Jesus' teachings took the form of parables, McFague makes the stronger assertion that for Christians, parables offer *"the only legitimate way of speaking of the incursion of the divine into history."*[35] In her view, Jesus did not merely tell parables about God and the kingdom of God, but more crucially, Jesus was *"himself* the parable of God. . . . [He] *was* the kingdom."[36] McFague attempts to justify that view by arguing that it is not some sort of hypothetical construct *"applied to* literary genres of the Christian tradition," but is instead "a kind of reflection that arises *from* them."[37] Consequently, the story of Jesus as the parable of God lets us see how "the transcendent touches the worldly—only in and through and under ordinary life."[38] Thus for McFague, the structure of a specific kind of biblical narrative—parable—and the structure of reality are ultimately mirror images of one another.[39]

But McFague is not through yet. Pushing this understanding of biblical narrative even further, she maintains that it obliges us "to take the mundane story of Jesus . . . as *the* metaphor of all human movement." She explains that

> [For] the Christian, the story of Jesus is *the* story par excellence. For his story not only is the human struggle of moving toward belief but in some way that story *is* the unification of the mundane and the transcendent. . . . [It shows us] God's way of always being with human beings *as they are,* as the concrete, temporal beings who have a beginning and an end—who are, in other words, themselves stories.[40]

McFague thinks that narratives such as the story of Jesus 'grab' us precisely because of the isomorphic structure they share with all human experience:

> We all love a good story because of the basic narrative quality of human experience; . . . and a good story is *good* precisely because somehow it rings true to human life. Human life is not marked by instantaneous rapture and easy solutions. Life is tough. That is hardly a novel thought, but is nonetheless the backbone in a literal sense—the structure—of a good story. . . . In a sense, a good story, a true story, is "true to" the structure of human experience.[41]

In the end, this 'structuralist' account of McFague, like that of Frei before it, contends that the veracity of biblical narrative lies in its faithful depiction of the structure of reality. Shape of story and shape of experience ultimately go hand-in-hand.[42]

II. FOLLOWING THE STORY

Obviously, a story is more than its structural or formal elements. The way it is fleshed out is as vital as the skeleton it is given. As important as the question of *how* a story is presented is the question of *what* is revealed through its presentation. Paul van Buren and Irving Greenberg have in fact focused on that very question.

1. *Paul van Buren* (1924-   ) is an Episcopalian, Basel-trained professor of religious studies at Temple University, where his interests have recently turned to the theological necessity of an ongoing dialogue between Jews and Christians for a proper understanding of their shared biblical mission.[43] At the beginning of his book, *The Burden of Freedom* (1976), Van Buren states quite straightforwardly what he takes theology's task to be: "By 'theology,' then, I mean nothing more nor less than critical reflection by Christians about the One whom they believe has set them in this world, and about this world in which he has set them."[44] With similar plain-spokenness, the rest of the book lays out Van Buren's central conviction that due to an almost perverse refusal to listen seriously to the way the biblical narratives portray that One, theology's traditional conceptions of God, his freedom, and the consequent implications for human beings have all been "profoundly wrong and need to be reconstructed in a radically new way."[45]

Van Buren believes that all too frequently, theology has tended to treat God as a philosophical abstraction. By contrast, he contends that it is time to return God to his rightful theological—and logical—status, namely that accorded persons. Van Buren is not unaware that some will protest his insistence that we resume speaking of God and his freedom the way the Bible's stories do, i.e., in essentially personal terms. But that is precisely his point! Though such person-oriented talk of God may be "an extended or stretched use of language,"[46] it is nevertheless primarily through the biblical narratives' use of such language that we learn to speak of God at all. Van Buren grants that one may, of course, still opt to speak of God as being an "infinite Absolute" such that instead of being conceived as in any way personal, God subsequently becomes regarded as an "it." Yet as he dryly observes:

> How such an absolute abstraction can commit itself to a particular people, rescue them from slavery, get furiously angry with them, shed tears of love over them, I do not know, and I will leave to those who wish to carry on such a theology to see what they can come up with that commends itself. . . . If on the other hand we hear the biblical witnesses of . . . God . . . , then I do not see how we can avoid admitting that we are speaking of God as we speak of persons.[47]

In Van Buren's opinion, the only way for theology to get its story straight about the nature of God and his freedom—as well as our own—is to go back straightaway to those biblical stories which tell us about God and about ourselves:

> The whole story, from the call of Abraham to the appearances of the risen Jesus, and reflected back into a story of creation and a covenant with Noah and ahead into an unimaginable victory, is a story that opens up that mystery of God's freedom. The word we hear is that

this God, regardless of whatever ideas men may have about him, this God refuses to be without his creatures, without men and women. He refuses, that is, to be God without us sharing in all that he has to give us.[48]

In a very basic sense, these biblical narratives set the bounds and limits of God's freedom. Van Buren argues that in turning its back on that biblical notion of God's freedom, choosing instead some philosophical formulation of boundless or unqualified freedom, theology becomes faced with a whole barrage of insurmountable— and unnecessary—theoretical stumbling blocks. In the first place, as Van Buren rightly notes, the word 'freedom,' by its very use, seems to be a *relative* term, i.e., one always used with respect to some particular context or circumstance. Hence, the attempt to use it in a sense abstracted from all contexts and all circumstances so as to arrive at some sort of unqualified and 'absolute freedom' is, in Van Buren's words, "a move that takes us right out of how we speak English." More seriously, however, such a move turns the freedom of the personal God about whom we hear in the biblical stories into "the abstract condition of an eternal state of affairs."[49] Consequently, we abandon the biblical God who through his promises, covenants, and commitments has freely chosen to limit his freedom, thus taking responsibility for some things but not for others, and instead, we embrace the insoluble problems associated with worshiping a deity so free that everything from Hitler's holocaust to our own home-grown homicides must be seen as his—or its—responsibility.[50] Yet worst of all is that by accepting this false idealization of God's freedom, we simultaneously create a false image of what human freedom ought to be like as well—as though our ideal freedom should be the ability to do what we want, "though all the world can go to hell."[51] But as both the biblical narratives and Van Buren remind us, that kind of freedom belongs neither to God nor to human beings:

> The God of Abraham, Isaac, and Israel, the God of Sinai, and the God of Jesus Christ is the God of freedom in such a way as to prove his freedom by qualifying it to make room for the freedom of his creatures. He is free to make his freedom dependent on theirs, so that the realization of his freedom awaits the realization of the freedom of the sons and daughters of God.[52]

No matter what the tale this age and its theological bards may try to tell, the saga of the world's redemption which biblical narrative relates is, according to Van Buren, one which makes that redemption dependent on the mutual dependency between God and humankind.

2. *Irving Greenberg* (1933-   ) is a Harvard-educated Jewish scholar whose standing as a member of the Jewish studies department at CUNY and as director of the National Jewish Resource Center has given him the opportunity to reflect creatively on the survival of the Jewish people after the holocaust. In his article, "Judaism and History: Historical Events and Religious Change" (1977), Greenberg observes that most of human life has been measured by what might be called "the statistical norm of human existence":

The vast majority of all the human beings who ever lived have lived in poverty and oppression, their lives punctuated by sickness and suffering. . . .

Of the nameless and faceless billions, we know little and can say even less. Of the wealthy and the powerful and the creative whose records we *do* have, we can say that inescapable tragedies were built into their existence, including vulnerability and failures, separation from and loss of loved ones, and untimely death. Thus, most of humankind know the world as indifferent or hostile. Statistically speaking, human history is unredeemed, and human life is of little value.[53]

Judaism, however, disagrees with this assessment of human existence. It asserts, claims Greenberg, "that much of what passes for reality and history, the statistical norm of human existence, is really a deviation from the ultimate reality."[54] Judaism bases that assertion on an actual Jewish experience in history: the Exodus. Greenberg thus concludes that the Exodus is for Jews the normative perspective, the "orienting experience," by which "all of life and all other experience could be judged and oriented." As such, the Exodus narrative, a specific Bible story, provides an orientation to experience different from that offered by the story of Pharaoh and the Egyptian overseers or by any other story which gives a statistical norm version of human existence:

The Exodus is an "orienting experience" because [it] makes certain claims. There is a God who cares; human beings are His creatures and are valuable. The Exodus implies that no human power is absolute, for this God transcends human power. It follows that human power is conditional and temporary—at least until a time comes when there is a reality which is consonant with this model of perfection. That humans are meant to be free also follows from the Exodus experience. Exodus morality means treating people on the basis of freedom or value rather than by power and use, which, of course, has been the usual standard of behavior throughout history.[55]

Importantly, the Exodus does not claim that the world, by virtue of the redemption of Israel, has itself been fully redeemed. Slavery, genocide, poverty, and idolatry—the evil in the world—still exist the day after the Exodus as they existed the day before the Exodus.[56] But while the Exodus may not show that the world is fully redeemed at present, it does show *as history* that the world carries with it the possibility of being fully redeemable in the future. In Greenberg's words, the Exodus "is a statement of what *will be,* based on an experience already undergone." Therefore, says Greenberg, Jewish faith is not so much a matter of certitude as of testimony.[57]

Yet such testimony may be open to contradiction or even refutation. If the Exodus offers historical evidence for certain claims about the nature and direction of history, then the possibility must exist that other historical events can provide evidence to support contrary claims:

Defeats or disasters of the Jewish people weaken the effect of its testimony. Thus the credibility of faith is also dialectical. Faith is not pure abstraction, unaffected or unshaken by contradictory events; it is subject to "refutation." Yet it is not simply empirical either. A purely empirical faith would be subject to immediate refutation, but in fact, the people of Israel may continue to testify in exile and after defeat. . . . On the other hand, if redemption never came or if Israel lost hope while waiting for redemption, then the status quo would win and Jewish testimony would come to an end. Thus, faith is neither a simple product of history nor insulated from history. It is testimony anchored in history, in constant tension with it, subject to revision and understanding as well as to fluctuation in credibility due to the unfolding events.[58]

If the Jews were to disappear through, for example, genocide or assimilation, the claims of the Exodus story and of Judaism would thereby be shown to have been false. The Exodus story would be shown to have been not an orienting experience, but rather a dis-orienting experience that turned people away from a true understanding of the meaning of human existence.[59]

Moreover, even if subsequent events might not totally discredit the claims of the Exodus narrative, they may nevertheless force a revised interpretation of that story. Greenberg notes that the destruction of the Second Temple in 70 challenged certain prior, Exodus-based assumptions about the way God manifests his presence and power in history. In the Exodus story, God actively intervenes in history to rescue his people from their enemies "by a mighty hand and through an outstretched arm." But after the destruction, how could God possibly be called "great, mighty, and awesome"? (See Deu-

teronomy 10:17.) Greenberg's answer begins with a
citation of the Midrashic response of the Talmudic sages:

> This is His might—that He controls His urges. When
> the wicked flourish [for example, the Temple is
> destroyed], He is patient with them [that is, He gives
> them time and freedom to act; He does not intervene
> and stop them]. And this is God's awesomeness—were
> it not for the awe of God, how could this one
> people—the Jewish people—exist among all the other
> nations that are out to destroy it?[60]

Greenberg's own response continues:

> How is it known that God is, in fact, present after the
> Destruction? Only by a radical reinterpretation of His
> presence in the world: He controls Himself. He is the
> hidden presence, not the intervening presence. The
> only other way we know of His presence is that His
> people continue to exist in defiance of all logic and all
> force. This proves that behind it all there is a God who
> keeps the Jewish people alive.[61]

If "proves" sounds too strong here, then perhaps "offers
evidence" might be a happier choice of words. In any
event, however, Greenberg's point is that the rabbis
were committed to a reinterpretation of one part of the
Exodus story because of their more basic commitment to
the Exodus narrative as a whole. The historical event of
the Temple's destruction obliged those Jews bound to the
historically oriented Exodus narrative to reread history in
a way that took account of that new—and disastrous—

event in history. To do otherwise, "to go on speaking of God as if nothing had happened would be a lie. To go on with the same religious way of life would be a contradiction of the historical model of revelation, which demands that catastrophe be taken seriously in order that Judaism make credible—not merely pious—statements."[62]

On Greenberg's analysis, the possibility that the Exodus story may have to be revised or even discarded as false follows from the story itself. Thus, unless one is willing to admit that possibility, one does not truly understand how the story follows or what the story means.

III. ENACTING THE STORY

There is, of course, another sense in which one can follow a story; one can try to 'follow through' on a story's moral implications. One can take up the story in one's own life story. In this section, I will examine the work of two theologians who have explored the significance of biblical narrative for ethics.

1. *Stanley Hauerwas* (1940-   ) is a Texas-bred, Yale-educated Methodist who has taught for years at the Roman Catholic University of Notre Dame, and who has used that strategic appointment to address theological ethics in a style more classical and Thomist than Kantian or utilitarian. His writing has had three foci—character, vision, and narrative, all three of which are present in the following typical passage:

> The basis and aim of the moral life is to see the truth, for only as we see correctly can we act in accordance with reality. Even though the good can be embodied in our choices, we do not create it through our choices. However, we are not able to "see" the good simply by looking; to be man is to create and love illusion. . . . Our vision must be trained and disciplined in order to free it from our neurotic self-concern and the assumption that conventionality defines the real. Ethics is that modest discipline which uses careful language, distinctions, and stories to break [our] intellectual bewitchment.[63]

Contrary to the assumptions of many contemporary ethicists, Hauerwas does not believe that the moral life primarily consists in making one good decision after another. He does not think that the ethicist's work stops with an answer to the question of what makes some particular act good; he maintains instead that ethics must end up by answering what makes human beings good. In other words, ethics must speak about the character of the actor and not *just* about the character of his act. For Hauerwas, a person's character reflects the character of the story he is acting out as an agent who exists through time:

> [Our] moral lives are not simply made up of the addition of our separate responses to particular situations. Rather we exhibit an orientation that gives our life a theme through which the variety of what we do and do not do can be scored. To be agents at all requires a directionality that involves the development of character and virtue. Our character is the result of our

sustained attention to the world that gives a coherence
to our intentionality. Such attention is formed and given
content by the stories through which we have learned to
form the story of our lives. To be moral persons is to
allow stories to be told through us so that our manifold
activities gain a coherence that allows us to claim them
for our own. The significance of stories is the significance
of character for the moral life as our experience itself, if it
is to be coherent, is but an incipient story.[64]

Reminiscent of Stuart Hampshire's remarks on similar
topics,[65] Hauerwas' comments here call attention to the
logical fact that to be an agent at all—indeed to be human
at all—requires that a person be able to act intentionally.
In turn, what one *intends in* the world depends on how
one *attends to* the world. After all, a person's image of the
world can greatly affect his sense of his own place in the
world. As Wittgenstein put it, "The world of the happy
man is a different one from that of the unhappy man."[66] As
Hauerwas puts it, the way we have come to see the world
is the result of the way we have been trained to regard the
world in the light of the narratives we have heard:

> We neither are nor should we be formed primarily by
> the publicly defensible rules we hold, but by the stories
> and metaphors through which we intend the variety of
> our existence. Metaphors and stories suggest how we
> should see and describe the world—that is how we
> should "look-on" ourselves, others and the world—in
> ways that rules taken in themselves do not. Stories and
> metaphors do this by providing the narrative accounts
> that give our lives coherence.[67]

By allowing a particular story to direct our attention to the world in some specific way, we let it direct our activity in the world in a certain manner. As the story shapes our understanding of reality, it simultaneously qualifies the way we relate to reality. Thus, stories have a didactic quality like that evoked by the case-study method typically used in business and law school settings. As that method assumes that an appropriate response to a case depends upon a prior apt description of it, these stories too work on a similar premise. They first attempt to answer the question, What is the case of being human in the world? and then on the basis of that description of the facts of life, they suggest a plan for the most appropriate way to respond to life. Additionally, it is important for us to remember that the case-study method does not simply accept a givenness about the facts of a case, but rather seeks out the options and potentialities inherent in the case so that the current legal or business practice and climate might be transformed. Likewise, paradigmatic stories, through their moral implications, not only describe the world the way it is at present, but also suggest how it ought and might be changed in the future. Hauerwas writes:

> [Our] moral language does not just describe what is; it describes how we ought to see and intend the world. . . . Our metaphors and stories entice us to find a way to bring into existence the reality that at once should be but will not be except as we act as if it is. Morally the world is always wanting to be created in correspondence to what is but is not yet.[68]

By articulating a certain vision of the world, narratives provide us with a way of articulating what we are doing in the world. Such articulation, manifested in both linguistic and institutional form, gives us the skill to intend our behavior in the world so that 'the good' may be achieved.[69]

One of the consequences of Hauerwas' theory is that moral disputes are often the result not of a conflict between principles but of a clash between stories. What in fact *counts* as a principle or as a moral issue depends on the context supplied by these stories. For example, it may make all the *moral* difference whether the removal of a fetus is described as an 'abortion' or as an 'embryotomy,' and the mere 'brute facts' alone cannot settle the issue. Only some narrative, speaking about the meaning of human life, can enable us to speak about what to do with the fetus' life—and our own. For example, the present paradigmatic secular story trains us to regard our lives—and our bodies—essentially as our *possessions* for which we are ultimately answerable only to ourselves and the purpose of which is to be utilized in the pursuit of self-fulfillment and happiness. Thus, an unwanted pregnancy which might possibly interfere with such happiness, can, through a purely personal and private decision, justifiably be remedied by removing the fetus much as one might similarly remove an unwanted, bothersome appendix. By contrast, Hauerwas contends that the biblical narratives which inform a Christian moral vision teach us to understand that life is a gift whose preciousness suffering does not diminish. Such a story gives a special place to the care of the weak and unprotected, a care which extends even—and perhaps paradigmatically—to the fetus.[70] As Hauerwas says summing up the matter, "The choice of our vocabulary is a moral act."[71]

Hauerwas goes on to say that religious faith "comes to accepting a certain set of stories as canonical": "[We] discover our human self more effectively through these stories, and so use them in judging the adequacy of alternative schemes for humankind."[72] Consequently, the oft-posed dilemma between morality and religion proves to be misleading (if not altogether meaningless),[73] and asking, "Why have a canonical story?" is like asking, "Why be good?" Our only response can be "to point to the endemic tendency of men and women to allow certain stories to assume that role [i.e., of canonical story], just as ethicists remind us of the assessments we do in fact count on to live our lives."[74] Hauerwas' own central conviction is that Christian faith, ethics, and life all center on the "canonical story" of Jesus Christ: "Christian ethics is the systematic investigation of the astounding claim that the world and our self is only rightly seen and intended in the light of what God has done in the person and work of Jesus Christ."[75] For Hauerwas, the character of this one life story reflects the character of the world and ought to be reflected in the character of those who hear that story and live in this world.

2. *John Howard Yoder* (1927-   ) is an American Mennonite church historian and ethicist, trained at Basel, whose research in the Anabaptists of the sixteenth

century has given him a sharply nuanced standpoint from which to criticize the self-understanding of Bible-believing present-day communities. His book, *The Politics of Jesus* (1973), is a forthright statement of what it means to 'follow through' the moral consequences of the Christian story. At the outset of that book, Yoder puts the issue squarely:

> I propose to read the Gospel narrative with the constantly present question, "Is there here a social ethic?" I shall, in other words, be testing the hypothesis that runs counter to the prevalent assumptions: the hypothesis that the ministry and the claims of Jesus are best understood as presenting to men not the avoidance of political options, but one particular social-political-ethical option.[76]

Methodologically, Yoder sets himself two tasks: (1) to sketch an understanding of Jesus and his ministry that proves significant for social ethics, and (2) to "state the case for considering Jesus, when thus understood, to be not only relevant but also normative for a contemporary Christian social ethic." Yoder readily admits that his enterprise depends upon the successful completion of both these tasks. Were he to find, for example, that "Jesus, whoever he was, is no model for social ethics," the various details of Jesus' life and ministry would thereby become irrelevant for further ethical reflection. Alternatively, were the investigation to reveal that Jesus showed no political concerns, or that though concerned, he showed no originality in his responses, then "it would be pointless to ask about the meaning of his stance for today."[77]

Informed both by New Testament studies and by theological ethics, Yoder's work is guided by a very careful methodology. In the past, theological ethics has often been done as a 'process of extraction,' i.e., of taking some teaching of Jesus out of the larger context of the Gospel narratives. In turn, this isolated teaching (or collection of such teachings) becomes the basis for whatever ethical proposals the theologian might have to make. But as Yoder correctly perceives, that approach assumes that "the only way to get from the gospel story to ethics, from Bethlehem to Rome or to Washington or Saigon, [is] to leave the story behind."[78] In order to avoid the kind of mistake—the mistake of treating the story of Christ as some sort of 'super-fable'[79]—Yoder continually keeps sight of the Gospel narratives, thereby keeping his moral claims continually in touch with them. Rather than simply focus on some teaching of Jesus in isolation from the larger narrative context, Yoder attends "more [to] the events than [to] the teachings, more [to] the outlines than [to] the substance." This method enables Yoder to avoid the theological trap of having to choose between *Historie* and *Geschichte*—between the historic and the historical Jesus:

> Fortunately for our purposes, this is a question we need not answer in a general, methodological way, since it happens—or *is* it just happenstance?—that the particular Gospel materials we have been looking at are generally conceded to be those points at which the historic and the historical most nearly coincide; the place where there is the least distinction between what the critic thinks must actually have happened and what

the believing witnesses reported. There is widespread debate about the sense in which the resurrection reports can be called "history," or about how much the sayings and parables have evolved when we find them in their Synoptic settings. The doubts have not the same depth or breadth when we turn to the narrative skeleton of the Gospels, according to which Jesus gathered disciples, proclaimed the imminence of the kingdom, and was executed accused of insurrection.[80]

What then are the fruits of Yoder's labors? No longer can the Christian ethicist justifiably confront the believer with the classical theological disjunctions: the Jesus of history *or* the Jesus of dogma; the prophet *or* the institution; the catastrophic kingdom *or* the inner kingdom; the political *or* the sectarian; the individual *or* the social.[81] By contrast, Yoder's analysis of the Gospel narratives leads him to conclude that to confess Jesus as Messiah is to take up an ethic of the cross which reconciles all these disjunctions—and indeed, all the world:

> Jesus was not just a moralist whose teachings had some political implications; he was not primarily a teacher of spirituality whose public ministry unfortunately was seen in a political light; he was not just a sacrificial lamb preparing for immolation, or a God-Man whose divine status calls us to disregard his humanity. Jesus was in his divinely mandated . . . prophethood, priesthood, and kingship, the bearer of a new possibility of human, social, and therefore political relationships. His baptism is the inauguration and his cross is the culmination of that new regime in which his disciples are called to share. Men may choose to consider that kingdom as not

real, or not relevant, or not possible, or not inviting; but no longer may we come to this choice in the name of systematic theology or honest hermeneutics. *At this one point* there is no difference between the Jesus of *Historie* and the Christ of *Geschichte*, or between Christ as God and Jesus as Man, or between the religion of Jesus and the religion about Jesus (or between the Jesus of the canon and the Jesus of history). No such slicing can avoid his call to an ethic marked by the cross, a cross identified as the punishment of a man who threatens society by creating a new kind of community leading a radically new kind of life.[82]

In short, Jesus did not simply *have* a social ethic; he *was* a social ethic, as, in Yoder's view, a close and honest reading of the Gospel narratives plainly shows.

Additionally, Yoder claims that Jesus' social ethic is one radically different from any currently abroad in the world. Even calling it 'pacifism' tends to be misleading. According to Yoder, Jesus' 'moral program' is not the kind of pacifism which opposes killing while still believing that "with the proper nonviolent techniques you can obtain without killing everything you really want or have a right to ask for." Such pacifism glibly supposes that violence is to be eschewed simply because there are other less dangerous ways to impose one's will on others. But Yoder asserts that the kind of 'pacifism' entailed by Jesus' story rests on the conviction that "what Jesus renounced is not first of all violence, but rather the compulsiveness of purpose that leads men to violate the dignity of others."[83] What justifies a truly Christian social ethic is not the belief that one can have all one's legitimate ends without resort to violence. Rather, its justification is that "our readiness to renounce our legitimate ends whenever they cannot be attained by legitimate means itself constitutes our participation in the triumphant suffering of the Lamb."[84] A Christian social ethic marked by the cross is marked first of all by the renunciation of the self-centered compulsiveness which cries for the legitimacy of its own claims. For an ethic of the cross, there is only one legitimate claim, namely, the call to "our social obedience to the messianity of Jesus."[85]

At the same time, however, an ethic of the cross does not imply that any and every suffering, such as unforeseeable illness or unpredictable calamity, is in and of itself redemptive. Instead, the believer's 'cross'

> . . . must be, like his Lord's, the price of his social nonconformity. . . . [It] is the end of a path freely chosen after counting the cost. . . .
>
> Representing as [He] did the divine order at hand, accessible; renouncing as he did the legitimate use of violence and the accrediting of the existing authorities; renouncing as well the ritual purity of noninvolvement, his people will encounter in ways analogous to his own the hostility of the old order.[86]

Therefore, the church's primary ethical directive is to be herself—to be *the church*. She is neither to attack the powers of the world nor to be seduced by them. On the contrary, her very existence testifies that they have already been conquered. In Yoder's view, it is absolutely imperative that the church follow this most basic of all moral imperatives: "the very existence of the church is her primary task. It is in itself a proclamation of the Lordship of Christ to the powers from whose dominion the church has begun to be liberated."[87] While Yoder concedes that such an ethic may make the church appear ineffective in the eyes of the world, he nevertheless believes that for the church to adopt any other ethic would be for it—by its very existence—to discredit its story's moral claims about the world in plain sight of the world. Such an act would be both a betrayal of the politics of Jesus and a perversion of the story of Jesus. One suspects that for Yoder, there could be no act ultimately more immoral than that.

Having surveyed the positions of various writers on the implications of biblical narrative for theology, we are now in position to begin to raise some critical questions about the validity of their claims. As I previously discussed their work according to the typologies of "structuring the story," "following the story," and "enacting the story," I will now begin a critical examination of that work using these same categories as a focus for my inquiry.

IV. STRUCTURING THE STORY: CRITIQUE

While Frei and McFague are clear in stressing that the structural shape of the biblical narrative plays a crucial role in shaping our understanding of reality, they are nevertheless far from clear in answering whether 'reality' can shape stories in kind. Can new 'facts' or 'experiences' ever force us to reshape or revise our stories, and if so, how? The responses provided by Frei and McFague prove to be less than satisfactory.

Although Frei's observation that biblical narrative has a

"history-like" character is helpful, it is also extremely misleading if it would imply that the 'historical facticity' of certain parts of that narrative is unimportant. For as Hauerwas so cogently points out:

> [Frei's] suggestion would be disastrous if it is an attempt to make irrelevant whether Jesus in fact did not exist and act in a way very much like the way he is portrayed in the gospel accounts. For the demand that what Jesus was not be different than how we have come to know him in the gospels is not based on some external demand of historical truth, but rather because the very nature of the story of Jesus itself demands that Jesus be the one who in fact the church said and continues to say he is.[88]

Whatever else may bear on the relationship between truth and narrative theology, surely any such theology must at least be true to the terms set forth by the narrative on whose basis it makes its claims. In this sense, no justifiable narrative theology can avoid the fact that a story must at least be *true to itself*. For the biblical narratives which portray a historically conditioned reality, the historical facticity of the events narrated in those stories must affect the truth of any claims which have them as their basis. For stories such as these, the question of 'whether it really happened' cannot be ignored without theological peril. Frei's answer to that question remains ambiguous.

For her part, McFague makes it virtually impossible even to raise such questions. Since her epistemological and ontological points are but mirror images of one another, any critical distinction between story and reality collapses. Thus, she easily moves from saying on the one hand that "metaphor follows the way the human mind *works*," to claiming on the other that "the self has a priority [over the world]. In a real sense, what the world *is* is what we say it is and we say it is what *we* are."[89] Yet people have said all sorts of things about the world which are true neither to the world nor to themselves. McFague's thesis not only closes off the possibility of asking about the truth of our storied claims, it forecloses any chance of adjudicating among conflicting conviction sets reflecting rival stories. After all, what justification is there for taking "the mundane story of Jesus . . . as *the* metaphor of all human movement"?[90] Why not take some other "mundane story" as that metaphor? Unless there is some attempt to delineate more clearly the relationship between story and reality, between stories and the truth of claims which they generate, then the appeal to the importance of the use of narrative in theology will appear to be only a new way of sidestepping the age-old question of the relationship between truth and religion.[91]

V. FOLLOWING THE STORY: CRITIQUE

While the authors in the first group were primarily concerned with the importance of narrative for understanding reality, those in the second group were fundamentally interested in the importance of *understanding* some particular narrative for understanding reality. Their project was to show that a specific understanding of a specific narrative led to a specific conception of the meaning of life. At bottom, their task was hermeneutic. However, as G. E. Wright rightly perceived some twenty-five years earlier, "as the Bible contains no system of theology, it likewise contains no self-conscious hermeneutical methodology."[92] Indeed, one of the main points of issue between Jews and Christians has been an essentially hermeneutical one: does the story of Jesus *follow* the Exodus story by being its natural continuation and culmination—or is it rather a terrible misreading of that story? Referring to this dispute concerning the messianity of Jesus and the redemption of the world, Van Buren comments that the Jews say:

> It didn't happen, and it hasn't happened yet. And must we not concede that they do have a point? Nineteen and a half centuries have passed and the world has become more complex, but hardly more liberated. I think we must be much clearer than we have been in speaking to Judaism and say that in the sense in which Judaism has awaited the Messiah, Jesus was not the Messiah.

Having said that much, however, Van Buren continues by saying,

> I do not think we can leave it at that, for the very fact of our being here, Gentiles who worship Israel's God, points to the fact that Jesus was a prophet and more than a prophet. What happened with his coming forces us to say to Judaism that their conception of the Messiah has to be adjusted to whatever new thing that God does. . . . the God of Israel is free in his mystery to do more than one new thing, and on this the witness of the Scriptures is clear. Again and again, Israel, Judaism and the Church have been sure that they had God's plan all

figured out, only to be surprised and sometimes shocked into acknowledging the mystery of his freedom.[93]

But having now let Van Buren have his say, *we* must nevertheless say that his remarks, instead of resolving the issue between Jews and Christians, only sharpen it all the more. For certainly, at some basic level, the disagreement hinges on whether God through the work and person of Jesus Christ was freely "in his mystery" doing one more "new thing," or whether, as Jews contend, the work and person attributed to Jesus could only be ascribed to an altogether new—and false—god, whose ways are so mysterious as to make it totally impossible to identify him with the Lord of the Exodus. In fact, this disagreement between Christians and Jews is reflected in the very nomenclature given by Christianity to the two major parts of its canon, namely, the Old Testament and the New—a nomenclature which Judaism does not use.

Furthermore, even if one (such as Greenberg) sticks to one particular canon, selects from it one particular narrative (such as the Exodus), and calls it the dominant biblical story for the proper understanding of the whole of history, what finally justifies the choice of that story over any of the canon's other stories for the title and role of 'the dominant story'? Why not choose instead, for instance, the story of the binding of Isaac, or the story of Jacob wrestling with the angel? Greenberg does not answer. Nor does he answer what one is then to do with these stories or with those parts of the Jewish canon which are apparently non-narrative, e.g., Psalms and Proverbs. Similarly, Greenberg cannot merely remark that histori-

cal circumstances forced the Talmudic sages to reinterpret the Exodus story without also showing what justified
their particular reinterpretation. Clearly, that kind of
challenge may arise in a clash between two conflicting
religious traditions, each with its own 'reading' of the
story. Historically, however, that challenge has arisen
more often from within the same tradition as first one
group and then another takes issue not so much with the
basic canon as with some 'canonical' reading of it. The
narrative theologians have claimed repeatedly that 'the
facts' are not simply 'out there' waiting to be read off the
surface of reality but instead are read through the lenses
of some story. Yet surely, someone could also justifiably
claim that stories such as the biblical narratives are
likewise not simply out there waiting to be read but are
always read through the lenses of some tradition or from
the perspective of some standpoint within a tradition.

In fact, the question of what justifies a particular reading
of a story may be even more crucial than the question of
what justifies the claims made on the basis of that reading: it
is certainly more fundamental. What is needed, therefore,
is some hermeneutic for following a story properly.
Without one, the narrative theologians are vulnerable to
the kinds of charges made by George Stroup:

> In too many instances, those theologians who have
> attempted to develop a concept of narrative have
> avoided the unavoidable—the question of how narrative
> functions hermeneutically. . . . [It] is incumbent on
> those who insist that narrative is the primary genre in
> the biblical text to describe hermeneutically what it

means to "understand" the text. . . . How does biblical
narrative alter and transform the personal-identity
narratives of individuals and communities? It is not
sufficient to assert simply that biblical narratives have
this remarkable kind of power. A successful and compelling appropriation of narrative by theology demands
a description of "the hermeneutics of [biblical]
narrative."[94]

Stroup's points about the centrality of an adequate
hermeneutic for narrative theology are ones which cannot
be circumvented. As academic theologians have long
scorned the crude hermeneutic moves of the 'uninitiated'
who have tried to prove their case by citing some random
biblical verse, the narrative theologians must now ask
themselves whether they might not also be engaged in
just the same kind of theological dumb show, only this
time hurling stories at one another instead of verses.

VI. ENACTING THE STORY: CRITIQUE

Whatever critical questions have been asked of the
theologians of the previous two groups must also be put to
the writers in this section. If their shared central thesis is
that virtue depends on vision and that life stories must
embody canonical stories, then surely, they too must
address the issue of the relationship between stories and
truth-claims as well as the issue of the hermeneutic
involved in following a story correctly. And as one might
expect, the field of ethics draws attention to these
concerns in a particularly intense way.

For example, Hauerwas is one of the few figures who

has focused on the issue of truth for a narrative-based theology in any kind of direct or sustained fashion. However, he generally fails to spell out explicitly the hermeneutic on whose basis he makes his various theological and ethical claims. For instance, Hauerwas forms his case against the moral justifiability of suicide by arguing if life is indeed a gift, then suicide is an act of the most supreme ingratitude.[95] Although one can certainly make a case for Hauerwas' account of the biblical portrayal of life, that case, however, is not the only one which we can make on the basis of the biblical narratives. For example, one might argue that the Genesis depictions of Adam as steward of the garden and of Abraham as partner in the covenant teach us to regard our lives more basically as *trusts*.[96] In that light, suicide becomes morally reprehensible because it is fundamentally a betrayal. Obviously, life-as-gift and life-as-trust mean suicide is morally wrong, and clearly, each of these two visions may have a place for the other. But importantly, they each at bottom reflect a distinctively different ethical foundational notion. While life-as-gift calls forth a moral outlook rooted in unbounded generosity and gratitude, life-as-trust evokes an ethical stance informed by reciprocally binding obligations and commitments. Have not Judaism and Christianity in fact reflected this very difference in emphasis, the one stressing the primacy of God's concern for justice, the other of God's regard for freely given love?[97] Without a more explicit hermeneutic, Hauerwas' moral claims, whatever else their merits, cannot help but appear to be on somewhat shaky ground.

By comparison, Yoder's analysis seems hermeneutically sound; unfortunately, it fails to show much regard for some conception of human existence apart from that displayed by the story. As a consequence, Yoder's implied claim that Jesus' story alone offers an appropriate human social ethic seems crucially unsupported. Surely, the *mere narration* of a story is not enough to justify its position as the basis for one's moral behavior. One must make some attempt to give reasons why that story ought to hold that position in one's own life—or in anybody else's. Otherwise, there is only the kind of relativism that makes moral argument across 'story-lines' altogether impossible. Unless there are some criteria for judging the adequacy of various storied claims which are not themselves totally dependent on any one story alone, then all we are left with is the rather dismal prospect of saying to one another (of *shouting* at one another?), "I've got my story; you've got yours. That's all there is to it!" If a narrative theology cannot adequately address this kind of problem, then whatever suspicion there may be surrounding the legitimacy of the use of narrative for theology will have been well-founded.

In summary, this chapter has tried to present a survey of some of the main themes of narrative theology. In so doing, it has also attempted to raise three critical issues which any narrative theology must face: (1) the relationship between stories and experience—the question of truth; (2) the hermeneutic involved for understanding stories rightly—the question of meaning; and (3) the charge of moral relativism—the question of rationality.

These are topics which any study of the justifiability of a narrative theology must meet head on, and therefore, these are the questions which we will confront in the next chapter, the chapter whose title asks a question central to this study, "How Can a Narrative Theology Be Justified?"

VI

'REVIEWING THE STORY':
HOW CAN A NARRATIVE THEOLOGY BE JUSTIFIED?

In a sense, this chapter's subtitle might be thought of as the superscription for the study as a whole. For the question of how a narrative theology can be justified, a question which will be the explicit focus of this chapter, has in reality also been before us in one form or another in all the book's previous chapters. Our analysis of Fletcher, Cone, and Christ in chapter 1 called our attention to the fact that the intelligibility and significance of our moral and religious convictions presuppose some larger narrative framework. By closely examining the work of Braithwaite, Dunne, and Stevenson in chapter 2, we saw that the appropriate understanding and assessment of the claims made on behalf of certain narratives depend on distinguishing properly among different narrative genres, such as fable, myth, and history. The third and fourth chapters, dealing with biography and autobiography, reminded us that some kinds of narratives—life stories—not only aspire to 'ring true' to common aspects of human experience, but also claim to be true to the experience(s) which they portray. Moreover, those life stories which seem to be the embodiments of the 'paradigmatic stories' of various religious communities can become the focus for significant theological reflection. To that extent, such stories help us recognize that at least part of the justifiability of a religious conviction lies in the justifiability of a life lived. Finally, in the previous chapter, we explored biblical narratives as paradigms for understanding—and transforming—human life. Our discussion there raised anew, with greater clarity and vigor, three critical issues which had been present all along in our investigation of the justifiability of the use of narrative for theological purposes: the meaning, truth, and rationality of a narrative theology. This chapter will now tackle those issues head on.

What might the process of justifying a narrative theology be like? In the past, theologians have used a variety of methods to justify their proposals. Several have grounded their claims in an appeal to divine revelation;[1] some have invoked criteria of validity used in other disciplines, such as science;[2] others have appealed to some common intuition or shared, self-evident truth;[3] still others have tried to show the merits of their own claims through a process of elimination, pointing out the defects in all rival accounts.[4] We would venture too far afield of our present concerns to discuss the relative strengths and weaknesses of each of these different justificatory procedures—or to discuss the ways that similar problems of justification have been faced by thinkers in other areas, such as epistemology[5] and ethics.[6] However, recalling what we said in our study's introduction about the relationship between a theology and its convictions, we might now say that in general, the justifiability of any theology depends on the justifiability of those convictions which that theology embraces. Thus, if a narrative theology is one whose convictions arise from, are informed by, and ultimately point back to some narrative, then we need a method or scheme that will enable us to state clearly and assess critically those very kinds of convictions. Happily, the work of James Wm. McClendon, Jr., and James M. Smith in *Understanding Religious Convictions* suggests the sort of approach we need for the task ahead.

A JUSTIFICATORY PROCEDURE

Using John Austin's theory of speech-acts as a foundation, McClendon and Smith construct a model for analyzing the justifiability of religious utterances—and of the convictions which they may express. The justifiability (or "happiness") of such utterances (and convictions) depends on the extent to which they fulfill a certain limited, specifiable range of conditions which arise from the issuance of the utterances themselves.[7] To make matters somewhat clearer, let us, along with McClendon and Smith, consider the utterance, "Please pass the bread."[8] What kinds of conditions must be satisfied if that utterance is to count as a *happy request?*

In the first place, there must be some linguistic convention common to both speaker and hearer alike such that "Please pass the bread" *counts as a request*.[9] That is, were someone to say instead, "Bread, dammit!" his utterance might be considered an *order*, a *command*, or a *demand* that the bread be passed, but it will not normally be justifiably taken as a *request* for bread because, quite simply, there is no convention in the language to the effect that "Bread, dammit!" is *a way of performing the speech-act of requesting*. Thus, at this level of the *primary conditions of justification*, we need a sentence whose utterance is a conventional linguistic device for making a request.

However, while the utterance of a sentence under a certain linguistic convention is primary since such conventions constitute the language and make linguistic meaning possible, nevertheless, language is not a self-contained activity but comes to grips with a *world* which language alone cannot replace.[10] Consequently, in the second place, a justifiable request for bread must not only satisfy certain linguistic conditions, it must also fulfill the requirements of some possible state of affairs which such a request logically presupposes. For a request for bread to be in any way justified, there must at the very least be some bread available, someone who wants or needs it,[11] and someone capable of passing it.[12] Hence, for our speaker's utterance to be deemed justified at this level, it must so describe or represent the relevant state of affairs (e.g., what it is the speaker wants) that these *representative conditions* can be fulfilled.

There remains, however, a third set of conditions which must be met in order for a request for bread to be justified. As Austin showed, speech-acts are what they are not simply because through them we *say* something, but in uttering them, we also *do* something. In that sense, speech-acts have the capacity to affect both persons and circumstances. Thus, in terms of our example, we need to remember that *requests* are always made *of someone for something*. That fact helps explain why, for example, if after having 'requested' bread and then having it offered, a person were to push the bread away, his fellow diners would understandably wonder whether what they had heard was in fact a genuine request. These *affective conditions*, just like the primary and representative conditions before them, must be observed if the justifiability of an utterance, be it a request for bread or some other speech-act, is to be defended.

What might all this mean for the justification of religious utterances and the convictions they express? Once again, let us follow the lead of McClendon and Smith, and consider as an example the utterance, "God led Israel across the Sea of Reeds." Let us also suppose that that utterance has been issued by some member of the Jewish or Christian tradition as a "confession of faith." For such an utterance to be judged a happy confession, various primary, representative, and affective conditions must be satisfied. The primary conditions require here that in order for this utterance to count as a *confession*, the speaker must take up and display a stance consistent with just that sort of utterance, namely faithful witnessing: (1) to what has happened in the life of the speaker's community, and (2) to what has therefore happened in the speaker's own life as well. Certainly, if this utterance were issued within the context of a worship service, its utterance in that context would go a long way in helping justify it as a confession at this level of the primary conditions. By contrast, were that utterance set within some other framework, e.g., that of a biblical archaeologist sitting in his study and mulling over possible excavation sites, then it could no longer justifiably be taken as a confession, but as a guess or supposition instead.[13] In turn, the representative force of our confession necessitates, among other things, that in a certain historical context, a certain event (being led across the Sea of Reeds) occurred to a certain people (Israel); that furthermore, this event is attributable to the God acknowledged in this context; and obviously, that this God exists. Hence, if Israel never crossed the Sea, or if the crossing was attributable to some other deity such as the Egyptian god Osiris, or if the God acknowledged in the confession simply does not exist, then that confession, *no matter what the sincerity with which it's uttered*, is unjustifiable as it stands. Its justifiability at this stage depends on *meeting* the representative conditions—and not on merely *believing* them. Finally, to be justified in his confession of faith, the speaker must convey to his hearers that he has the kind of affect appropriate to that kind of utterance and conviction. "Awed gratitude" might be a candidate for that sort of affect.[14] If, on the contrary, the speaker were to issue that utterance with an attitude of bored indifference, his utterance *qua* confession would be "affectively unhappy."[15]

In short, the process of justification demands a successful passage through the various primary, representative, and affective dimensions of speech-acts and the convictions which they may express, and that demand is one which applies to both religious and nonreligious utterances alike. Part of the attractiveness of this analytical model is that it enables us to pinpoint where and how a religious conviction, like any other kind of deeply held belief, can go off the track. Too often, past discussions of the justifiability of religious utterances and convictions have focused on the representative conditions alone, or alternatively, they have abandoned those conditions while attending only to the primary and affective dimensions. As the work of McClendon and Smith has demonstrated, all three dimensions are equally crucial to the task of justification.

Earlier, I said that the analysis offered by McClendon and Smith might suggest a serviceable methodological scheme for our own inquiry about the meaning, truth, and rationality of a narrative theology. I believe that that kind of scheme is now at hand. An analogy could be made likening the issue of meaning to the conditions surrounding the primary level of justification, the question of truth to the representative conditions, and the problem of rationality to the affective conditions.[16] By following this analogy through wherever possible, we might just be able to sketch out a 'map' to help guide us through the complexities involved in justifying a narrative theology.

I. PRIMARY CONDITIONS/MEANING

To ask about the primary conditions of justifications is to address the question of meaning. Such conditions remind us that before we can evaluate the *truth* of what was said or the *consequences* of what was said, we must first understand the meaning of what was said. Remembering our previous discussion, we recall that in general, the primary conditions oblige us to make sure that something that counts as a sentence in our common language has been uttered, and that moreover, there is a convention in the language to the effect that this sentence counts as a way of performing this or that particular speech-act. In terms of our analogy with a narrative theology, the primary conditions required for justification would therefore minimally be that the convictions embraced by that theology have indeed arisen from something that counts as a narrative in our common language; moreover, since there are conventions in the language which help class narratives according to various literary genres, our primary conditions further require that to be justifiable, a narrative theology's convictions must be appropriate to *the kind of story* which that theology claims as their ground.[17]

Through their detailed study of narrative, Robert Scholes and Robert Kellogg can help us bring into focus a number of the issues now before us. They note, for instance, that for something to be justifiably deemed a 'narrative,' no more and no less is needed than "the presence of a story and a story-teller." Narrative is thus separated, for example, both from drama which lacks a teller and from lyric which lacks a tale. By 'story' Scholes and Kellogg mean the interaction between character and action. Stories, therefore, may be differentiated from chronicles, diaries, and the like which fail to have "two elements essential to the narrative art: selectivity and movement."[18] Consequently, from the standpoint set by the narrative, we follow the contingencies surrounding persons and events through time. What follows in the course of a narrative does not follow along the lines of a well-constructed syllogism but instead follows from the way the narrative builds, takes shape, and then unfolds. To fashion something in which all the events follow with the kind of logical necessity with which deductions follow premises is to concoct something so far removed from our concept 'story' that we might hesitate to classify it even as a *bad* story: after all, one cannot *narrate* a syllogism. The connections found in narratives are neither those of logical necessity nor those of the mere sequence of 'one damned thing after another,' but those of such interconnectedness that we want to ask, we *have* to ask, "And then what happened next?" At the very least, any justifiable use of narrative for theology must be one which respects the integrity of such narrative connections, neither breaking down the relevant narrative into a mere 'systematic formulation' nor breaking it up into isolated statements taken out of context.[19] Any attempt at theological abstraction must take seriously the fact that it is a narrative from which the abstracting is done. Such abstraction must not treat the narrative as a shell which may be discarded once the 'theological pearl' has been extracted. And that is one of the primary conditions which no justifiable narrative theology may ignore.

But there are other primary conditions that must be met as well. In his article, "The Structure of Historical Narrative," Hayden White stresses that the skills for understanding the meaning of a narrative are dependent on certain linguistic and communal conventions. Now these are the very kinds of things we have dubbed "primary conditions." White compares mastery of such skills with attaining "both lexical and grammatical competence in a foreign language [such that one] finally grasps the rules of syntax that permit him to formulate, and to understand, sentences uttered in that language."[20] As understanding a language is a prior condition of speaking it, being able to follow a story is a prior condition of being able to tell one. White goes on to explain that the various literary traditions of each culture provide the themes and motifs which "encode" narratives as recognizable instances of specific types of stories. Just as there are certain cultural conventions which assure that images in a painting will be 'read' one way rather than another (so that, e.g., even in a two-dimensional painting, one figure will be understood to be standing *behind* rather than *beside* another; this is a canon of post-Renaissance Western culture but not that of ancient Egypt), so, too, there are communally dependent style-guides for storytellers in every society. "Plot-structures charge the phases of a story with different affective valencies or weights, so that we can read the change in continuity (or the reverse) figured in a story as a consummation, a culmination, or a degeneration—that is to say, as a drama with Comic, Tragic, or Ironic significance, as the case may be."[21] Thus, stories, like other linguistic phenomena which arise within communal contexts, are manifestations of both *glossai* and *ethnoi,* languages and peoples.[22] In a larger sense, stories stand within a whole narrative tradition. Referring to oral epics as an example, Scholes and Kellogg describe the relationship between tradition and story this way:

> The tradition is seen to consist rather of a "grammar" than of fixed elements. It is a grammar superimposed on the normal grammar of the spoken language; but like that grammar it is learned from below the level of consciousness and carries with it profound restrictions on both the apprehension and the conceptualization of the external world. Evolution of thought has to take place within the double set of restrictions imposed by linguistic structure as it is ordinarily conceived and by the "grammar" of the traditional wisdom.[23]

The linguistic and social phenomenon called tradition thus functions like a literature teacher who shows the as-yet untutored and fumbling student how to appreciate a narrative for the kind of story it is and so be able to discern its meaning.

For theological purposes, this task is vitally important. The narrative theologian must make sure to distinguish properly among the various kinds of narrative, e.g., fable, myth, historical account, so as to be able to make out the meaning proper to each kind. In this regard, one of the mistakes of fundamentalists and secularists alike is the failure to draw distinctions among the different narrative genres present in the Bible, the fundamentalists accepting them all as histories and the secularists rejecting them all as myths.[24] In committing this mistake, both groups ride roughshod over one of the basic primary conditions. Scholes and Kellogg draw attention to the need of trying to understand a story on its own terms:

> A fixed text will tend to survive its native milieu and be forced to make its way in alien surroundings. Not only will its language become archaic and obsolete, but the assumptions about man and nature and about the proper way to tell a story, upon which the tale is built, will also recede farther and farther from the assumptions of living men. . . .
>
> To understand a literary work, then, we must first attempt to bring our own view of reality into as close an alignment as possible with the prevailing view in the time of the work's composition.[25]

Whatever meaning a theologian may claim a narrative to have for the community of his day, he must *at least initially* try to get straight about what the narrative meant to those who first told it in days gone by.[26]

However, while such a step is an important one on the road toward justification, it is in the end only a first step. For a narrative theology to be justified, one must attend closely to a whole history of tradition which reaches from the past down to the present. Obviously, at a very basic level, there are traditions already present *in* various religious texts. Yet equally present and fundamental is that tradition which *shapes* and *interprets* those texts as canonical scriptures. As literary traditions of composition and criticism set the bounds for the proper understanding and status of certain kinds of narratives, religious traditions for their part establish the parameters for the appropriate interpretation and standing of others. For

Jews and Christians at least, tradition was what designated a particular corpus of diverse stories as one sacred scripture, thus assigning those stories a normative position which they otherwise would not have had. Furthermore, by forming those stories into a canon, tradition not only staked a claim for them, but also made that claim in a quite specific way. It claimed *'these-stories-in-this-order'* as providing the correct context for a justifiable understanding of any individual part within the larger body of Holy Writ. In assenting to these points, one need not necessarily opt for a 'Catholic,' as opposed to a 'Protestant,' view of tradition. Brian Wicker, for instance, uses the Tower of Babel story as a starting point to illustrate the way the process of shaping meaning is already at work in the Bible itself:

> Taken simply by itself this story could be interpreted in two ways. In one way, it could be understood as the story of Yahweh's spiteful interference with, and cruel destruction of a work with which the Babylonian people are legitimately occupied in their ordinary lives. On this view, Yahweh is jealous of man's competition. . . .
>
> On the other view, however, the meaning is just the opposite. The people are stupidly trying to compete with Yahweh who after all made them in the first place. They can do nothing at all without him. They deserve to be taught a lesson. Far from being cruel and spiteful, Yahweh is simply showing to the people what happens when they attempt to defy his almighty power. He is really kind, and even compassionate. In other words, what seems to them a cruel outrage is just the far-seeing wisdom of a loving parent.[27]

Which interpretation is correct? Only by reading the story which follows the Babel narrative can the question be decided. That story tells of the election and blessing of Abraham, indicating that despite all the evil that has transpired, God has not vindictively left human beings to their own devices, but is still unconditionally and lovingly involved in human history. To be sure, there is still plenty of material in Genesis that could provide the grist for an interpretation of Yahweh as cruel and spiteful. One might cite Genesis 12 where Yahweh afflicts an unsuspecting Pharaoh for unwittingly seducing Sarah. What justification is there then for claiming that these stories mean to portray God in a favorable light? Wicker answers: "We can only reply, the attitude of the author, or authors, who have so arranged the material of Genesis (and the other Biblical material that belongs with it) that we are prevented, if we read it *as a whole*, sensitively and intelligently, from taking up the "spiteful" interpretation."[28] Thus, by placing these narratives within a larger canonical context—in this case, the arrangement of narratives we call "Genesis"—tradition sets the limits— the primary conditions—for a justifiable interpretation of their meaning. To take these stories 'out of context' is to run the risk of seriously misunderstanding them *in the eyes of the community whose traditional context it is*. In such a case, members of that community might well argue that though one may have read an ancient document, one has not yet come face to face with a story told *in Scripture*.

Tradition further determines what ought to be considered the proper understanding of its sacred stories by its selective use of them in preaching, ritual, and liturgy. Those stories so used tend to gain a priority and dominance over others within the canon.[29] For example, in Jewish tradition, references to the Exodus narrative appear repeatedly in the liturgy while the same liturgy never alludes to the biblical stories about Adam and Eve. Consequently, in the light of this Exodus narrative, the kind of redemption about which Judaism understands the rest of Scripture primarily to be speaking is that of a liberation from the people's enemies and oppressors. By contrast, a Christian tradition dominated by the story of the Fall might rightly be expected to understand the redemption promised by Scripture as liberation from one's own sins. Stanley Hauerwas has depicted the relationship between tradition and narrative in the following manner:

> Tradition . . . as the memory sustained over time by ritual and habit . . . sets the context and boundaries for the discussion required by . . . stories. As Kermode has recently reminded us [in *The Genesis of Secrecy*], the way to interpret a narrative is properly through another narrative, indeed a narrative is already a form of interpretation, as the power of a narrative lies exactly in its potential to produce a community of interpretation sufficient for the growth of further narratives.[30]

We ought to and must remember that each tradition is itself a story, a story not only about some narrative told by some community, but moreover, about that community as well. Indeed, one of the basic claims for tradition is that as the communal and linguistic institution which is the composer, editor, and teller of the tale, it is in the best position to lay out the primary conditions for a justifiable understanding of its meaning. In this regard, while religious faith may hinge in part on the trustworthiness of God and on the narratives which tell of him, such faith depends at least implicitly as well on trust in that human institution called tradition which speaks of both.

Some might find this statement maddening. They might be inclined to protest, "Away with the relative vantage points set by some tradition or other! Let's just approach the stories as they stand. That's the right way to understand them and take up a theological position most in accord with them." But as David Kelsey has shown,[31] while that proposal is easily made, it's not so easily acted on. Kelsey's major thesis is that no theologian simply approaches the biblical text in an unmediated fashion. Rather he or she approaches it with considerations derived from both a pre-text and a con-text:

> Conditions necessary for discourse to be intelligible, open to reasoned elaboration, and capable of argued defense; culturally conditioned limits to what is seriously imaginable; the structure of "tradition": these are three types of limit imposed on the range of ways a theologian might imaginatively characterize the *discrimen* by which he criticizes and proposes reforms of current churchly forms of speech and action.[32]

These pretextual and contextual considerations operate as the fundamental determinants, the primary conditions, for deciding which way the texts themselves will be construed. Such determinations serve as the guideposts the theological venture will take by first marking out what course the argument will take:

1) What aspect(s) of scripture is (are) taken to be authoritative?

2) What is it about this aspect of scripture that makes it authoritative?

3) What sort of logical force is ascribed to the scripture to which appeal is made?

4) How is the scripture that is cited brought to bear on theological proposals so as to authorize them?[33]

Kelsey concludes that there is no 'objective' perspective or 'neutral' vantage point in virtue of which a person can contend that his or her own theological position is the one which *really* accords with scripture such that all others are faithless to its meaning. "On the contrary, . . . our thesis is that any [statement] put that way is meaningless. Rather, it is our concern to find ways in which to state what it *means* in each case to say that scripture is 'authority' for this theological position."[34]

Kelsey helps support his thesis by sketching out the very different ways that different theologians have used biblical narrative to authorize their theological proposals. According to G. E. Wright, for instance, the authoritative meaning of biblical narrative lies in its interpretation of events in ancient Palestine. In turn, certain conceptual keys are suggested by which we can interpret the meaning of historical events in our own time. By contrast, Karl Barth takes the narratives in scripture to be rendering an agent to whom the reader or hearer is called to make the response "appropriate to the unique personal

individuality of just this agent, viz., worship of the Lord."
These two distinct ways of construing the meaning of the
biblical narratives carry in their wake quite disparate
ways of justifying the theological claims they generate:

> Where scripture is authoritative in that it proposes
> concepts [Wright], there theology's task is to analyze the
> "logic" of the concepts proposed. In that case, scripture
> bears on theological proposals very directly, for the
> latter are best seen as remarks about the conceptual
> "content" of scripture. It seems quite fitting to see such
> theological proposals as "translations" of scripture's
> content. But where scripture is authoritative in that it
> renders a character [Barth], then its function is not to
> provide the concepts that theology discusses, but to
> make the Risen Lord vividly present at least in
> imaginative memory and anticipation of his "real"
> presence. . . . In such cases it is very misleading to see
> theological proposals as "translations" of scripture's
> "content." The "content" is a person, not a set of
> concepts, not even about this person. "Proposing
> concepts" and "rendering an agent" are irreducibly
> diverse functions that scripture may fill as "authority"
> each of which brings with it a quite different order of
> phenomena for which it is authority, and, accordingly,
> quite different ways in which scripture serves to
> authorize theological proposals.[35]

Kelsey's work has at least two significant implications
for our own work here. First, by showing that biblical
narratives have been used theologically in a variety of
ways, Kelsey's study suggests that although it is not
logically impossible, it hardly seems likely that all (these)

narrative theologies can be justifiable interpretations of those particular stories. While any rich and complex narrative may have a whole range of valid interpretations of its meanings(s), there are nevertheless some interpretations which simply do not and will not fit. To ignore that fact is to ignore once again the primary conditions required for a justifiable narrative theology.

Second, Kelsey's work can help us appreciate more fully some of the differences among the narrative theologians we examined in the previous chapter. For example, both Hauerwas and Greenberg believe that at least some of the significance of biblical narrative comes from what might be called its 'orientational dimension.' These two theologians differ, however, about the focus of that orientation. Hauerwas takes a narrative which depicts a self—Jesus—and makes a 'theological proposal'[36] which focuses on character as the orientation of the self in its community: "[My] basic thesis [is] that Christian ethics is best understood as an ethics of character since the Christian moral life is fundamentally an orientation of the self."[37] For his part, Greenberg understands the Exodus narrative as portraying an event. Thus, the orientational focus is not so much the 'individual' human self as all of human history. Accordingly, Greenberg's theological proposal is to take the Exodus as an orienting experience, i.e., "a norm by which all of life and all other experience could be judged and oriented. It became the interpretative key by which all events were understood."[38]

One way of accounting for this difference between Hauerwas and Greenberg would be to point out the obvious fact that the two men come from religious traditions which, though related, are clearly different. That does not mean that a theologian such as Hauerwas or Greenberg has his own 'hidden theological agenda' for which he uses some narrative as a convenient 'proof.' It does suggest, however, that no theologian gets his understanding of the meaning of a narrative independent of any perspective whatsoever. To the extent that one's hermeneutic perspective has its roots in some tradition (religious or otherwise), and to the extent that each tradition is a narrative of sorts, one's choice of stories for theological significance as well as one's understanding of what significance such stories have will themselves be narrative-dependent. In the end, traditions such as these establish the various primary conditions for the proper theological understanding of the meaning of a narrative.[39]

In summary, no matter what else one may want to claim for the justifiability of the use of narrative for theology, one must at least fulfill the necessary primary conditions for such justification, namely: (1) that what is used as the basis for theological reflection is a narrative and not, e.g., some discursive philosophical system or some randomly selected passages; (2) that whatever narrative is used has been properly identified and subsequently used as the kind of narrative it is, e.g., a myth and not an historical account; and (3) that whatever narrative is used has been correctly understood within the context of meaning provided by the communal tradition which claims it as its own.

II. REPRESENTATIVE CONDITIONS/TRUTH

If we have now succeeded in indicating how a narrative theology might be justified at the level of the primary conditions we must nevertheless recall that there are two other levels of conditions for justification that still need to be scaled. Hence, for example, while it is one thing to ask whether a narrative theology's convictions justifiably follow from the story claimed as their fundamental ground, it is something else again to ask if and how those convictions might be true. Yet that question cannot be properly addressed unless we first remember what the previous section had to say about the importance of identifying and classifying narratives according to their appropriate genres; the failure to distinguish adequately among various literary kinds can generate convictions which are unjustifiable at the level of the primary conditions. Similarly, the representative force of a narrative theology's convictions will vary from genre to genre, and here too, any attempted justification of a narrative theology must carefully take note of that fact. Thus, in the case of convictions for which some historical account is claimed as ground, the representative conditions will require appropriate attention to matters involving the 'historical facticity' of persons, events, and the like. By contrast, convictions based in fictions, fairy tales, and fantasies will lack that kind of representative force—and that is something *true by definition*. One might characterize the truth of convictions arising from stories such as these as being of a mimetic nature. For convictions rooted in stories such as fables, the requisite representative conditions will be met only if their moral point is indeed justifiable, e.g., that it really is true that 'honesty is the best policy.' As for convictions based in primeval myths, it is not at all clear how or what representative conditions might have to be met given the fact that such myths tell of 'events' which occurred in another spatiotemporal dimension, outside our world and prior to its very creation.

At the risk of being repetitious, I say again that as before in the case of the primary conditions, we are now once more put on notice to be careful to classify each narrative according to its proper genre. As we noted previously, one of the confusions shared by both a self-righteous fundamentalism and a self-satisfied modernism is the common disregard of the distinctive types of narrative found in the Bible and the correspondent failure to assign the representative force most appropriate to each. Certainly, even for the most sensitive and discerning reader, it is difficult at times to sort out the different kinds of stories that may be embedded within the same larger biblical narrative; history, legend, and allegory, for example, are all to be found in 'the story of Joseph.' Yet while it is true that the biblical narratives seldom if ever explicitly identify themselves as myths, fables, histories, etc., it is also true that neither do most other narratives. As we acquire the skills to tell a story, we must likewise acquire the skills to tell one story from another. By being able to identify a narrative in terms of ·the motifs, themes, and style it displays, one may be better able to identify the sort of representative conditions which will have to be fulfilled if a narrative theology is to be justified.

As an illustration, we could consider how we might go about trying to meet the representative conditions of a narrative theology which claims the story of the Exodus as its base. Using an example slightly different from one we looked at earlier, suppose we examined the conviction expressed by the confession, "God saved Israel at the crossing of the Sea of Reeds." The necessary representative conditions required for justifying that conviction might look like this:

1. In a certain historical context, a certain event (being saved at the crossing of the Sea of Reeds) happened to a certain people (Israel).
2. This event is attributable to the God referred to in this context.
3. This God exists.   •

There are obviously a number of ways our conviction could prove unjustifiable at this point. If, for example, the Israelites had crossed at the *Red Sea* (as some older versions have it), or if some group of people other than the Israelites were the ones who made the crossing, then our claims here would be unjustified for just these reasons. Importantly, if at some level the story of the Exodus is intended or taken as an historical account, then historical disciplines such as biblical criticism, archaeology, and the like have vital roles to play in determining the validity of some of the convictional claims arising from that story. Clearly, the validation of historical claims, and particularly of those about persons and events in antiquity, is a far from simple task. It involves the weighing of diverse data from many fields by means of various warrants so that a probable hypothesis can be constructed—and a probable event reconstructed. Therefore, the judgment of the veracity of historical claims rarely takes the form of a flat yes or no. As Van Harvey has written in *The Historian and the Believer:*

> Our assertions and claims . . .cannot simply be classified as either true or false, but have a certain degree of probability attached to them. [This degree of probability] reflects the trained judgment of the historian, the degree to which he is prepared to stake his authority on a certain utterance. . . .
>
> The historian's assent, so to speak, possesses a texture.[40]

While deciding whether the sea referred to is the Sea of Reeds or the Red Sea may be a relatively simple thing to do, assessing whether those who came out of Egypt were a *people called Israel* (and not just a ragtag band of social outcasts called *"Habiru"*) may be a good deal more difficult, and the answer is likely to be far more ambiguous.

However, the strictly historical task pales when compared to the broader theological one. Even if we could definitively answer that, yes, all the 'historical' events portrayed in the Exodus narrative actually happened, and that therefore, at least in this sense our conviction stands justified, could we then with equal justifiability state that these events can also be attributed to the God referred to in the narrative, and that, furthermore, this God exists? Significantly, only by attending to that narrative itself can we hope to give any answer at all, for it is precisely during the course of that narrative, within the context of that narrative, that we learn both what this God is like and what evidence of his existence is like. At the very least, assessing the 'truth-claims' of a narrative theology depends on *listening attentively* to the story which informs it:

> God spoke to Moses and said to him, "I am YHWH. I appeared to Abraham, to Isaac, and to Jacob as El Shaddai, but by my name YHWH, I did not make myself known to them. I also established my covenant with them to give them the land of Canaan, the land in which they lived as sojourners. Now I have heard the moaning of the Israelites whom the Egyptians have enslaved, and I have remembered my covenant. Say therefore to the Israelites: "I am YHWH, and I will bring you out from under the burdens of the Egyptians, and I will deliver you from this bondage, and I will redeem you with an oustretched arm and with great acts of judgment. And I will take you for my people and I will be your god, and you shall know that I, YHWH, am your god who brought you out from under the burdens of the Egyptians. I will bring you into the land which I swore to give to Abraham, Isaac, and Jacob, and I will give it to you for a possession, I, YHWH!' " (Exod. 6:2-8)

If a theologian takes the Exodus narrative as the basis and the focal point for his claims, then his being able to know whether the events described in the story are attributable to the God referred to in the story depends at some basic level on his *coming to know* this God for the god he is through the course of the events unfolded *in* the story. Additionally, his being able to know whether this God exists depends in part on his *knowing what* kinds of events *the narrative depicts* as counting for, testifying to, or signifying that existence. This God, therefore, is and must be revealed neither primarily through 'history,' nor fundamentally through 'the rendering of an agent,' but more basically, through *the narrative itself.* Consequently, no matter what the justificatory procedure might be for fulfilling the representative condition that the crossing of the Sea be attributable to this particular deity, that procedure must never lose sight of the narrative within whose context we learn of *this God* in the first place.

Thus, for instance, according to the Exodus narrative, the god portrayed is one who makes promises—and keeps them: "The Israelites were groaning under the bondage and cried out; and their cry for help from bondage rose up to God. God heard their moaning, and God remembered his covenant with Abraham and Isaac and Jacob. God looked upon the Israelites, and God took notice of them" (Exod. 2:23-25; see also Genesis 15:13-14; Exodus 3:6-21; and, of course, the previously cited verses in Exodus 6). In the context of the narrative, then, Israel's crossing of the Sea is to be understood as one of the events through which Israel comes to know YHWH as that kind of promise-keeping deity. Therefore, one engaged in trying to justify the conviction, "God saved Israel at the crossing of the Sea of Reeds," might reasonably argue that both the event of the crossing and the deliverance it entailed were exactly the kinds of things that could *prima facie* be ascribed to the sort of being who faithfully carries out the promises he makes.

Attacking the problem of justification at this stage from a slightly different angle (though still one with a narrative vertex), a person might say that to ask whether Israel's deliverance at the Sea is attributable to YHWH is like asking, "Is that the kind of thing that YHWH would do?" Pressing his point further, one might add that were we to try to answer this sort of question in relationship to some other event (Y) and some other figure (X), one of the first things we would likely do would be to look at X's past behavior over time [41] such that we might be able to decide whether Y was the kind of thing that X could have been expected to do. That is, we would seek out a narrative context in which Y would either fit or be in some way out of place. The argument would continue that that is what must be done here in our case too. For a conviction set or theology which claims the Exodus narrative as its ground, the way that narrative unfolds the character of God through time is something that cannot justifiably be ignored. To put the matter even more strongly, one might say that a genuine Exodus-based theology cannot justifiably speak of God in terms of some timeless and unchanging *essence*, but rather in terms of a *character* developed over time. For someone else to be dissatisfied with this argument and to ask whether Israel's safe passage through the Sea might not have been attributable to another deity or whether it might have been attributable to no deity at all (but instead to Moses' leadership or to natural forces alone) is already for him or her to ask for another context, i.e., another narrative, in which the event might reasonably be set. In any case, a narrative theologian could rightly contend that the event *qua* isolated occurrence cannot even *begin* to answer such a question.

How might one answer the question, Does the God portrayed in the narrative exist? He might begin his response by importantly noting that, according to the *conditions set by the narrative itself,* answering this question depends on first knowing what is to count as evidence of God's existence:

> And YHWH said to Moses . . . "I will harden Pharaoh's heart that I may multiply my signs and wonders in the land of Egypt. When Pharaoh will not listen to you, I will lay my hand upon Egypt and bring out my ranks, my people, the Israelites, from the land of Egypt by great acts of judgment. The Egyptians will know that I am YHWH, when I stretch out my hand over Egypt and bring out the Israelites from the midst." (Exod. 7:1, 3-5)

Thus following the lead of the story, a narrative theologian might claim with some justification that this God's existence is signified by the existence of certain phenomena designated in the story as judgments, wonders, and signs. He might then support his claim by pointing out several crucial features of such phenomena. First, *as signs,* they point to something beyond themselves. But second, again *as signs,* they do not carry their own meaning. They do not themselves say how they are to be read or understood. Our theologian might be likely then to go on to say that only the larger context of the narrative can show how to do that, and in making that point, he would be once again calling attention to the narrative as setting the proper context for the correct interpretation of *these events as ascribable to this deity*. In essence he would be saying that for a theology whose perspective is informed by the Exodus narrative, and not some transcendental principles of metaphysics, these events become the necessary conditions for YHWH's becoming known. Thus, for example, he might support his thesis by citing what God tells Moses to say to Pharaoh before the advent of the seventh plague:

> "Let My people go to worship Me. For this time, I will send all My plagues upon you, and your courtiers, and your people, in order that you may know that there is none like Me in all the world. By now, I could have stretched forth My hand and stricken you and your people with pestilence, and you would have been effaced from the earth. Nevertheless, I have spared you for this purpose: in order to show My power, and in order that My fame may be recounted throughout all the earth." (Exod. 9:13-16)

Moreover, a narrative theologian could conceivably argue that conversely, had these events, these signs—this God's existence—been readily intelligible, there would have presumably been no need for the story to run its course through ten plagues *and* the crossing of the Sea in order that both the Egyptians and the Israelites would come to know of the reality of YHWH:

> And the Israelites went into the Sea on dry ground, the waters forming a wall for them on their right and on their left. The Egyptians came in pursuit after them into the

Sea, all of Pharaoh's horses, chariots, and horsemen. At the morning watch, YHWH looked down upon the Egyptian army from a pillar of fire and cloud, and threw the Egyptian army into panic. He locked the wheels of their chariots so that they moved forward with difficulty. And the Egyptians said, "Let us flee from the Israelites, for YHWH is fighting for them against Egypt." . . .

Thus YHWH delivered Israel that day from the Egyptians. Israel saw the Egyptians dead on the shore of the Sea. And when Israel saw the wondrous power which YHWH had wielded against the Egyptians, the people feared YHWH: they believed in YHWH, and in his servant Moses. (Exod. 14:22-25, 30-31)

Summing up, our narrative theologian might observe, that according to this story, *knowing that* God exists depends on *know how* to understand his 'sign-language,' a skill taught through the narrative itself.[42] And through that observation, the theologian would thus remind us: (1) that failure to attend to what the narrative has to say can lead to a failure to hear the kinds of claims it has to make, and (2) that in order to be considered true, convictions whose reputed basis is some narrative, whether biblical or otherwise, must at least be true to that narrative on its own terms.

As the final point of his argument for justifying our conviction ("God saved Israel at the crossing of the Sea of Reeds") at the representative level, a narrative theologian might ask us to consider the terms of that crossing as they are portrayed in Exodus 15, the oldest description of the event:[43]

> Pharaoh's chariots and his army
> He [i.e., God] has cast into the Sea;
> And the pick of his officers
> Are drowned in the Sea of Reeds.
> The depths covered them;
> They went down into the depths like a stone. . . .
> You send forth Your fury, it consumes them like stubble.
> At the blast of Your nostrils the water piled up
> The floods stood straight like a wall;
> The deeps froze in the heart of the Sea. . . .
> You made Your wind blow, the Sea covered them;
> They sank like lead in the majestic waters.

At the outset, a narrative theologian might astutely note that whatever else the verses are describing here, they are at the very least depicting a violent *storm* which destroyed the Egyptian host. He might point out that some Israelites clearly took that natural event as a sign of God's saving power and were moved to exclaim:

> I will sing to YHWH, for he has triumphed gloriously;
> Horses and driver he has hurled into the Sea.
> YHWH is my strength and my might,
> He has become my salvation.
> This is my God, and I will glorify him,
> The God of my fathers, and I will exalt him.
>   (Exod. 15:1-2)

However, an astute narrative theologian would also note the possibility that an Israelite could have crossed the sea, turned around, and seen the Egyptians being drowned in the churning waters, and then said to himself, "Gee, I don't understand it. I listened to the weather report before we left Goshen, and they didn't predict rain." For that Israelite, the crossing of the Sea would have lacked the significance that it had for the composer(s) of Exodus 15—or of the rest of the Exodus narrative. But our narrative theologian would admit that that kind of alternative response to the events referred to in the Exodus story remains a possibility due to the very conditions laid down by the story itself. For the kind of God that the story portrays and the kinds of events that it ascribes to him leave room for rival understandings—for rival convictions—about the significance of what has taken place. Returning to what he has said earlier, our theologian might reiterate once more that the narrative refers to those events as signs, and that as events, their significance is not ambiguous, while as signs, their meaning is not self-evident. As both events and signs, they gain their significance, meaning, and *representative force* only through the narrative in which they are set. And here, our theologian might offer some comments by Stanley Hauerwas as instructive:

> To point to the story character of religious convictions may . . . help us to avoid some of the misleading ways that religious convictions are often thought to be true or false. For example, questions like does God really exist . . . are sometimes taken as the central questions that determine the truth or falsity of religious convictions . . . , but it is inappropriate to single them out as *the* issues of religious truth. For the prior question is how the affirmations of God's existence . . . fit into the story of the kind of God we have come to know in the story of

Israel. . . . The emphasis on story as the grammatical
setting for religious convictions is the attempt to remind
us that [religious] convictions are not isolatable 'facts,'
but those 'facts' are part of a story that helps locate what
kind of 'fact' you have at all.[44]

And so, our narrative theologian might wrap up his case
by saying, "There is simply no way to get around it: the
truth of a narrative theology cannot be assessed in total
disregard of the narrative which that theology claims as
ground of its convictions."

And here, *I* must say that as with any narrative, and
certainly with the Exodus narrative, there is no
guarantee, no *necessity*, that everyone will grasp the
significance of the events portrayed or the truth of the
storied claims which they are meant to signify. Obviously, Pharaoh never does. But to acknowledge that is
to acknowledge no more and no less than any literature
teacher already knows. No matter how diligent the
teacher, no matter how well-told the story, there will
always be some students who will fail to 'get it.' There will
always be some students who will miss it for what it is and
who will fail to appreciate the kinds of things it has to say.
In aesthetic terms, the ability to grasp the truth(s)
displayed by a story might be called 'sensitivity'; in
religious terms, it could be called 'grace.'

III. AFFECTIVE CONDITIONS/RATIONALITY[45]

We come now to the final set of conditions which must
be met if a narrative theology is to be justified—namely,
those at the affective level. Such conditions help explain

why it is, for example, when someone has finished telling his friends a story intended as a humorous anecdote, if they simply *stand there*, there is something very unhappy indeed about his then claiming, *insisting*, that the story is really a funny one.[46] As we might expect from our discussion of the other levels of justification, both the affective conditions and what counts as satisfying them will vary from narrative to narrative. Typically, a fundamental conviction of a narrative theology such as one based on the Exodus is not only that its claims are true to what happened in the Egypt of the distant past, but also that its story has the capacity to ring true to the lives of those who hear it in the present so that the story might *come true* for them as well. For such a narrative theology there is the conviction that when such stories are told through preaching, ritual, or liturgy, there exists not only the intention that they have that sort of transformational dimension,[47] or the fact that that intent is so understood by those hearing these stories, but that furthermore and perhaps most importantly, without such stories being told and heard, the hoped-for transformations affecting both persons and events would never come to pass.[48] In fine, there is the conviction that such stories operate on the most basic *affective* level possible: they have the power *to affect* our lives. It is just at this level of the affective conditions that a Hauerwas can assert, "The test of each story is the sort of person it shapes."[49]

And that is exactly as it should be, for here we have the affective conditions for justifying a narrative theology writ large. After all, whether in regard to our 'paradigmatic stories,' or to Hauerwas' "canonical" stories, or to

Greenberg's "orienting-experience" stories, we have throughout the course of this study repeatedly heard the theological claim that such stories can, do, and ought to affect our lives. Referring to the powerful implications of the "dangerous memory" engendered and sustained by the Gospel narratives, J. B. Metz has put the matter this way:

> Christianity as a community of those who believe in Jesus Christ has, from the very beginning, not been primarily a community interpreting and arguing, but a community remembering and narrating with a practical intention—a narrative and evocative memory of the passion, death, and resurrection of Jesus. The logos of the cross and resurrection has a narrative structure. Faith in the redemption of history and in the new man can, because of the history of human suffering, be translated into dangerously liberating stories, the hearer who is affected by them becoming not simply a hearer, but a doer of the word.[50]

In this sense, there can be no greater test of the justifiability of a narrative theology's convictions *at the affective level* than to examine the capacity of those narratives which are their basis to affect human lives, and additionally, to study those lives which have been affected by those stories. No doubt some will be surprised by a claim as stark as this, but as Stanley Cavell has said in reference to similar claims set forth in ethics:

> Questioning a claim to knowledge takes the form of asking "How do you know?" or "Why do you believe

that?", and assessing the claim is, we could say, a matter of assessing whether your position (as Austin put it, your "credentials and facts", your learning and perception) are adequate to the claim. Questioning a claim to moral rightness (whether of any action or any judgment) takes the form of asking "Why are you doing that?", "How can you do that?", "What *are* you doing?", "Have you really considered what you're saying?", "Do you know what this means?"; and assessing the claim is, as we might now say, to determine *what* your position is, and to challenge the position itself, to question whether the position you *take* is adequate to the claim you have entered. The point of the assessment is not to determine *whether* it is adequate, where *what* will be adequate is itself *given* by the form of the assessment itself; the point is to determine *what* position you are taking, that is to say, *what position you are taking responsibility for*—and whether it is one I can respect. What is at stake in such discussions is not, or not exactly, whether you know our world, but whether, or to what extent, we are to live in the same moral universe. What is at stake in such examples . . . is not the validity of morality as a whole, but the nature or quality of our relationship to one another.[51]

Certainly, there are some lives, just as there are some stories, that seem to be able to 'grab' us. That is, there *are* lives which as embodied stories have the power to reach out and seize the investigator and transform his life so that he, too, comes to take up and take on the narrative as his own. Such is the stuff of which conversions are made. By contrast, a narrative which can no longer generate the kind of conviction(s) on which people stake their lives is, in a very real sense, a lifeless story—and ought to be judged accordingly. The justifiability of a narrative theology at the affective level perhaps has been best summed up by Herbert Fingarette, who writes:

> When an orientation is not taken, the claims generated by it are not valid. For the validity of such images comes in their operation. In particular, it comes when they function as the central, dominating, organizing images of a man's life. Let such an image cease to dominate a man's life and, as a *spiritual* conception, it ceases to be. The validity or invalidity of such a vision is not like the truth or falsity of a proposition in science; it is like winning or losing a race.[52]

Yet it is exactly at this point that those who base theology—and ethics—on narrative draw the most criticism from those who view such a foundation as shaky rational ground, which, resting on a vicious relativism, rationalizes any and all behavior whatsoever and thus reduces theological and moral argument to total irrationality.[53] However, these critics, whether theologians or ethicists, are not without their own problems of justification—and precisely because they have failed to see how to make the appropriate connections between the requisite affective conditions and the necessary primary and representative ones. Using their own terms, the ethicists might say that they are, for their part, at a loss to show how if an ethical claim is emotive (i.e., expressive of personal feeling, attitude, or commitment), it can be universal (i.e., necessarily binding on every human being, regardless of place or time), yet if not universal, then how justifiable as a rationally supportable claim about what one ought to do. A similar quandary has confronted theologians. Are religious convictions merely expressions of individual private belief (thus shifting the burden of justifiability from the truth of one's convictions to the strength with which one holds them), or are justifiable convictions self-evidently, axiomatically, necessarily true—no matter who, or even *if*, anybody at all believes them? Thus a basic challenge for a narrative theology, a challenge raised perhaps most intensely at the affective level, will be the test of such a theology's ability to resolve these apparently so-daunting (post-enlightenment) problems of the discontinuity between, e.g., truth and commitment, or between particular and universal. To the extent that a narrative theology can join questions of 'praxis' to those of meaning and truth, it will have a rational basis, and to just that extent, be justifiable.

By this time, I suppose it will come as no surprise to anyone to say that what counts as meeting a narrative theology's affective conditions of justification—and thereby giving some indication of its rationality—will vary from narrative to narrative. But here we must be careful. We must differentiate between the general *concept* 'rationality' and various *conceptions* of rationality. Failing to make such a distinction, we will most likely fall into the classical trap of feeling that we either have to choose the view that there can legitimately be only one universal standard of rationality applicable to all, or else embrace the position that each culture, society, etc., has its own particular canons of rationality which can neither judge nor be judged by the canons of rationality of others 'outside' that group. Happily, Alasdair MacIntyre, a philosopher who has given great attention to the narrative background of many of our important beliefs, has also given us a way to avoid that trap.

First, as MacIntyre has pointedly observed, "Rationality is nobody's property."[54] By that, he means that there are certain recognizable formal criteria of rationality in all recognizably human societies. Although the task of evaluating the convictions of another culture requires that we first understand them (and this is but to remind us once again of the importance of the primary conditions), a prior condition for such understanding is our being able to differentiate among the various kinds of speech-acts present in that culture—things determined by both logic and language. Consequently, MacIntyre very judiciously notes that we shall not be able to make this sort of differentiation

> except on the assumption that the laws of logic are embodied in the linguistic practice of the community which we are studying. If we cannot identify negation and such laws as . . . embodied in this practice, I do not understand how we can be confident in our identification of the speech-acts of assertion and denial. . . . So far as this element in rationality is concerned then, there is no question of *us* judging the rationality of alien cultures in terms of *our* criteria. For the criteria are neither *ours* nor *theirs* but simply *the* criteria, and logic is the inquiry which formulates them.

MacIntyre further notes that the rationality of some belief is never determined in isolation from all the other beliefs to which it may be related and on which it most likely depends. To speak, therefore, of the 'rationality' of some belief is always at the very least to speak of it against a larger background of beliefs. Thus, once again "the distinction between *ours* and *theirs* . . . breaks down. If we indict others for contradiction or incoherence, the contradiction or incoherence is a feature of *their* beliefs, but the standard of contradiction must be the same for them and for us."[55] Hence, no matter what story a theology may invoke, there are certain formal criteria of rationality, e.g., consistency, comprehensiveness, coherence, which it will have to observe if any notion of justifiability is likewise to be invoked. So were someone, for example, to claim as the basis for his convictions a story which he has correctly understood as truly portraying the actual occurrence of something which has in fact made all human beings equal, there would be something unjustifiable—and irrational—about his convictions at the affective level if he then were to discriminate against some of those human beings due to their race. In general terms, the irrationality and corresponding unjustifiability of such convictions could be attributed to inconsistency. In our terms, those convictions must be deemed crucially untenable with those on the primary and representative levels.[56] In any case, one of those post-enlightenment puzzles about the relationship between truth and commitment has just been solved, and a partial claim has thus been staked out for the rationality of a narrative theology.

But having discussed these formal characteristics of the

concept of rationality and the reasons why any justifiable narrative theology must display them, are we then left with an account whose validity, by being grounded in such general and abstract features of logic and language, thus eliminates theology's need for narrative altogether? On the contrary—such a fact makes narrative needed all the more! Though such formal criteria may be necessary conditions for justifying any convictions which we may hold, they are not in themselves sufficient conditions of justification, for being merely formal criteria, they do not and cannot go very far in telling us which convictions are worth holding. Such guidance can come only from the kind of tapestry of beliefs, experiences, and perspectives woven together by the sorts of narratives that bind the disparate elements of our lives into some type of intelligible pattern. If narratives speak of anything, they speak of relations, and primarily of those between persons, their convictions, their actions, and their worlds. Narratives help school us in imagining what might follow from our taking up and acting on one set of convictions rather than another. As David Tracy has said, "Human beings need story . . . to disclose to their imaginations some genuinely new possibilities for existence; possibilities which conceptual analysis, committed as it is to understanding present actualities, cannot adequately provide."[57] Through narratives we can follow through and gauge the possible consequences of embracing some particular conviction(s) and/or pursuing some course of action. In this respect, narratives offer us a relatively safe way to explore our 'options' without our first having to experiment with our own lives. Hence, the kind of rational assessment which narratives foster is, in Hauerwas' words, "less a matter of weighing arguments than of [seeing] how adopting different stories will lead us to become different sorts of persons."[58] In this regard, the story of, e.g., one particular person or people may quite justifiably suggest a whole universe of meaning and significance for the lives of others. And it is in just this regard that another of the classical theological (and ethical) riddles can be solved—and a very solid case thereby made for the rationality of a narrative theology.

As we have been arguing throughout this study, whatever notions we may have about, e.g., God, ourselves, the world, have gained whatever intelligibility and significance they may have from the context of some narrative. As we found in our investigation of Braithwaite and Fletcher, ignoring that fact can render a theology's convictions unjustifiable. Starkly put, it's not simply that a theology's convictions have got some story-context; it's that they've *got to have* some story—or else be unintelligible and/or insignificant. Lacking some place for narrative, a theology cannot possibly meet the conditions of the primary, representative, and affective levels of justification. Since our convictions about God, ourselves, and the like gain their sense and import within the broader context of some narrative, the primary conditions of justification require that to understand such convictions properly we must attend to the narrative from which they take their meaning. The attempt to justify or explain a conviction without this kind of narrative-based understanding leads either to an explanation of a different conviction or to explaining that conviction away. Again, if theological convictions are to be justified at the level of the representative conditions, questions of their truth and falsity cannot be asked—or answered—in total isolation from the narratives in which these convictions have arisen. Instead, such questions and answers (and the concomitant attempts at justification) must be commensurate with the form (genre) and content of the story which has engendered those convictions in the first place. Finally, whatever affective dimensions a theology's convictions are supposed to have in terms of entailing certain kinds of attitudes and actions, a justifiable theology must make some room for narrative as a way for following how the meaning and truth of our convictions might result in commitments that could affectively transform our lives and the world which we inhabit. The plain fact is that for describing that kind of enterprise, i.e., one which is purposeful but not necessary, we have no other way than stories.[59] In short, while what counts as the rational justification of a theology may vary from story to story, one thing will nevertheless always remain constant: the only totally unjustifiable theology will be one which claims to be wholly non-narrative.[60]

Now for those who would claim a narrative basis for theology, this conclusion cuts two ways. On the one hand, it obviously strengthens and defends the justifibility of a narrative-rooted theology against the onslaughts of those who would cast theology in a framework completely independent of the perspective of any narrative whatsoever. On the other hand, though, it means that for adjudicating between rival conviction sets suggested by competing narratives, there is no neutral standpoint either. After all, every stand-*point* is just that, and every evaluation of the claims generated from some narrative takes place from the vantage point of some other narrative that has already been previously adopted.

Surprisingly, even one as sympathetic to narrative theology as Hauerwas can at times forget this critical caveat. While at one point, he rightly says that "[there] is no story of stories, i.e., an account that is literal and that thus provides a criterion to say which stories are true or false,"[61] he elsewhere unaccountably formulates a "list of working criteria," which, though he admits is incomplete and ambiguous, he nevertheless presents as containing those features which "[any] story we adopt, or allow to adopt us, will have to display":

> (1) power to release us from destructive alternatives;
> (2) ways of seeing through current distortions;
> (3) room to keep us from having to resort to violence;
> (4) a sense for the tragic: how meaning transcends power.[62]

Hauerwas has been roundly and rightly criticized at this juncture, for other than the bare assertion of these criteria, he fails to support his claim for their necessity.[63] Not only is it unclear why these criteria are ones that any justifiable narrative theology must employ, but also it is equally unclear, at least upon initial inspection, how such criteria are related to narrative in general. Perhaps the solution lies in the fact that these 'criteria' are not linked at all to 'narrative-in-general,'—but rather to one specific narrative—the story of Christ. Thus, ironically, almost despite himself, Hauerwas has ended up demonstrating his more basic and pervasive thesis that every justifiable theology must have reference to some narrative in order to display the 'grammar,' the logic—the rationality—of its convictions.[64]

But if a theology free of the perspective of any narrative is not a possibility, are we then left with only a hard perspectivism or vicious relativism? Does discourse between rival narrative theologies thus become impossible, such that our story lines may well become our battle lines? For once, our answer can be brief and unequivocal: no. In support of that answer, we may cite Van Harvey as one who has argued that although we as human beings may indeed occupy our own relative standpoints, nevertheless, *as human beings*, we have the capacity to transcend those standpoints so as to be able to enter imaginatively into the standpoint(s) of others—even though these standpoints may be alien to us and even though, while thus having come to *understand* them, we may still be unable to *accept* them.[65] Quite perceptively, Harvey has seen that those who deny this possibility of our "self-transcendence," claiming instead a "Hard Perspectivism" or sheer relativism, nonetheless are forced to offer support for that possibility by the very statement of their own position.[66] For our work here, one of the important implications of Harvey's position (which he calls "Soft Perspectivism")[67] is that while theological agreement "across story lines" is not inevitable, neither is rational discourse between those representing rival

narrative theologies impossible. Making a similar observation about moral discourse and argument, Stanley
Cavell has remarked:

> But suppose that it is just characteristic of moral
> arguments that the rationality of the antagonists is not
> dependent on an agreement emerging between them,
> that there is such a thing as *rational disagreement* about
> a conclusion. *Why* assume that "There is one right thing
> to be done in every case and that that can be found out?"
> Surely the existence of incompatible and equally
> legitimate claims, responsibilities, and wishes indicate
> otherwise? . . . Then how is the rationality of the
> answers to be determined? By the argument, no doubt;
> and perhaps the argument is such that it could establish
> rationality in the absence of agreement—though
> agreement *may*, it is to be hoped, supervene. Without
> the hope of agreement, argument would be pointless;
> but it doesn't follow that without agreement—and in
> particular, apart from agreement arrived at in particular
> ways, e.g., bullying, and without agreement about a
> conclusion concerning what ought to be done—the
> argument was pointless.[68]

Cavell's point is that it is possible after all for two people
to disagree morally, and yet for each of them to be rational
in that disagreement. Our point is that it is possible for
two (or more) people to disagree theologically, and yet for
each of them to be rational in that disagreement. But our
even stronger point—and one crucial to our pluralistic
world—is that just as there may be more than one
justifiable ethic, so too, there may be more than one

justifiable theology—just so long as there are the required narrative foundations, the requisite fulfillment of the conditions at each of the levels of justification, and the necessary attention to the formal criteria of rationality.

All of this will probably mean that our answer to the question of whether a certain theology is justified will most likely *not* take the form of a simple yes or no. Rather, our assessment will, in all likelihood, involve a more textured and nuanced response, judging a narrative theology to be perhaps fully justified in some respects, totally without justification in regard to others, while being to some extent justifiable at other levels. And that is how it should be, for if there is any justification at all for us human beings telling and hearing stories, it lies in the ability of these stories to train us to take note of subtle shades of meaning, to open us to the various ways the world might reasonably be envisaged, and to sensitize us to the richness and complexity of the diverse possibilities for our lives.

VII

'MAKING A LONG STORY SHORT':
SUMMARY AND CONCLUSION

In some stories the final chapter not only reviews and ties together all that has gone before, but it also suggests how the story might continue. My intention in this, the concluding chapter of our study, is somewhat similar. I intend to summarize some of the study's findings regarding the justifiability of a narrative theology, and in so doing, I hope to indicate some of the study's implications for the ways narrative might be used for theology in the future.

Our work began with an examination of situation ethics (chapter 1), and its purpose in starting there was twofold: (1) to demonstrate the importance of explicitly attending to the background context against which theology and ethics are done, and (2) to begin to show why and how that context must be given by some broader, more encom-

241

passing narrative. As the moral life is richer than the mere following of rules, so, too, it is far more complex and nuanced than any 'decisionist' theory of ethics would imply. Neither 'the facts' nor our 'experiences' come to us in discrete and disconnected packets which simply await the appropriate moral principle to be applied. Rather, they stand in need of some narrative which can bind the facts of our experience together into a coherent pattern, and it is thus in virtue of that narrative that our abstracted rules, principles, and notions gain their full intelligibility. Theologians and ethicists who ignore the central position that narratives occupy in human life must do so at their own peril—and to their own detriment, as our examination of Fletcher showed.

Moreover, that conclusion should serve as a critical caveat for those who, like Braithwaite, want to treat narrative as the mere chaff surrounding the more precious theological kernels, so that once the desired principle or proposition has been extracted, the narrative 'husk' may be discarded. But that kind of attitude is unjustified on two counts. First, it wrongly regards narrative as a kind of intellectual crutch needed by the less perceptive. Second, and perhaps more serious, it tends to view all narratives as fables, i.e., as stories with detachable meanings. But there *are* narratives whose meaning cannot be stated apart from the story, whose meaning cannot be gotten except through the story, whose meaning *is* the story. By assuming that all stories are in some sense fables, thinkers such as Braithwaite unjustifiably equate narratives with falsehood, thus unreasonably precluding any further discussion about a story's worth. Yet as our discussion in chapter 2 pointed out, different narrative kinds or genres must be recognized for what they are and for the different kinds of claims and meanings that they have. Consequently, a theology such as Dunne's or Stevenson's that fails to get right about the specific kind of narrative base it has will most likely go wrong on whatever proposals it has to make. In purely logical terms, that kind of error could be labeled a category mistake; in terms of narrative, it might be called a misreading of the story.

Clearly, there are narratives that lack detachable 'points' or 'morals' and that additionally make claims to being true. In chapters 3 and 4, we considered biographies and autobiographies as examples of such stories. We found that life stories are theologically significant for several reasons. A life story may be seen as the individual's embodiment of the larger paradigmatic story of his or her community. As such, that life may stand as a validation, challenge, or critique of that community's convictions, and as McClendon's work suggested, on this level at least, the justifiability of a conviction may very well lie in the justifiability of a life lived. However, if that kind of theological 'test' is to be made, then life stories must be allowed to, as it were, speak for themselves; theological analysis must avoid imposing some sort of reductionist, non-narrative framework such as that used by Fowler. Futhermore, the issue of the truth of stories must not be limited to the capacity to portray certain events with accuracy, for both life stories and the paradigmatic stories which they reflect raise the question of truthfulness, the ability to face reality without resort to self-deception. Justifiably held convictions must be rooted in some narrative which gives us the capacity to step back from our current engagements and spell out what we have been doing from a broadened perspective, hence enabling us to integrate our lives in a more coherent and comprehensive fashion than before. As the autobiographical writings of Campbell and Wiesel illustrated, the convictions generated by certain stories may be vindicated or invalidated to the extent that those stories can reach out, sustain, and transform the lives of those who hear them and who then go on to claim them as their own. In that respect, some narratives not only help explain to us what has come before, but also show us how we ought to proceed.

Traditionally, biblical narratives, such as the Exodus or the Gospel accounts of Christ, have been regarded as being those kinds of stories, and obviously, these biblical narratives have the most direct import for theology. In chapter 5, we explored the views of a number of contemporary thinkers who have stressed the necessity of attending closely to such narratives in the doing of theology. While these figures disagree on the exact locus and nature of the theological significance of the biblical narratives, on the proper way of employing them theologically, and on the criteria for theologically assessing them, they generally concur that these narratives reflect the primary structure of existence, make basic claims about the truth of that existence, and display the ways whereby such existence may be fundamentally affected and transformed. These narrative theologians not only understand such stories as being true portrayals of past events, but also as ringing true to some common aspect(s) of human experience, thereby providing the basis on which human beings might more truthfully live their lives. And here the question could be asked, How can these or any narrative-based theologies be justified?

Chapter 6 took up this question explicitly. As we had come to see throughout the course of our investigation, part of the problem of justifying a narrative theology lay in the inability to develop a procedure for systematically assessing whatever narrative-grounded convictions might be put forth. I suggested an analytic model in some ways analogous to the one presented by McClendon and Smith as a means of generating such a procedure. The model calls on the narrative theologian to distinguish carefully among the primary, representative, and affective conditions of justification. For example, in evaluating the work of those theologians primarily concerned with biblical narrative, one could say, for instance, that while the narrative theologies of Frei and McFague were to some extent justifiable at the primary level through their attention to the meaning entailed by the specific narrative kinds involved, they nevertheless were inadequate at the representative level due to their failure to address adequately the question of the truth-claims stemming from those stories, and that furthermore, their theological proposals will to that extent stand unjustified, no matter what might be their merits on the remaining affective, 'transformational' plane. By contrast, one might judge that the work of Van Buren or Greenberg, while fulfilling the necessary representative and affective conditions, falls short at the primary level by ignoring the question of what constitutes a justifiable hermeneutic. One could go on to say that Yoder's thesis seems fine at the primary and affective levels, but it needs more work—and support—as far as the representative conditions are concerned. As for Hauerwas, one might observe with some justice that in his concentration on the notion of truthfulness, he too often makes the affective dimension of convictions do much of the work of justification, thus failing to show sufficient regard for the demands of the primary and representative conditions. If nothing else, these remarks should help us realize that very rarely can we answer whether a certain narrative theology is justified with a flat or simple yes or no. More positively, this approach provides us with a way of articulating precisely how and where a narrative theology stands in need of justification.

Furthermore, this approach let us see that quite importantly, what counts as meeting the various conditions of justification will vary from story to story, and that in any case, every assessment of the justifiability of a narrative theology will itself be narrative-dependent. We concluded that such narrative-dependency need not result in a vicious relativism since justification across story lines was still a possibility. More significantly, however, our view does suggest that there can be *rational disagreement* among those holding convictions reflecting rival stories, and moreover that there can thus be more than one justifiable theology. In short, while our account of theological justification does allow a great deal of latitude, it still insists on the observance of certain 'constants': (1) that any justifiable theology have a narrative foundation; (2) that every theology's convictions be justified at the level of the primary, representative, and affective conditions; and (3) that justification requires a theology to meet certain formal criteria of rationality.

And now, we are indeed in the position of the storyteller who has finished relating his tale. Whatever responses and questions his hearers have to make will reflect on the power of what he has had to say and on the skill with which he has said it. Such questions and responses may in fact shape the future telling of that story and may even determine whether in fact it ought to be told again. But ultimately, the power of a narrative—and the justifiability of a theology—depend on that kind of give-and-take, as any storyteller or theologian knows.

NOTES

CHAPTER I

1. James Wm. McClendon, Jr., *Biography as Theology: How Life Stories Can Remake Today's Theology* (Nashville: Abingdon, 1974), p. 188.

2. Stanley Hauerwas, with David Burrell and Richard Bondi, *Truthfulness and Tragedy* (Notre Dame, Ind.: University of Notre Dame Press, 1977), p.8.

3. Johann Baptist Metz, *Faith in History and Society*, trans. David Smith (New York: The Seabury Press, 1980), p. 148.

4. Stephen Crites, "Myth, Story, History," in *Parable, Myth, and Language*, ed. Tony Stoneburner (Cambridge: Church Society for College Work, 1968), p. 68.

5. Carol P. Christ, *Diving Deep and Surfacing* (Boston: Beacon Press, 1980), p. 1.

6. *Ibid.*, cf. p. 82.

7. *Ibid.*, cf. pp. 13-14, 51-52.

8. *Ibid.*, pp. 13, 129.

9. *Ibid.*, pp. 51-52.

10. *Ibid.*, cf., e.g., pp. 129-31 where Christ speaks of the possibility of women's spiritual and social quests coinciding.

11. *Ibid.*, p. 137, footnote 18.

12. James H. Cone, *God of the Oppressed* (New York: The Seabury Press, 1975), pp. 30-31, 34.

13. Cone uses the notions of 'blackness' and 'whiteness' in both a literal and a symbolic sense. For instance, he says of Jesus Christ that his

> blackness is both literal and symbolic. His blackness is literal in the sense that he truly becomes One with the oppressed blacks, taking their suffering as his suffering and revealing that he is found in the history of our struggle, the story of our pain, and the rhythm of our bodies. . . . To say that Christ is black means that God, in his infinite wisdom and mercy, not only takes color seriously, he takes it upon himself and discloses his will to make us whole—new creatures born in the spirit of divine blackness and redeemed through the blood of the Black Christ. . . .
>
> Maybe our white theologians are right when they insist that I have overlooked the *universal* significance of Jesus' message. But I contend that there is no universalism that is not particular. Indeed their insistence upon the universal note of the gospel arises out of their own particular political and social interests. As long as they can be sure that the gospel is *for everybody,* ignoring that God liberated a *particular* people from Egypt, came in a particular man called Jesus, and for the particular purpose of liberating the oppressed, then they can continue to talk in theological abstractions, failing to recognize that such talk is not the gospel unless it is related to the concrete freedom of the little ones. My point is that God came, and continues to come, to those who are poor and helpless, for the purpose of setting them free. And since the people of color are his elected poor in America, any interpretation of God that ignores black oppresson cannot be Christian theology. The "blackness of Christ," therefore, is not simply a statement about skin color, but rather, the transcendent affirmation that God has not ever, no not ever, left the oppressed alone in struggle (pp. 136-37).

14. *Ibid.*, pp. 116-18, 118-19.

15. *Ibid.*, pp. 47, 30, 106-7.

16. Cf., e.g., John Howard Yoder's position in his *Politics of Jesus*, discussed in chapter 5 below.

17. Cone, *God of the Oppressed,* pp. 219, 222.

18. Much has already been written about Fletcher's book, and a good deal of cogent criticism has been brought against it. In particular, the following sources provide fruitful ways of pursuing the 'situationist debate': James M. Gustafson, "Context Versus Principles: A Misplaced Debate in Christian Ethics," *Harvard Theological Review,* 58 (1965), 171-202; Gene Outka and Paul Ramsey, eds., *Norm and Context in Christian Ethics* (New York: Charles Scribner's Sons, 1968), especially Donald Evans', "Love, Situations, and Rules," and Richard McComick's, "Human Significance and Christian Significance"; Robert L. Cunningham, ed., *Situationism and the New Morality* (New York: Meredith Corporation, 1970), particularly the "Introduction" with the extensive bibliography on situationism given there and the section entitled "The Fletcher-McCabe Debate." Well aware of the many contradictions and incoherencies already correctly pointed out in Fletcher's work by others, I will nonetheless try to go on and present Fletcher's account at its strongest and in its best light and work from there.

19. Joseph Fletcher, *Situation Ethics* (Philadelphia: The Westminster Press, 1966), p. 26; for Fletcher, this concern is *agape*.

20. John Searle, *Speech Acts* (New York: Cambridge University Press, 1969), pp. 34, 35.

21. Fletcher, *Situation Ethics,* pp. 58, 59.

22. *Ibid.*, p. 49.

23. *Ibid.*, p. 33.

24. *Ibid.*, pp. 143, 84.

25. G. E. M. Anscombe, *Intention* (Ithaca: Cornell University Press, 1969), pp. 37-38.

26. Fletcher, *Situation Ethics,* pp. 142, 143.

27. Stanley Hauerwas, *Vision and Virtue* (Notre Dame, Ind.: Fides Publishers, 1974), p. 23.

28. Fletcher, *Situation Ethics,* p. 110.

29. *Ibid.,* p. 95.

30. *Ibid.,* p. 113.

31. *Ibid.,* pp. 153, 154.

32. Edmund Pincoffs, "Quandary Ethics," *Mind* 80 (1971), 554.

33. Fletcher, *Situation Ethics,* p. 42.

34. Pincoffs, "Quandary Ethics," p. 570.

35. Fletcher, *Situation Ethics,* p. 157.

36. Again, Stanley Hauerwas' critique of Fletcher in *Vision and Virtue* provides excellent insights into how these themes might be and need to be developed in Fletcher's own analysis.

37. James Wm. McClendon, Jr., and James M. Smith, *Understanding Religious Convictions* (Notre Dame, Ind.: University of Notre Dame Press, 1975), p. 7.

38. For a helpful typology outlining some of the ways various theological enterprises might be characterized, see David Tracy's *Blessed Rage for Order* (New York: The Seabury Press, 1975), pp. 22-42.

39. McClendon and Smith themselves present a more elaborate—and cumbersome—definition of theology:

> the discovery, examination, and transformation of the conviction set of a given community, carried on with a view to discovering and modifying the relation of the member convictions to one another, to other (non-convictional) beliefs held by the community, and to whatever else there is (p. 192).

40. Technically speaking, there is a difference between narrative and story. Thus, Robert Scholes and Robert Kellogg

define 'narrative' as "all those literary works which are distinguished by two characteristics: the presence of a story and a story-teller"; by contrast, they say that 'story' is a "general term for character and action in narrative form" (*The Nature of Narrative* [London: Oxford University Press, 1966], pp. 4, 208). However, in keeping with common English usage, I shall frequently use these two terms interchangeably.

41. Cf. McClendon, *Biography as Theology*, p. 178.

42. Cf. Hauerwas, *Truthfulness and Tragedy*, p. 15. Additionally, many of our disputes and clashes arise from the fact that both as communities and as individuals, we are rarely the bearers of just one story alone. As Alasdair MacIntyre has pointed out, in a secularized, pluralistic society such as ours, we are heirs to many different stories, and each of us consequently bears within himself or herself fragments from many different narratives, e.g., the story of modernity, the American story, the Christian story. Consequently, our lives are often fragmented, involving partial commitments and limited responses as we act on the basis of first one, and then another, of these 'story-pieces.' See MacIntyre's "How Virtues Became Vices: Values, Medicine, and Social Context," in *Evaluation and Explanation in the Biomedical Sciences*, ed. H. T. Englehardt and S. Spicker (Utrecht, Holland: Reydal, 1975). Thus, the caveat of Michael Novak is quite cogent here:

> Some writers use the concept story as though there were only one story a person is living out. . . . This . . . is naive. Usually, a human life is a tangle of stories. Our conscious lives, at different depths, are divided by contrary impulses. We may be trying to pattern our lives on some favorite model or some vivid ideal. . . . Meanwhile, our inner lives are theaters of conflict. We are inhabited by many stories at once: by cover stories, by stories to which we only aspire, by stories that would seduce us, and by stories that others have learned through living with us to find reliable, even though we have not put them into words.

The concept story, then, points to the tangled nests of our inner lives. It is not designed to simplify them. It obliges us to sort out many different dramatic threads (*Ascent of the Mountain, Flight of the Dove*, rev. ed. [New York: Harper & Row, 1978], pp. 222-23).

Yet having cited Novak's pertinent observations, it is also germane here to recall Crites' observations (p. 2 above) that a person's sense of his own identity seems largely determined by the sort of story that he takes himself to have been acting out during the course of his life. Although something that could be called '*the Christian story*' is probably only rarely embodied in the life of a community or of an individual as a pure type, nevertheless, both communities and individuals frequently have in the past and still do in the present stake their lives on ostensibly *Christian convictions*. A basic claim of narrative theologians is that such convictions (and the lives which display them) are dependent at some fundamental level on narrative categories for their significance and justifiability. Thus, in this study, when I speak of 'paradigmatic narratives' such as 'the Christian story,' I do so in order to call attention to this theme (and analytic tool) present throughout recent narrative theologies.

43. I feel that the need for such a 'map' is particularly urgent at present and believe that that urgency is due to two factors.

First, much of what has been written heretofore about the diverse implications of narrative for theology has lacked any sustained or unified mode of presentation. A good deal of what has been said about 'narrative theology' has appeared episodically in individually distinct and separate essays. So, for example, there are: Crites' seminal and influential essay, "The Narrative Quality of Experience," *Journal of the American Academy of Religion*, 39 (September 1971); the collection of essays on the subject of story and religion edited by James B.

Wiggins, *Religion as Story* (New York: Harper & Row, 1975); and the wide-ranging essays on the significance of narrative for theology and ethics written at various times by Hauerwas and eventually gathered together in such books of his as *Truthfulness and Tragedy* and *A Community of Character* (Notre Dame, Ind.: University of Notre Dame Press, 1981). A possible exception is George Stroup's book, *The Promise of Narrative Theology* (Atlanta: John Knox Press, 1981). Even so, this book gives only a cursory discussion of the work of many of the figures currently doing narrative theology while ignoring altogether the work of several other important writers in the field. I suspect that what accounts for the relative lack of breadth (and depth) in Stroup's treatment of the subject is the fact that his book's true primary concern is not narrative theology *per se* but rather, "the existential problem of Christian identity and . . . the confusion in Christian theology about the meaning of revelation" (p. 17). At any rate for the most part, there has been up to now no coherent, detailed survey which systematically examines the work of those engaged in doing narrative-based theology.

Second, a large part of what has been written about narrative theology has failed to be sufficiently critical in spirit. The following books, for instance, make various claims about the import of narrative for theology, but generally lack a methodology capable of dealing adequately with the critical issues involved: Gabriel Fackre, *The Christian Story* (Grand Rapids: Eerdmans Publishing Co., 1978); John S. Dunne, *Time and Myth* (Garden City, N.Y.: Doubleday & Co., 1973), and *The Way of All the Earth* (New York: The Macmillan Co., 1972); and Sallie M. TeSelle, *Speaking in Parables* (Philadelphia: Fortress Press, 1975). I will discuss these books later.

This study is intended as a remedy to both these current problems; I fear that without such a remedy, 'narrative theology' will become just one more theological fad and that whatever significant contributions it may have to make will be lost as 'styles change.'

CHAPTER II

1. It is interesting to note how much more 'respectable' the word 'narrative' sounds compared to the word 'story.' Although this may have to do in part with the fact that the word 'narrative' comes from an Old French rather than an Anglo-Saxon root, it may also be connected with the way in which 'story' and 'fiction' have become tied in our language.

2. R. B. Braithwaite, *An Empiricist's View of the Nature of Religious Belief* (Cambridge: Cambridge University Press, 1955), pp. 16, 24.

3. *Ibid.*, pp. 23-24.

4. *Ibid.*, p. 27.

5. Cf. James Wm. McClendon, Jr., and James M. Smith, *Understanding Religious Convictions*, p. 28; and Terrence W. Tilley, *Talking of God* (Paramus, N.J.: Paulist/Newman Press, 1978), pp. 34-35.

6. John Dunne, *The Way of All the Earth*, p. 169.

7. Stanley Hauerwas, "Jesus: The Story of the Kingdom," *Theological Digest*, 26 (Winter 1978): 307; emphasis added.

8. Braithwaite, *An Empiricist's View*, p. 26.

9. McFague, p. 13. McFague originally published *Speaking in Parables* under the name of TeSelle. We will examine her work more fully later.

10. Braithwaite, *An Empiricist's View*, pp. 25-26.

11. Dunne, *The Way of All the Earth*, p. 53.

12. *Ibid.*, p. 39. Dunne cites Jung, *Answer to Job*, trans. R. F. C. Hull (New York: Meridian, 1960), p. 185. Cf. also pp. 136-37, where Dunne, drawing on Karl Jaspers, gives the following schematic formulation of developmental turning points in time:

mankind		individual
The beginning of time.	=	The beginning of life.
Transition from prehistory to history (invention of writing).	=	Going from immediate through existential to historical consciousness.
Enlightenment and revelation experiences giving rise to world religions.	=	Experimenting with truth.
Transition from history to world history "which has been taking place in our times as the different civilizations and religions of the world enter into communication with one another and their stories become one story. . . ."	=	Individual's process of passing over into standpoints other than his own and then coming back to his own.
End of time.	=	End of life.

13. John Dunne, *Time and Myth,* p. 50.

14. Dunne, *The Way of All the Earth,* p. 72.

15. *Ibid.,* p. 128; emphasis added.

16. Mircea Eliade, *Myth and Reality,* trans. Willard R. Trask (New York: Harper & Row, 1963), p. 77.

17. *Ibid.,* pp. 78-79, 82.

18. *Ibid.,* pp. 8, 18, 11.

19. W. Taylor Stevenson, *History as Myth* (New York: The Seabury Press, 1969), p. 17; quotes from Eliade, *Myth and Reality,* p. 18.

20. *Ibid.,* pp. 17-18, 31.

21. Mircea Eliade, *The Myth of the Eternal Return,* trans.

Willard Trask (Princeton: Princeton University Press, 1954), pp. xiii-xiv; emphasis added.

22. *Ibid.*, p. xiv.

23. *Ibid.*, pp. 35, 5, 92, 48.

24. *Ibid.*, p. 104.

25. *Ibid.*, p. 143.

26. *Ibid.*, p. 86.

27. Erich Auerbach, *Mimesis* (Princeton: Princeton University Press, 1963), pp. 4, 9. For a particularly insightful work discussing the significant implications of the literary style of biblical narratives for understanding their meaning, see Robert Alter's extremely valuable and remarkable book, *The Art of Biblical Narrative* (New York: Basic Books, 1981).

28. Eliade, *Myth and Reality*, p. 2.

29. Stevenson, *History as Myth*, p. 16.

30. Ludwig Wittgenstein, *Philosophische Untersuchungen, Philosophical Investigations*, German original with English translation by G. E. M. Anscombe and R. Rhees (New York: The Macmillan Co., 1953), S. 217.

31. Obviously, it does not necessarily follow from this contingent fact that *neither* is right.

32. Stevenson, *History as Myth*, p. 16.

33. Steven Crites, "The Narrative Quality of Experience," p. 305.

34. Eliade, *Myth and Reality*, p. 163.

35. G. E. Wright, *God Who Acts* (London: Regnery, 1952), p. 126.

36. *Ibid.* Wright has Tillich in mind here as well as Bultmann.

37. In the later New Testament books, where Christian thought confronts a sophisticated use of Greek μυθος, the writers are at pains to reject the applicability of μυθοι to the

story they have to tell. See for example: I Timothy 1:4; 4:7; II Timothy 4:4; II Peter 1:16.

CHAPTER III

1. Crites, "The Narrative Quality of Experience," p. 309.

2. James Wm. McClendon, Jr., *Biography as Theology*, p. 178.

3. *Ibid.*, p. 37.

4. James W. Fowler et al., *Trajectories in Faith: Five Life Stories* (Nashville: Abingdon, 1980), p. 9.

5. McClendon, *Biography as Theology*, pp. 14, 30, 31.

6. *Ibid.*, pp. 32, 29.

7. *Ibid.*, pp. 96-97. McClendon draws his basic notion of the importance of images for theological reflection from Austin Farrer's *The Glass of Vision*. However, he substantially enlarges on Farrer's theme and, in places differs from Farrer's own understanding of the significance of images theologically. See *Biography as Theology*, pp. 93-96.

8. *Ibid.*, pp. 31, 152, 191, 101.

9. *Ibid.*, p. 191.

10. *Ibid.*, pp. 38, 192.

11. *Ibid.*, pp. 190, 102.

12. *Ibid.*, p. 193.

13. *Ibid.*, p. 194.

14. *Ibid.*, p. 195. See the book written by McClendon with James M. Smith, *Understanding Religious Convictions*, for a more detailed treatment of the nature of religious convictions as well as for a theory of the process of justification of such convictions. I shall refer to this book later.

15. Fowler et al., *Trajectories in Faith*, p. 17.

16. *Ibid.*, pp. 19, 20, 21.

17. *Ibid.*, pp. 18, 24, 187.

18. Additionally, there is a "pre-stage" of "Undifferentiated

Faith," corresponding to the individual's preconceptual and prelinguistic orientation to the world during infancy; cf. p. 24.

19. Fowler et al., *Trajectories in Faith*, pp. 24, 25, 26.

20. *Ibid.*, p. 28.

21. *Ibid.*, p. 29.

22. *Ibid.*, p. 31.

23. *Ibid.*, p. 35.

24. *Ibid.*, p. 89.

25. *Ibid.*, p. 32.

26. *Ibid.*, p. 17; emphasis added.

27. *Ibid.*, p. 32.

28. Peter R. L. Brown, *Augustine of Hippo* (Berkeley: University of California Press, 1969), p. 9.

29. *Ibid.*, p. 100. Although my references here and elsewhere will be only to Brown's book directly, I would urge the reader to see Brown's own cititations of Augustine's writings as well as of other documentary sources for fuller bibliographical attestation of these points.

30. *Ibid.*, p. 147.

31. *Ibid.*, pp. 175, 176, 147.

32. Fowler et al., *Trajectories in Faith,* p. 23.

33. Brown, *Augustine of Hippo,* p. 149.

34. *Ibid.*, p. 165.

35. *Ibid.*, p. 173.

36. *Ibid.*, p. 177.

37. *Ibid.*

38. Fowler et al., *Trajectories in Faith,* p. 187-88.

39. *Ibid.*, p. 30.

40. Brown, *Augustine of Hippo,* p. 324.

41. *Ibid.*, p. 278.

42. Fowler et al., *Trajectories in Faith,* p. 31.

43. Brown, *Augustine of Hippo,* p. 224.

44. *Ibid.*

260 NOTES FOR PAGES 87-89

45. *Ibid.*, pp. 236-37.
46. *Ibid.*, p. 206.
47. *Ibid.*, p. 364.
48. *Ibid.*, p. 430.
49. Fowler et al., *Trajectories in Faith*, p. 31; emphasis added. Cf. also the previously cited essay by Katherine Herzog on Anne Hutchinson which seems to have as its theoretic basis a perspective shaped at least as much by feminism as by the putatively value-free faith-development approach. For example, Herzog writes that the three major controversies of the seventeenth century in the Massachusetts Bay Colony—Anne Hutchinson in 1636, the Quaker persecutions of the later 1650s, and the witchcraft trials of 1692—were all instances of "struggles between male authority and powerless women." According to Herzog, Hutchinson became the focus of much of the talk of witchcraft, thus "providing for the men in the colony a way to make sense of this remarkable woman who defied traditional female behavioral boundaries" (p. 75). In Herzog's view, Hutchinson as a religious figure gained much of her prominence at the time due to her "outspoken embodiment of a radical individuative-reflective faith [which] threatened the male-dominated synthetic-conventional society to its very roots" (p. 84). In making claims such as these, Herzog relies explicitly on the work of the English anthropologist, I. M. Lewis, whose concepts, "Spirit Theology" (which "speaks particularly to women") and "peripheral religion" (which "is often a type of protest by the oppressed members of society, usually women"), seem to Herzog to illuminate much of Anne's religious growth as well as the hostility of the Bay Colony toward her. In the end, one is unsure, therefore, whether the true methodological and conceptual basis for Herzog's understanding of Hutchinson's life is drawn from Fowler and the faith-developmentalists, or from feminism and Lewis. If

Herzog would answer "Both," then she needs to make explicit how and why such a 'marriage of methods' is not only possible, but necessary.

50. *Ibid.*, p. 17.

51. *Ibid.*, p. 189.

52. *Ibid.*, p. 187.

53. McClendon, *Biography as Theology*, p. 175.

54. *Ibid.*, p. 91.

55. *Ibid.*, p. 90.

56. To be fair, I must add that although this criticism certainly seems valid when applied to McClendon's purely 'theoretic' chapters, its validity varies among those chapters which deal with specific biographies. For example, while the criticism does apply to McClendon's treatment of King, the images in Jordan's life story do seem to move and develop over the years.

57. Crites, "Myth, Story, History," p. 300. My use of the term "image-stream" differs, however, from the use made of it by Crites. While he has in mind the images of memory which he sees as coming in a kind of "cinematic" succession, I am thinking instead of images *qua* metaphors or scientific models which are continually refined and modified in the light of new experiential data and/or other subsequently developed models which serve to complement them.

58. McClendon, *Biography as Theology*, pp. 201, 203.

59. Fowler et al., *Trajectories in Faith*, p. 186.

60. Quoted in Brown, *Augustine of Hippo*, p. 433.

CHAPTER IV

1. Roy Pascal, *Design and Truth in Autobiography* (Cambridge: Harvard University Press, 1960), p. 71.

2. McFague, *Speaking in Parables*, p. 157.

3. This is a technical term whose meaning I will make more explicit later. It is taken from Herbert Fingarette's book, *Self-Deception* (New York: Humanities Press, 1969). I will bring out the nuances of this term in detail.

4. Crites, "The Narrative Quality of Experience," p. 299.

5. Pascal, *Design and Truth,* p. 69.

6. *Ibid.,* pp. 187-88.

7. Stuart Hampshire, *Thought and Action* (New York: Viking Press, 1959), pp. 135, 119, 149, 72, 198.

8. Barrett J. Mandel, "Full of Life Now," in *Autobiography: Essays Theoretical and Critical,* ed. James Olney (Princeton: Princeton University Press, 1980), p. 60; hereafter referred to as *Autobiography,* ed. Olney.

9. Pascal, *Design and Truth,* p. 189.

10. Jean Starobinski, "The Style of Autobiography," in *Autobiography,* ed. Olney, pp. 77-78.

11. James Olney, *Metaphors of Self* (Princeton: Princeton University Press, 1972), pp. 152, 196.

12. *Ibid.,* p. 195.

13. Pascal, *Design and Truth,* p. 78.

14. Georges Gusdorf, "Conditions and Limits of Autobiography," in *Autobiography,* ed. Olney, p. 41.

15. Pascal, *Design and Truth,* p. 15.

16. Fingarette, *Self-Deception,* pp. 50, 140.

17. *Ibid.,* p. 40.

18. *Ibid.,* p. 41.

19. *Ibid.,* p. 38. Fingarette clarifies this point about the discontinuity between vision and consciousness by saying that consciousness can involve senses other than sight (we can be conscious of smelling or tasting something even when our eyes are closed), and by adding that, "we may concentrate so intently on our thoughts that even with eyes wide open, we are not conscious of seeing anything" (p. 37).

20. *Ibid.,* p. 43.

21. *Ibid.*, pp. 47, 143.

22. *Ibid.*, pp. 73, 53, 88.

23. *Ibid.*, pp. 48, 143.

24. *Ibid.*, pp. 141, 149; emphasis added.

25. Herbert Fingarette, *The Self in Transformation* (New York: Harper & Row, 1963), pp. 37, 73, 86, 43, 22-23.

26. *Ibid.*, pp. 38, 23, 20.

27. *Ibid.*, pp. 35-36.

28. *Ibid.*, pp. 42-43, 61, 62.

29. *Ibid.*, pp. 105, 106.

30. *Ibid.*, p. 164; Fingarette, *Self-Deception,* p. 149.

31. Fingarette, *The Self in Transformation,* pp. 164, 101, 64.

32. *Ibid.*, p. 55.

33. Hampshire, *Thought and Action,* p. 213-14.

34. Pascal, *Design and Truth,* p. 183.

35. Olney, *Metaphors of Self,* p. 43.

36. *Ibid.*, pp. 42-44.

37. I have drawn this notion of "becoming a story" from the work of Stanley Hauerwas, and I will return to explicate it at greater length in the next chapter when I take up an examination of Hauerwas' thought as a whole.

38. Fingarette, *The Self in Transformation,* p. 60.

39. Will D. Campbell, *Brother to a Dragonfly* (New York: The Seabury Press, 1977).

40. *Ibid.*, p. 5.

41. *Ibid.*, pp. 11, 50, 49, 43, 38.

42. *Ibid.*, p. 13.

43. *Ibid.*, p. 87.

44. *Ibid.*, pp. 95, 98.

45. *Ibid.*, pp. 112-13.

46. *Ibid.*, pp. 199-200.

47. *Ibid.*, p. 201.

48. *Ibid.*

49. *Ibid.*, p. 203.

50. *Ibid.*, pp. 220, 221.

51. *Ibid.*, pp. 220, 222.

52. *Ibid.*

53. *Ibid.*, pp. 223-24.

54. *Ibid.*, pp. 222, 249-50.

55. *Ibid.*, p. 225.

56. *Ibid.*, pp. 13-15.

57. *Ibid.*, p. 266.

58. *Ibid.*, p. 261.

59. *Ibid.*, p. 262.

60. *Ibid.*, p. 267.

61. *Ibid.*, p. 268.

62. See Pascal, *Design and Truth*, p. 177, for an elaboration of some of the differences between autobiography and the autobiographical novel.

63. Elie Wiesel, *The Town Beyond the Wall*, trans. Stephen Becker (New York: Atheneum, 1964), pp. 67-68.

64. Elie Wiesel, *One Generation After*, trans. Lily Edelman and Elie Wiesel (New York: Avon Books, 1970), pp. 184, 223-24.

65. *Ibid.*, pp. 223, 224.

66. Cf., e.g., Exodus 32:11-13 and Numbers 13:13-17 where Moses makes exactly this point to God!

67. Midrash on Psalms (Midrash Tehillim), on Psalm 123:1.

68. Elie Wiesel, *Night*, with a foreword by Francois Mauriac, trans. Stella Rodway (New York: Avon Books, 1960), p. 76.

69. Wiesel, *One Generation After*, p. 51; cf., e.g., Exodus 13:8 where the importance of the telling of the Jewish story is clearly set forth by its being explicitly commanded. In later Jewish tradition, this verse becomes the basis of the recital of

the *Haggadah* (literally: narration) at the Passover Seder.

70. Or, for that matter, of the Christian.

71. Elie Wiesel, *A Jew Today*, trans. Marion Wiesel (New York: Random House, 1978), pp. 9, 198-99.

72. Wiesel, *Night*, pp. 65-66.

73. *Ibid.*, pp. 118, 119, 124.

74. Elie Wiesel, *Dawn*, trans. Frances Frenaye (New York: Avon Books, 1961), p. 94.

75. *Ibid.*, pp. 78-79.

76. *Ibid.*, p. 112, 126.

77. Wiesel, *The Town Beyond the Wall*, pp. 148-49.

78. *Ibid.*, pp. 151, 163.

79. *Ibid.*, pp. 172, 177.

80. Wiesel, *A Jew Today*, p. 187.

81. Wiesel, *One Generation After*, p. 191.

82. Wiesel, *A Jew Today*, pp. 106, 49.

83. See, e.g., Deuteronomy 23:8-9: "You shall not abhor an Egyptian, for you were a stranger in his land. The children that are begotten of them may enter into the congregation of the Lord in the third generation."

CHAPTER V

1. H. Richard Niebuhr, *The Meaning of Revelation* (New York: The Macmillan Co., 1941), p. 34.

2. Besides the above-mentioned *Meaning of Revelation* and *The Responsible Self*, which we will also have occasion to refer to in the present chapter, see as well Niebuhr's *Christ and Culture* (New York: Harper & Brothers, 1951); *Radical Monotheism and Western Culture* (New York: Harper & Brothers, 1960); *The Advancement of Theological Education*, written with Daniel Day Williams and James M. Gustafson (New York: Harper & Brothers, 1957). As secondary sources on Niebuhr, cf. James Fowler, *To See the Kingdom: The*

Theological Vision of H. Richard Niebuhr (Nashville: Abingdon, 1974), and Paul Ramsey, ed., *Faith and Ethics: The Theology of H. Richard Niebuhr* (New York: Harper & Brothers, 1957).

3. In addition to Wright's *God Who Acts* which is discussed in detail in this chapter, see also the following books by the same author: *The Challenge of Israel's Faith* (Chicago: University of Chicago Press, 1944); *The Old Testament Against Its Environment* (Chicago: Henry Regnery Co., 1950); *The Book of the Acts of God* (Garden City, N.Y.: Doubleday & Co., 1957).

4. For example, Karl Barth, who is not usually classed as a 'narrative theologian,' often shows himself to be attentive to the implications and nuances of the Gospel stories' portrayal of Jesus. In fact, in the indented 'sub-sections' of *Church Dogmatics*, such as those found in IV:2, "The Royal Man," Barth as much as *tells* that story himself.

5. H. Richard Niebuhr, *The Responsible Self*, with an introduction by James M. Gustafson (New York: Harper & Row, 1978), p. 107.

6. *Ibid.*, p. 60.

7. Niebuhr, *The Meaning of Revelation*, p. 32.

8. *Ibid.*, pp. 68, 69.

9. *Ibid.*, pp. 48, 47, 61.

10. *Ibid.*, p. 127.

11. Wright, *God Who Acts*, p. 38.

12. *Ibid.*, cf. pp. 44, 67, 83, 109.

13. *Ibid.*, p. 85.

14. *Ibid.*, pp. 39, 44, 54-55.

15. *Ibid.*, cf. p. 127.

16. *Ibid.*, p. 116.

17. *Ibid.*, cf. pp. 123ff.

18. *Ibid.*, p. 116; emphasis added.

19. Brevard Childs, *Biblical Theology in Crisis* (Philadelphia: The Westminster Press, 1970), p. 52. In this book, Childs traces the development of a theological position which he calls "The Biblical Theology Movement." He follows it from its rise in the early forties to its decline in the midsixties. Although at its height, the movement embraced such diverse figures as Niebuhr, Wright, Floyd V. Filson, Otto Piper, John A. Mackay, H. H. Rowley, and James D. Smart, at its center was the shared conviction that the biblical narratives provided the proper locus for significant theological reflection.

20. James Barr, *Old and New in Interpretation* (New York: Harper & Row, 1966), p. 18. Childs (p. 65) calls Barr's work "the final blow" to the biblical theology movement.

21. Hans W. Frei, *The Eclipse of Biblical Narrative* (New Haven: Yale University Press, 1974), p. 130.

22. *Ibid.*, pp. 5, 6.

23. *Ibid.*, p. 10. The terms "realistic" and "history-like" are used by Frei to refer to certain kinds of narratives. Obviously, terms like these need some further explication, and that will be provided a little later on in my discussion of Frei's work.

24. *Ibid.*, pp. 1, 2, 3.

25. *Ibid.*, p. 4.

26. *Ibid.*, pp. 7, 8.

27. *Ibid.*, p. 128. Frei is referring here to what he takes to be the central claim of Christianity, namely, that "Jesus is the Redeemer."

28. *Ibid.*, p. 230.

29. *Ibid.*; emphasis added.

30. *Ibid.*, pp. 27, 280, 323.

31. *Ibid.*, p. 27.

32. Frank Kermode has some very interesting observations about how the *re-shaping* of a story may reflect the reshaping of a sense of reality. In *The Genesis of Secrecy,* says that

[the] novel. . . is a form of narrative inconceivable as anything but a book in the modern sense; it requires, in principle, that we be able to turn back and forth its pages. A novel written on a roll would be something else. So it is of interest that the Christians, from a very early date, preferred the codex to the roll. The Jews, upon whom the end of time had not come, whose prophecies of a Messiah were unfulfilled, kept to the roll, but the Christians, having the desire to establish consonance between the end of the book and the beginning, needed the codex, and not only used it for their own books but transferred the Old Testament to the same form. . . . [A] new view of the history of the world entailed a new system of retrieving and ordering information about it. ([Cambridge: Harvard University Press, 1979], pp. 88-89).

Reflecting on the rather 'open-ended' quality of much modern fiction, Kermode notes:

The fiction of transition is our way of registering the conviction that the end is immanent rather than imminent; it reflects our lack of confidence in ends, our mistrust of the apportioning of history to epochs of this and that. Our own epoch is the epoch of nothing positive, only of transition. Since we move from transition to transition, we may suppose that we exist in no intelligible relation to the past, and no predictable relation to the future. (*The Sense of an Ending* [London: Oxford University Press, 1967], pp. 101-2.)

33. It was during her marriage to TeSelle that she wrote *Speaking in Parables*. Thus, in citing that work for bibliographical purposes, I refer to her as Sallie TeSelle; on all other occasions, however, I shall use the name "McFague."

34. McFague, *Speaking in Parables,* pp. 13, 56, 58.

35. *Ibid.,* p. 76; cf. also pp. 56, 77, 78-79.

36. *Ibid.,* p. 82. See also Frederick H. Borsch, *God's Parable* (Philadelphia: The Westminster Press, 1976), for a similar thesis.

37. *Ibid.,* p. 10.

38. *Ibid.*, p. 3.

39. The structural 'parallels' between narratives, religious traditions, and the world is also one of the major themes of Wesley Kort's book *Narrative Elements and Religious Meaning* (Philadelphia: Fortress Press, 1975). Kort's basic question is, "Why do narratives so often and so easily complicate and enrich themselves with meanings that are religiously suggestive or apparently religious?" His answer to that question is:

> [T]hey do because the elements of narrative stand to the characteristics of religion like two walls of a canyon stand to each other, separated but with structural matching points. It is for this reason that religious power and meaning have so often in the past, and in the present still can be, expressed in stories, and, more to the point of this discussion, that consciousness of the elements of narrative . . . can lead to images and ideas which indicate counterparts in religious life and thought. . . . Between narrative and religion, then, there exists an open area, so to speak, in which the two can extend themselves or across which a theorist can cast some lines. This area is indicated by a narrative when an element is reflected upon, complicated, and enriched; from the other side, this area is indicated when religious life and thought are described in terms of general characteristics such as those I have used, characteristics which at one time are both less than religious and suggestive of components of a human world. The words I have used in the titles to chapters in this study indicate possible moments of convergence in this area: otherness, paradigm, process, and belief (p. 111).

40. McFague, *Speaking in Parables*, pp. 125, 139.

41. *Ibid.*, p. 138.

42. Another writer who draws attention to the structural similarities between story and world is Brian Wicker. Indeed, the very title of his book, *The Story-Shaped World* (Notre Dame, Ind.: University of Notre Dame Press, 1975), reflects Wicker's contention that the structure of the narratives we tell

gives a structure to the realities we perceive. In regard to biblical narrative, Wicker offers an analogy to help make his point. As a movie projector casts an image onto a blank wall, so, too, a story such as the kind found in the Bible casts its image onto a previously undifferentiated and unformed world. Thus, for example, in the biblical stories,

> the figure Yahweh is not only a character in the story but also, at the same time, a person who really exists. The complex relation thus involved implies that the structure of the story in which this character appears is projected on to the real world to give *it* a structure which otherwise it would not have. [This analogy] illustrates the thesis that the sacred story gives "chaos" a shape or "nisus." For without the story, as [the analogy] indicates, there would be no shape to reality: it would only be a blank wall. It is not until the structure of the story is projected on to this blank wall that we can recognize that the wall too exhibits the same structure (p. 96).

Wicker himself has a Thomist theory of analogy which enables him to make this sort of link between story and world (cf. p. 99). For a somewhat similar Thomist understanding of the role that analogy plays in linking language and word, see David Burrell's *Analogy and Philosophical Language* (New Haven: Yale University Press, 1973), p. 224. There Burrell writes:

> Analogous expressions . . . come into play precisely at those points where one wishes to speak of language itself or of the relation between language and the world, and yet realizes that one must have recourse to a language. At these points we need expressions that function within our language but whose serviceability is not restricted to their role within the language. . . . The fact that these expressions own a proper use within each language framework and yet are also used in every framework is what suggested their identification as transcendentals. . . . Moreover, this very account presupposes some capacity to single out distinct "languages" and so employs the scheme of *unity*.

For the role of analogical language in theology, see Burrell's remarks on pp. 266 and 287. Finally, the reader should look at Burrell's article on Wicker, etc., "Stories of God: Why We Use Them and How We Judge Them," in *Is God God?* eds. Axel Steuer and James Wm. McClendon, Jr., (Nashville: Abingdon, 1981).

43. Cf. his *Discerning the Way* (New York: The Seabury Press, 1980) in which van Buren investigates the implications of such dialogue for reconstructing Christian theology. His concerns there are not without precedent; Van Buren has long been interested in ways for doing such theological reconstruction. See, for example, his *The Secular Meaning of the Gospel* (New York: The Macmillan Co., 1963), and *The Edges of Language* (New York: The Macmillan Co., 1972).

44. Paul M. van Buren, *The Burden of Freedom: Americans and the God of Israel* (New York: The Seabury Press, 1976), p. 4. In a fundamental way, this book may be seen as Van Buren's contribution to the American bicentennial.

45. *Ibid.*, p. 7.

46. *Ibid.*, p. 18.

47. *Ibid.*, pp. 21-22. In a similar (though far less sophisticated) way, Gabriel Fackre has also observed that the "storyline" of the Gospel and Old Testament narratives force us to conceive of God the way we conceive of persons. In his book, *The Christian Story* (Grand Rapids: Eerdmans Publishing Co., 1978), p. 232, Fackre comments that the New Testament narratives in particular disclose a

> God [who] . . . is a subject. The events . . . traced rise out of a Self that purposes and chooses. . . . [And] the deeds done to consummate the intention bespeak freedom, awareness, and self-direction. Here is the living, willing Spirit and therefore the *personal* God.

48. *Ibid.*, p. 28.

49. *Ibid.*, p. 24.

50. *Ibid.* Van Buren quickly and instructively adds: "The biblical writers were certainly aware of evil, but apparently they realized that for some strange reason God could not, or at least did not, always act to rescue" (p. 24).

51. *Ibid.*, p. 44.

52. *Ibid.*, p. 9. The whole passage is in italics in the original.

53. Irving Greenberg, "Judaism and History: Historical Events and Religious Change," in *Perspectives in Jewish Learning*, vol. 1, eds. Stanley Kazan and Nathaniel Stampfer (Chicago: Spertus College Press, 1977), p. 43.

54. *Ibid.*

55. *Ibid.*, p. 44.

56. *Ibid.*, p. 45.

57. *Ibid.*, p. 47. In *Ascent of the Mountain, Flight of the Dove*, Michael Novak gives a more theoretical and general account of what Greenberg has called an "orienting experience." Novak's own term is "cultural story," and he believes that this kind of story performs several functions: it provides a normative guide for living; it serves as an illuminator of certain aspects of a people's experience; it offers meaning and significance to that experience by taking some events out of the people's past in order to make them the basis for its aspirations for the future; it functions as a selector of goals by giving a community a direction and framework for action; lastly, it operates as a 'style guide' for proper responses in concrete situations. In short, a cultural story, in Novak's view, is one which holds out a paradigm for understanding the truth and meaning of existence. (Cf. pp. 104-8). See also *The Rise of the Unmeltable Ethnics* (New York: The Macmillan Co., 1972) where, using Mark Zborowski's clinical study, *People in Pain*, Novak provides a wonderful example of the way that cultural stories affect individual life stories. There Novak shows how the

reactions of hospitalized patients from different ethnic groups is but a retelling of their groups' different cultural stories.

58. *Ibid*.

59. The logical merits (or demerits) of the so-called "Falsificationist Challenge" aside, Greenberg has apparently answered it here by specifying at least one state of affairs—i.e., the disappearance of the Jewish People—that could falsify the claims of Judaism, thereby giving those claims meaningful status according to this 'empiricist' view of meaning.

60. Greenberg, "Judaism and History," p. 57; brackets in original.

61. *Ibid*.

62. *Ibid*., pp. 57-58.

63. Stanley Hauerwas, *Vision and Virtue*, p. 102. This book represents a kind of link between the various stages of Hauerwas' thought. The earliest stage is reflected in *Character and the Christian Life: A Study in Theological Ethics* (San Antonio: Trinity University Press, 1975), in which Hauerwas' central focus is the notion of character; in *Vision and Virtue*, that notion is complemented and expanded by Hauerwas' calling attention to the importance of images, metaphors, and vision for the formation of character. His *Truthfulness and Tragedy*, written with Richard Bondi and David Burrell, elaborates both these themes by adding to the discussion the significance of narrative for each of these other two elements. Among other things, narrative provides a way of articulating the movement—the development—of both character and vision through time. As might be gathered from the title of Hauerwas' most recent collection of essays, *A Community of Character: Toward a Constructive Christian Social Ethic*, Hauerwas has been currently engaged in spelling out the social dimensions and implications of his previously formulated notions of character, vision, and narrative.

64. *Ibid.*, p. 74.

65. Cf. my discussion of Hampshire in chapter 4.

66. Ludwig Wittgenstein, *Tractatus Logico-Philosophicus: The German Text of Ludwig Wittgenstein's Logisch-philoso- phische Abhandlung,* trans. D.F. Pears and B. F. McGuinness (New York: Humanities Press, 1961), S. 6.43.

67. Hauerwas, *Vision and Virtue*, p. 71.

68. *Ibid.*, p. 73.

69. *Ibid.*, cf. pp. 17, 19, 20.

70. Cf. Hauerwas, *Vision and Virtue*, "Abortion and Normative Ethics" and "Abortion: The Agent's Perspective" as well as *Truthfulness and Tragedy*, "Memory, Community, and the Reasons for Living: Reflections on Suicide and Euthanasia."

71. Hauerwas, *Vision and Virtue*, p. 172.

72. Hauerwas, *Truthfulness and Tragedy*, pp. 38, 39.

73. Hauerwas, *Vision and Virtue*, cf. p. 3.

74. Hauerwas, *Truthfulness and Tragedy*, p. 39.

75. Hauerwas, *Vision and Virtue*, p. 102.

76. John Howard Yoder, *The Politics of Jesus* (Grand Rapids: Eerdmans Publishing Co., 1973), pp. 22-23.

77. *Ibid.*, p. 23.

78. *Ibid.*, p. 25.

79. One thinks here of Braithwaite's error; cf. chapter 2 above.

80. Yoder, *The Politics of Jesus*, pp. 25, 104-5.

81. *Ibid.*, cf. pp. 106-14.

82. *Ibid.*, pp. 62-63.

83. *Ibid.*, pp. 243-44. See also Yoder's *Nevertheless: A Meditation on the Varieties and Shortcomings of Religious Pacificism* (Scottdale, Pa.: Herald Press, 1971), and *The Original Revolution: Essays on Christian Pacifism* (Scottdale, Pa.: Herald Press, 1971).

84. *Ibid.*, p. 244.

85. *Ibid.*, p. 98.

86. *Ibid.*, pp. 97, 98.

87. *Ibid.*, p. 153. For a far different appraisal of both the conditions of liberation and the "politics of Jesus," see Robert McAfee Brown's *Theology in a New Key* (Philadelphia: The Westminster Press, 1978). With regard to Yoder's contention that the 'powers' of the world have been vanquished by Christ and thus need not be actively attacked by the church, Brown answers from the point of view of liberation theology that "far from being the kind of world that we wish it were . . . we discover that our world is a *world of conflict,* in which major forces are polarized and apparently unable to work together. The most frequently described polarity is that between *the oppressors and the oppressed* " (p. 67). Brown goes on to challenge Yoder's critique of liberation theology in a direct way:

> The . . . critique . . . charges that liberation theology's *use of the Bible* is too selective, and that a small group of passages becomes normative for the rest. John Howard Yoder questions the emphasis on the exodus motif in liberation theology. The exodus he insists, is not the only Biblical image nor is it necessarily the central one, and the Bible's message is twisted when everything else is interpreted in its light. Yoder presses for more attention to other images, such as Bethel, and suggests that even the exodus story is not necessarily a helpful model for Christian engagement today, since it proposes walking away from the scene of trouble. . . .
>
> Dialogue about these concerns needs to continue. But we need to remember, as the dialogue proceeds, that *all* Christians read the Bible 'selectively,' and that the tendency to develop a working 'canon within a canon' was not invented in Lima or Montevideo. . . . The goal is not to have one bias win out, but to subject all biases to the closest approximation of the Scriptural bias we can corporately discern, recognizing that liberation theology may be closer to the Biblical message than we are (p. 116).

These passages touch on a critical issue for narrative theology—the criteria for a justifiable hermeneutic for the use of narrative in theology. This is an issue to which we will have occasion to return at the end of this chapter and one which will raise important questions for the chapter to follow.

88. Hauerwas, *Truthfulness and Tragedy*, p. 72.

89. McFague, *Speaking in Parables*, pp. 56, 148.

90. *Ibid.*, p. 125.

91. Cf., e.g., James Wiggins, ed., *Religion as Story*, in which, despite the number and variety of thinkers represented, the issue of the relationship between narrative and truth is never seriously raised or treated.

92. Wright, *God Who Acts*, p. 64.

93. Van Buren, *The Burden of Freedom*, p. 107.

94. George Stroup III, "A Bibliographical Critique," *Theology Today* 32 (July 1975), 141-42. Clearly, I share many of Stroup's other concerns about the justifiability of narrative theology as well; cf. his *Promise of Narrative Theology*.

95. See Hauerwas, *Truthfulness and Tragedy*, pp. 107-9.

96. While Hauerwas refers to the notion of life as involving trust, he uses 'trust' in the sense of 'faith' or 'confidence' (see *Truthfulness and Tragedy*, p. 110). I, however, am using 'trust' in the sense of 'commission' or 'charge.' Thus, the notion that I am trying to get at is best expressed by saying, *not* that 'life involves trust,' but rather that 'life *is* a trust.'

97. Though clearly, Judaism gives an important place to love in its conception of God, just as Christianity's conception involves a central notion of God's justice.

CHAPTER VI

1. E.g., Barth, *Church Dogmatics*.

2. E.g., D. C. MacIntosh.

3. E.g., Tillich.

4. For an approach somewhat similar to this, along with a useful typology outlining other theological strategies, see David Tracy, *Blessed Rage for Order: The New Pluralism in Theology* (New York: The Seabury Press, 1975).

5. As helpful and different ways of looking at the problems of justifying claims to knowledge, see: Stanley Cavell, *The Claim of Reason* (New York: Oxford University Press, 1979) where, for example, he sees the philosopher's search for proof about the objective character of the world 'out there' as an almost abnormal (pathological?) obsession (cf. p. 238); Nicholas Wolterstorff, for his part, has shown in his book, *Reason Within the Bounds of Religion*, that the search for self-evident, indubitable foundations as the ultimate justification of epistemological claims is, in the end, a quest in search of a phantom; Thomas Kuhn, in his influential book, *The Structure of Scientific Revolutions* (Chicago: University of Chicago Press, 1962) has pointed out that the notion of the totally objective, neutral, detached scientist at work in his laboratory is after all a science-fiction. Although Cavell, Wolterstorff, and Kuhn have very different basic concerns, they are all nevertheless agreed about two things: (1) knowledge of the world is possible, but (2) such knowledge can be neither gained nor justified from a totally unconditioned, non-perspectival position.

6. For a useful introduction to a variety of ways of justifying moral claims, see Bernard Williams' instructive little book, *Morality: An Introduction to Ethics* (New York: Harper & Row, 1972).

7. McClendon and Smith use the term "happy" instead of Austin's more cumbersome locution, "felicitious." See *Understanding Religious Convictions*, p. 10.

8. *Ibid.*, cf. pp. 59ff.

9. Actually, the *first* thing which McClendon and Smith single out for consideration is what they call "Preconditions":

"The speaker . . . and some hearer know a common language (in this case, English); both speaker and hearer are conscious and free from relevant physical impediments so that speaker's sound-production and hearer's hearing of speaker are normal" (p. 59). Although such preconditions are obviously important, they are somewhat tangential to our immediate concerns here, and hence, in my discussion, I shall merely presuppose them.

10. *Ibid.*, cf. p. 63.

11. E.g., the speaker doesn't already have it in his hands.

12. E.g., there is a hearer who isn't totally paralyzed.

13. Cf. *Understanding Religious Convictions*, p. 67.

14. *Ibid.*, cf. pp. 74ff.

15. *Ibid.*, p. 87. For a more detailed, step-by-step account of the justificatory procedure entailed by the confession, "God led Israel across the Sea of Reeds," see pp. 65-66.

16. At this point, the parallels between what we are doing and what McClendon and Smith have done will be at their greatest distance. For their part, McClendon and Smith have in mind what Austin called "the perlocutionary act," i.e., the act by which various psychological or physical effects are brought about, such effects being closely related, both linguistically and logically, to the speech-acts which are intended to produce them. For my part, while I certainly would not deny that similar 'connections' surround narrative-based convictions, I will nevertheless be using the category of affective conditions primarily as a way of focusing on the justification of the 'transformational' claims of a narrative theology. Most certainly, one of the classical concerns of theology has been to show how the expression of religious convictions, through the self-involving character of such convictions, can affectively transform the lives of the communities and individuals who hold them. Traditionally, this kind of analysis came under the rubric of "practical theology." By bringing up the notion of

"rationality" at this level, I mean to call attention to the need for sketching out a procedure for justifying—for *giving reasons* to support—a narrative theology's convictions about the kinds of transformations that can and ought to be made in human life. Clearly, the issue of rationality applies to the other two levels of justification as well, but I believe that by approaching that issue at the level of the affective conditions, we will gain a kind of 'spring-board' for making some wider observations later on about the relationship between rationality and a narrative theology as a whole.

17. How 'happy' would it be, for instance, to hold convictions which one claims to be absolutely historical in nature, but which nevertheless have their base in a story which begins, "Once upon a time . . ."?

18. Scholes and Kellogg, *The Nature of Narrative*, pp. 4, 208, 211.

19. For an example of the former mistake, see Fowler's *Trajectories in Faith* (chapter 3 above); for an example of the latter, see Fletcher's *Situation Ethics* (chapter 1 above).

20. Hayden White, "The Structure of Historical Narrative," *Clio*, 1 (June 1972), 16.

21. *Ibid.*, pp. 17-18.

22. Cf. McClendon and Smith, *Understanding Religious Convictions*, p. 108, regarding the tie required between linguistic and cultural institutions for even so simple a speech-act as "happy bread requesting."

23. Scholes and Kellogg, *The Nature of Narrative*, p. 25.

24. As we have seen before in chapter 2, Braithwaite is one who is certainly guilty of this kind of blunder, treating all religious stories as being in essence fables.

25. Scholes and Kellogg, *The Nature of Narrative*, p. 83.

26. No doubt, some, such as Paul Ricoeur, might object to

this statement, even with the limits indicated by the italicized words, "at least initially." They would claim by contrast that the hermeneutical, theological task does not require an understanding of the original meaning of the story to those who first told and heard it. Instead, their contention is that the story as now fixed text, bears its own meaning available *as is* to anyone who can read (or hear). See, e.g., Ricoeur's *Interpretation Theory* (Fort Worth: Texas Christian University Press, 1976). But for a different assessment, namely, one which says that meaning is and must be closely tied to use (as opposed to the views of both Ricoeur and any others who might try instead to link meaning to notions of 'sense' and 'reference'), see the remarks of one of the foremost philosophers of language, William P. Alston in his book, *Philosophy of Language* (Englewood Cliffs, N. J.: Prentice-Hall, 1964), especially chapters 1 and 2. I suspect that in part, Ricoeur's position reflects a certain tension he feels between a text's *meaning* and *meaningfulness*. Happily, in the scheme used by McClendon and Smith, there is no such tension in the felicitous speech-act between primary and affective conditions; cf., e.g., the scheme laid out on page 60, under section 4.

27. Wicker, *The Story-Shaped World*, p. 89.

28. *Ibid.*, p. 91.

29. For those who would agree with this view of the role played by tradition *vis-a-vis* narrative, see, e.g., Gerhard von Rad, *Old Testament Theology* (New York: Harper & Row, 1962); D. A. Knight, ed., *Tradition and Theology in the Old Testament* (Philadelphia: Fortress Press, 1977). For views, which by contrast, deemphasize the role of tradition in favor of the claims of the completed canon as it stands, see, of course Barth, and Brevard Childs, *Introduction to the Old Testament as Scripture* (Philadelphia: Fortress Press, 1979). For a lucid presentation of the positions of both sides—along with some

preliminary suggestions about the needs and ways of reconciling them, see Bernhard W. Anderson, "Tradition and Scripture in the Community of Faith," Presidential Address presented at the centennial meeting of the Society of Biblical Literature, Dallas, Texas, November 6, 1980.

30. Hauerwas, *A Community of Character*, p. 59. Hauerwas is specifically referring here to "the Christian stories."

31. David Kelsey, *The Uses of Scripture in Recent Theology* (Philadelphia: Fortress Press, 1975).

32. *Ibid.*, p. 175. By *"discrimen,"* Kelsey, following Robert C. Johnson, means "a configuration of criteria that are in some way organically related to one another as reciprocal coefficients" (p. 160).

33. *Ibid.*, pp. 2-3.

34. *Ibid.*, p. 5.

35. *Ibid.*, pp. 149-50.

36. Hauerwas' "self" is always a social self.

37. Hauerwas, *Character and the Christian Life*, p. vii.

38. Greenberg, "Judaism and History," p. 44.

39. Some might find a problem with this observation: if 'traditions' establish the metes and bounds of justifiable narrative interpretation, *and* if 'traditions' are themselves narrative in character, isn't there an uncomfortable circularity here? Perhaps so—but only if one is looking for some narrative independent, non-perspectival vantage point from which to see *'the* meaning' of some narrative. As we pointed out in the last chapter, part of the historical clash between Judaism and Christianity has involved a conflict in vantage points over how properly to understand the Old Testament. However, while we may not be able to find a vantage point completely unconditioned by any narrative tradition whatsoever, we might at least search for one which has a place in it for other narratives and traditions not our own. As we pointed out in our discussion

of autobiography (chapter 4 above), the fact that some stories
seem to give us the ability to 'step back' and see what we have
been doing from a different perspective may be the narrative
equivalent of 'the universalizability principle,' and hence may
be a factor recommending their adoption.

40. Van Harvey, *The Historian and the Believer* (New York:
The Macmillan Co., 1966), p. 62.

41. I am purposely using the words 'behavior,' 'event,'
'figure' rather than 'action,' 'act,' 'person' so as not to raise (or
beg) any issues about conceiving of God in the way that we
conceive of (other) persons. However, I do believe that at least
so far as the Exodus narrative is concerned, there are good
reasons for such a conception. Cf., e.g., chapter 5 which sets
forth Paul van Buren's narrative-based theology which argues
for conceiving of God in personal terms.

42. Of course, as I said earlier, if these 'sign-events' never
happened, then at least at the representative level, our
Exodus-based conviction may well prove unjustified, but even
then, it would be important to remember that that unjustifiability would stem from the nature of the conditions
entailed *by the narrative itself*.

43. According to contemporary biblical scholarship, this
poetic description of the crossing reflects the earliest account of
that passage; the prose versions, such as the one found at the
end of Exodus 14, are later recensions of this older portrayal of
the event.

44. Hauerwas, *Truthfulness and Tragedy*, p. 73.

45. See note 16 above.

46. This example can serve to show how one of the
challenges commonly put to a narrative-based theology reflects
a certain mistaken assumption. That challenge typically takes
the form: must a justifiable narrative theology be based on a

'good' story? And of course, the mistaken assumption is that the same criteria of commendation can be applied to all stories (e.g., anecdotes, histories, fables, fantasies) in exactly the same way. In a sense, the challenger makes the same mistake as those who assume that all pieces of language do, and are meant to do, the same exact work, viz., 'describe.' According to that kind of 'linguistic theory,' how 'good' a word would be 'hello'? In other words, according to what we have been saying, what counts as a 'good story' will vary from genre to genre, and the affective conditions of justification partially provide us with a way of making discerning assessments of the relative values of narratives and the theologies which arise from them. I say 'partially' of course because such assessments must take note of the primary and representative conditions as well.

47. Thus reminding us once more of the importance of the primary conditions.

48. Cf. McClendon and Smith, *Understanding Religious Convictions*, pp. 60, 62-63.

49. Hauerwas, *Truthfulness and Tragedy*, p. 35.

50. Metz, *Faith in History and Society*, p. 212.

51. Cavell, *The Claim of Reason*, p. 268.

52. Fingarette, *The Self in Transformation*, p. 235. Again, another of the challenges frequently brought against narrative theologians is of the sort, "Do you mean to say that if the Nazis had won World War II, then the Nazi story (and the moral convictions it entails) would be therefore justified?" Part of the problem the narrative theologians have had in adequately responding to this challenge has been due to their failure to attend adequately to the three levels of justification and to distinguish among them accordingly. Had the Nazis triumphed, then on one level—*that which we are here describing as that of the affective conditions*—their convictions would have been justified. However, that still would not

necessarily have meant that their claims were therefore fully justified. How justifiable were they, for instance, in terms of the representative conditions, e.g., were the Jews really the ones responsible for the defeat of Germany in World War I? Moreover, it is not theologically unimportant in terms of a Jewish conviction set that the Nazis were defeated and that the Jews did survive them. Again, on the affective level at least, that fact may have something to say about the justifiability of a Jewish narrative theology.

53. See, e.g., J. Wesley Robbins' attack on Hauerwas, "Narrative, Morality, and Religion," *Journal of Religious Ethics* 8 (Fall 1980), 161-76.

54. Alasdair MacIntyre, *Against the Self-Images of the Age* (New York: Schocken Books, 1971), p. 253.

55. *Ibid.*, pp. 249-50.

56. Another way of saying this would be to stress the fact that whatever narrative-based convictions one chooses to take up in one's life, such 'uptake' must at least be consistent with the narrative which one claims to be their source. Hence, there would be something wrong about adopting a historically oriented narrative as the basis of one's convictions, i.e., one predicated on notions of novelty and evolution—and irreversibility—but then enacting those convictions in one's life as a mere *re*-enactment of what had gone before, that is, as though both they and one's life were merely part of some myth of the eternal return. To be sure, various religious rituals are in a sense such re-enactments, but only within a kind of larger context which *suggests* how our lives might be carried on from here. (And perhaps that is why it would seem odd to describe our whole life as but one 'ritual re-enactment.') So, for example, it is one thing to try to follow—or follow up—the story of Jesus in one's own life; it is quite another to try to *be* the story of Jesus as though by an almost mystical transformation, one could

become a perfect copy (a mere imitation?) of Jesus. Hauerwas, for instance, comes dangerously close at times to crossing this line. While he generally characterizes part of the force of Christian stories by saying (in Wittgenstein-like terms) that they are meant to give us the ability "to go on" (*Truthfulness and Tragedy*, p. 80), he sometimes slips and makes such statements as: "Any story that fails to provide institutional forms is powerless, for it is not enough merely to offer the story. One must know how to tell it in such a way that persons can *become the story*" (p. 97; emphasis added). That kind of bald assertion is simply unjustifiable given the kind of historically oriented narrative that the story of Jesus is. Perhaps Hauerwas might be better off saying that one should take up that narrative in such a way as to become another chapter in the ongoing, continuing story of Jesus Christ. For a very fine treatment of the affective dimension of narrative-based convictions, undertaken from a somewhat different perspective, see George Stroup's *The Promise of Narrative Theology*, Part III, "The Hermeneutics of Christian Narrative."

57. Tracy, *Blessed Rage for Order*, p. 207.

58. Hauerwas, *Truthfulness and Tragedy*, pp. 37, 35.

59. *Ibid.*, p. 76.

60. The field of ethics can provide an illuminating parallel regarding the need for some narrative context in order to give our notions, claims, convictions, etc., some sort of intelligible, rational, *justifiable* basis. Since the time of Kant, much of ethics has turned on the concept of 'the moral ought,' a notion whose justification, it is claimed, rests in its ability to generate non-perspectival prescriptions which are universally (and hence necessarily) binding upon any and all rational beings. Consequently, according to the argument presented, the rationality of this ought—and the prescriptions stemming from it—lie precisely in its 'objectivity,' i.e., in its autonomy from

the contingencies of any time or place—or story. As a result of this view, much of modern moral discourse and argument has typically become a matter of asking, "*Morally*, what ought *any person* do in such and such a situation?" of then answering, "Why, one *ought* to do thus and thus," and of justifying that answer if challenged, by responding with the virtually analytical retort, "Because, *morally*, that's simply what one *ought* to do!" If, however, one were at this point to press that challenge by asking further, "But *why?*" in all likelihood, his challenge would be greeted by either (1) a tautologous reiteration such as, "Because you just *ought* to! That's why!" or by (2) a look of disbelief that any *rational* person could fail to see a point so clear.

But how clear is it? What the challenger actually desires is some fuller account which shows why this 'moral ought' should have the significance and force assigned to it. Not surprisingly, that sort of intelligibility—and any attendant justifiability—can only come through an examination and understanding of the storied background from which 'the moral ought' derives. According to Alasdair MacIntyre, here is how that story goes:

> One way of seeing the history of ethics is this. The Greek moral tradition asserted—no doubt with many reservations at times—an essential connection between "good" and "good for," between virtue and desire. One cannot, for Aristotle, do ethics without doing moral psychology; one cannot understand what a virtue is without understanding it as something a man could possess and as something related to human happiness. Morality, to be intelligible, must be understood as grounded in human nature. The Middle Ages preserves this way of looking at ethics. Certainly there is a new element of divine commandment to be reckoned with. But the God who commands you also created you and His commandments are such as befits your nature to obey. So an Aristotelian moral psychology and a Christian view of the moral law are synthesized even if somewhat unsatisfactorily in Thomistic

> ethics. But the Protestant Reformation changes this. First, because human beings are totally corrupt, their nature cannot be a foundation for true morality. And next because men cannot judge God, we obey God's commandments not because God is good but simply because He is God. So the moral law is a collection of arbitrary fiats unconnected with anything we may want or desire (pp. 123-24).

On this view, the Reformation represented a turning point in the history (the story) of moral discourse. Out of it emerged the novel moral notion that moral rules are unconditional prescriptions which neither have nor need any further justification beyond themselves. From there, the storyline was (in part) taken up by Kantians who sought to establish morality on categorical imperatives which would thus ground the autonomy of ethics. And with that, 'the moral ought' had been born. MacIntyre cogently notes that only in "post-Protestant," increasingly secularized cultures does this 'moral ought' ever appear: "And it appears precisely in the period when the judgment that men ought to do so and so can no longer be supported by appeal to the nature that God created and the purposes toward which the commandments of God are directed" (p. 168). Ironically, however, this new 'moral ought' thus trades upon the prestige of the bygone theistically linked usages of 'ought' to make it appear as though it is criterionless, impersonal, universal, and non-perspectival, in short the secular ideal: man in God's place! But, concludes MacIntyre, this new 'ought,' cut loose from its previous narrative moorings which anchored its intelligibility and significance, has also lost its claims to rationality and justifiability as well: "Deprived of its [former] rationale, the use of this 'ought' . . . [is] in a real sense superstitious" (p. 169). Hence, in MacIntyre's view, the contemporary account of 'the moral ought,' which purported to tell a story to end all stories, ends up being the worst, most dangerous kind of story: a fiction mistaken as being absolutely true—and acted on as if it were. For a more extensive discussion of the storied background of contemporary moral theory—and the disastrous consequences for such theory due to its failure to attend to narrative—see MacIntyre's recent and quite important book. *After Virtue* (Notre Dame, Ind.: University of Notre Dame Press, 1981).

61. Hauerwas, *Truthfulness and Tragedy*, pp. 78-79.

62. *Ibid.*, p. 35. What makes Hauerwas' remarks here all the more perplexing is that in the very next sentence, he softens the starkness of his original assertin (and seemingly even contradicts it!) by conceding that "it is inaccurate, of course, to list these criteria as features which a story must display. For they envisage rather the effect stories might be expected to have on those who allow them to shape their lives." However, even this 'retrenched' position still suggests that there are certain, readily identifiable and independently statable features which must be present in "any narrative that can rightly commend our allegiance."

63. See, e.g., Robbins, "Narrative, Morality, and Religion," p. 175, and Gene Outka, "Character, Vision, and Narrative," *Religious Studies Review* 6 (April 1980), 116-18.

64. Hauerwas, *Truthfulness and Tragedy*, pp. 8, 9.

65. Harvey, *The Historian and the Believer*, p. 240.

66. *Ibid.*, p. 214. For a more detailed and sustained attack on the hard perspectivist position, see Roger Trigg, *Reason and Commitment* (Cambridge: Cambridge University Press, 1973). I should add, however, that I find Trigg's 'non-perspectivist' position (note the oddness of that last phrase!) in some ways equally untenable.

67. *Ibid.*, cf. pp. 240-42. See also McClendon and Smith in order to gain a fuller understanding of the precise implications of Harvey's work for our present concerns here.

68. Cavell, *The Claim of Reason*, pp. 254-55.